EXUBERANT ANIMAL

THE POWER OF HEALTH, PLAY AND JOYFUL MOVEMENT

Frank Forencich

FRANK FORENCICH

Bloomington, IN   authorHOUSE™   Milton Keynes, UK

AuthorHouse™
1663 Liberty Drive, Suite 200
Bloomington, IN 47403
www.authorhouse.com
Phone: 1-800-839-8640

AuthorHouse™ *UK Ltd.*
500 Avebury Boulevard
Central Milton Keynes, MK9 2BE
www.authorhouse.co.uk
Phone: 08001974150

First published by AuthorHouse 8/23/2006

ISBN: 1-4259-5663-7 (sc)

Printed in the United States of America
Bloomington, Indiana

This book is printed on acid-free paper.

For information, contact GoAnimal at 9112 32nd Ave. NE, Seattle, WA 98115.

WARNING:

Before beginning a program of physical inactivity, consult your doctor. Sedentary living is abnormal and dangerous to your health.

Let my words be bright with animals…

Joseph Brucha

Contents

PREVIEW: GETTING LAPPED

When I write, I feel like an armless and legless man with a crayon in his mouth.

Kurt Vonnegut

Long before I became a physical educator, I was a sick little kid, afflicted with a host of allergies, digestive problems and physical malaise. Nothing life-threatening, but enough to slow me down considerably. Weak and timid, I found little promise in physicality; books were my passion.

My earliest memory of physical incompetence was a fitness test in some early grade, a two-lap run/walk around the school track. I did not fare well. It's not often that a runner gets lapped in a two-lap race, but that's how I remember it. For one brief tantalizing moment, just prior to being lapped, I felt the thrill of victory as I led the pack around the far turn. But the illusion soon vanished and I eventually slumped across the finish line, thoroughly humiliated. My body had let me down.

The following year, my parents enrolled me in swimming classes, where I was also lapped with clockwork regularity. Inexplicably, I then joined a try-out for the high school water polo team, surely the last sport that I was qualified for. Fortunately for me, even a sport like water polo has room for non-swimmers: the shallow-end cage. I became a goalie, an ideal position for the hydrophobic and physically inept. Here at last was something physical I could do without getting lapped or drowning.

Over the next few weeks, the balls whizzed by my outstretched hands with regularity, but I did get my hands on a few errant shots. This modest success kept me coming back for practice every afternoon and, with so much time in the water, it was inevitable that I would actually swim a short distance each day. This regular movement began to have a therapeutic effect on my body and by the time I graduated from high school, I was as fit and healthy as my peers.

This transformation had a profound effect on my outlook and over the next decade I became an insatiable physical omnivore. I tried all the physical arts that I could. In particular, I dedicated myself to climbing and martial art. For the first decade of my adult life, all I cared about was movement and performance. I wanted to become stronger, faster and more endurant; I wanted to run long distances, climb big mountains and kick like Bruce Lee. This quest sustained me for a long time, but like many physical omnivores, I eventually got involved in teaching movement classes.

This changed everything. Suddenly I was forced into a position that demanded reflection and self-examination. What exactly was I teaching? Why is physical education important? What did physical performance mean for my students? As I studied various methods, I became frustrated with the fact that virtually every fitness and health care discipline treated the body as if it simply fell out of the sky. Hard as I looked, I could find no unifying context anywhere, no linkage between biology, human origins and physical exercise. Worse yet, I could find no fitness programs that linked humans with the millions of other species that inhabit this planet.

During my training I encountered, either through direct experience or research, dozens of martial art styles, yoga styles, sport training programs, strength training philosophies, rehabilitation practices, nutritional programs and mind-body disciplines. Many of them claimed to be the last word in training the body. And yet, not one of these disciplines addressed the historical reality of the human body or our animal heritage. It eventually became clear to me that if I was ever going to experience a movement program based on human evolution, play and functional fitness, I was going to have to do it myself.

I was excited about the prospects of describing a new philosophy of movement, but when I sat down to put my ideas onto paper, I was shocked to discover that once again, I was getting lapped. Not by fleet-footed jocks as before, but this time by writers—fast, wickedly intelligent writers who churned out books the way the other kids ran around the track. Whenever I set my fingers to the keyboard or browsed the bookstore, there they were, flying past me, brilliantly, powerfully and without fatigue. Suddenly I was ten years old again, cramping up on the backstretch, tripping over my own feet and watching in dismay as the pack disappeared around the far turn.

Fortunately, I've had some powerful allies who taught me some tricks, gave me some magic elixirs and pushed me back out onto the track whenever I started looking for a way out. My thanks and gratitude go first to Mom and Dad Forencich, my greatest and most devoted advocates. My brother Sam—my favorite exuberant—has inspired me at every turn. Susan Fahringer—my favorite neo-sister—and her family have stood with me throughout. In addition, I have enjoyed the support of these primal, practical and playful friends and mentors: Stuart Brown, Robert Sapolsky, Frank Lindsay, Steven Stanfield and Monica Donald, David and Debbie Bair, Troy Corliss, Peter Hercules, Deb Armstrong, Jennifer Lovejoy and Kurt Larson, Basin Ross Herbertson, Corey Jung, Robert Wood, Pat Kane, David Katz, Marc Bekhoff, Kevin Carroll, Skye Moody, Steve Myrland, Vern Gambetta, Paul Chek, Gary Gray, Lauren Muney, Steve Laskevitch, Gary Avischious, Rhonda Clements, Curt Rosengren, Ozzie Gontang, Corey Weathers, James Vaughan, Bill Matthews, Ibrahima Camara, John Hayden, Edward Mulhern, and my faithful readers of the GoAnimal newsletter. Special thanks to Jeri Helen for sculpting my words and polishing my manuscript.

A COPIOUSLY
BRANCHING BOOK

The affinities of all the beings of the same class have sometimes been represented by a great tree... As buds give rise by growth to fresh buds, and these if vigorous, branch out and overtop on all sides many a feebler branch, so by generation I believe it has been with the great Tree of Life, which fills with its dead and broken branches the crust of the earth, and covers the surface with its ever branching and beautiful ramifications.

Charles Darwin
The Origin of Species

Evolution is a copiously branching bush, not a ladder of progress; and although certain broad features are repeated from time to time, when and where individual twigs appear is quite unpredictable in our highly contingent world.

Stephen Jay Gould

These days, almost everyone's got a complaint about the condition of their body. For most of us, it's the familiar litany of woe: too fat, wrong shape, too weak, too wrinkled, too painful. We worry about our bodies endlessly, consumed with anxiety, desperate for a quick fix, appalled by the fact that we don't look or feel the way we want.

Driven by our discontent, we set out to study human health. We start out with some simple ideas about anatomy and physiology and at first, things go smoothly. But no matter how hard we try to stay on topic, things invariably seem to get messy and complicated. Even as we focus in on the body and its various systems, we tend to get dragged into a thicket of bushy, multi-disciplinary ideas.

We start out thinking we're studying muscle tissue or metabolism and suddenly realize that we're in a maze of cross-branches, some going to culture, some to history, agriculture or psychology. We try to evaluate fitness programs, but find ourselves lost in competing claims. We study diet programs for effectiveness, only to find that placebo effects complicate our work, drawing us into the world of mind-body influence and belief. We wonder about the prevalence of obesity and diabetes, but find that the incidence varies dramatically with social rank, thus drawing us into the world of culture and economics. No matter what our starting point, we always seem to wind up in the brush.

This bushy experience can be confusing and confounding, but it should really come as no surprise. Nature after all, is an incredibly bushy creature, spinning off an astonishing array of species, each with its own unique form and behavior. The biosphere is constantly growing and rearranging itself into new forms. Animal bodies are bushy too, growing new cells and tissues throughout life. The brain itself resembles a bush in both form and growth, constantly remodeling itself in response to changing patterns of use. And our exuberant spirit is bushy as well, generating a wild array of ideas, speculations and curiosities.

Bushiness can make our inquiry challenging, but it also makes it rewarding and endlessly fascinating. Ultimately, the bush gives us a curriculum of riches. In our biological age, the bush becomes an icon, not only of the healthy proliferation of species, but of exuberance, health and embrace. In such an environment, straight-line explanations become immediately suspect. Instead, we look for bushy philosophies, ideas that are well-rooted, but divergent and open-ended.

Of course, many of us are reluctant to enter the brush. In today's hyper-rational world, linear sequences are taken as evidence of ultimate knowledge and professional expertise. We expect people to lay down their ideas in linear patterns with distinct rankings, hierarchy and above all, order. But, as we are beginning to discover, neither evolution nor good ideas work this way. Good ideas don't proceed from point to point in sequential fashion; they split and splinter, branch and divide, just like species do. Simple ideas may sprout a few branches, but really good ideas become exceptionally bushy, generating thousands of conceptual sprouts that continue to grow as the discipline becomes ever richer.

MEET THE EXUBERANT ANIMAL

Exuberant Animal grows out of the trunk laid down in my previous book, *Play as if Your Life Depends on It*. In that work, I sketched out an evolutionary view of physical fitness and its three primary branches: the primal, the practical and the playful. The primal branch is that of human origins and the natural history of our bodies. The practical branch includes the study of functional movement–concepts such as balance, useful strength, core integration and efficient locomotion. The playful branch emphasizes joyful exuberance and pleasure in motion.

In *Exuberant Animal*, the idea is to take our interest in the human body and grow some additional branches, shoots and leaves. The branches you'll find in this book began life as a series of newsletters and are naturally diverse: some are sober, reasoned analysis, some are creative non-fiction, some are how-to, others are wild and passionate ravings on our physical predicament. (I will leave it to you to decide which is which.) Some are marked by gravity, others by levity. In any case, each branch will provide a different perspective on how your body works and give you some ideas on how to make it work better.

Throughout this book, we'll explore two main branches of human health: exuberance and animalhood. The animal side is our physicality, our flesh, our tissue. It's powerful, strong, endurant and primal. Exuberance is the psychospiritual branch, our joyful enthusiasm. It's creative, curious and playful. It seeks adventure, novelty and movement of all descriptions.

Of course, exuberance and animalhood are tightly interconnected and interdependent; each contributes to the other. In fact, it's almost impossible to address one without the other. The more exuberance you can generate, the happier your body will become. Likewise, the more vitality and performance you can bring to your tissue, the greater your enthusiasm for living. It's a perfectly virtuous circle that serves us well.

Unfortunately, exuberance and its close partners–passion and joy–are consistently underrated in mainstream studies of physical fitness, health and performance. These qualities are not given to easy measurement and tend to fall off the radar screen of our data-centric culture. We prefer our studies to be quantifiable and trackable. We want numbers that can be captured on spreadsheets and manipulated. Consequently, we now know more about lactic acid concentrations than we do about joy, more about body mass index than we do about passion, more about treadmill performance than we do about enthusiasm.

We study and test, research and measure, drilling our knowledge down to the deepest levels, and then we wonder why people find exercise so dull and unattractive. We strip human movement down to the sterile elements of anatomy, physiology and biomechanics and then complain that no one wants to participate.

EXUBERANT
JOYFUL
CREATIVE
CURIOUS
PASSIONATE   **ANIMAL**
PLAYFUL
                PRIMAL
                POWERFUL
                AGILE
                ENDURANT
                ADAPTABLE

Obviously, we're missing something fundamental. When we look at human movement from a broad perspective, we see that it's not only rich, it's positively bursting with juicy sensations, ideas and relationships that can drive us to life-long participation and transformation. Exuberance isn't a spin-off or a tangential benefit. It lies at the very core of what we're after. As Kay Redfield Jamison put it in her classic *Exuberance*,

> Psychologists, who in recent years have taken up the study
> of positive emotions, find that joy widens one's view of
> the world and expands imaginative thought. It activates.
> It makes both physical and intellectual exploration more
> likely, and it provides reward for problems solved or risks
> taken. Through its positive energies, it heals as well.

Unfortunately, modern living has put a damper on both sides of our exuberant animalhood. We are suffering in several ways. First is our epidemic of depression. According to the World Health Organization, depression is currently a major cause of disability and is projected to become a leading contributor to the global burden of disease. The frequency and severity of depression has been rising steadily over the course of the last 50 years. Closely related is the epidemic of stress; for many, stress either causes or exacerbates depression. But stress is rising across the board too. And of course, there's our well-documented epidemic of sedentary behavior and physical inactivity.

Naturally, the forces of depression, stress and inactivity feed off one another. Just as exuberance and animalhood create a virtuous circle of mutual reinforcement, depression and inactivity can lead us into a vicious cycle of disconnection, weakness and diminished physicality. Even the most casual observer of the human animal can see how this might work. A depressed spirit leads to physical apathy and more sedentary behavior, which leads to more depression and yet more physical malaise. Similarly, a weak or injured body can lead to a loss of enthusiasm and a diminished outlook.

THIS BUSHY BOOK

Because the spiritual and the physical are so intimately related, it hardly makes sense to talk about one without the other. In fact, any fragmented, single-sided approach seems doomed to failure. If we concentrate only on tissue, as a standard health-and-fitness prescription, we neglect the spirit. If we concentrate only on spirit, we miss our essential physicality. Specializations have their place, but they invariably lead to fragmentation.

Consequently, this book will embrace exuberance and animalhood together in a single conversation. As you read the essays in this book, you'll find a tight interconnection of mind and matter. If we're talking about the flesh, you can assume that the spirit is nearby. If we're talking exuberance, tissue is right there as well.

Being bushy by nature, this book will not give you a linear, step-by-step formula for health and fitness success. It won't provide you with a prescription or a checklist. It won't reveal a secret antidote for aging or a breakthrough discovery for instant weight loss. Instead, this bushy material will open your mind to new possibilities, relationships and ideas that you can adapt to suit your own purposes. Most importantly, the ideas in this book will help you develop a sense of depth and sustainability in your life of physical movement. You'll begin to realize that the world of the body is far more than one of sets, reps and calories. It is immensely rich and endlessly fascinating–an ideal life-long study.

THE STATE OF THE ANIMAL

Rapid changes in transport, work, and leisure activities
have led to a global collapse in physical activity levels.

Science Magazine editorial
"Global Chronic Diseases"
January 21, 2005

CATASTROPHE IN PROGRESS

It's not easy being an exuberant animal in this modern world. Last year I had the misfortune to visit Las Vegas where, in spite of my best efforts to do otherwise, I was forced to spend several nights in a casino hotel. It had been years since I had last set foot in one of these places and in the meantime, my brain had managed to repress the memory.

But now, the flashing lights, sounds and smoke all came back to me as familiar features. The scene was plenty engaging in it's own right, but what really grabbed my attention was the nature of the gamblers themselves, especially their bodies. These individuals were a spectacle of ill health, poster-children for the epidemic of obesity and atrophy that is sweeping not just North America, but the planet at large.

I stood in the center of the casino gaming area, stunned at the condition of these creatures. Disembodied, hypnotized by lights and the promise of instant riches, they pumped a steady stream of coins into hungry slot machines. The whole thing seemed like a grim laboratory experiment; I imagined a strain of lab animals bred specifically for obesity, nicotine tolerance, sedentary behavior and machine training. I scanned the ceiling for one-way mirrors and cameras, supposing I would spot a white-coated graduate student with a clipboard, but all I saw were security officers.

Incredibly, the gambling machines themselves actually seemed more alive, vigorous and vibrant than the individuals who were using them. Regular maintenance and professional care keeps them in good health and malfunctions, however minor, are attended to. Their function, after all, is of critical importance.

Many of the bodies I observed were so degenerated that, even if they were somehow provided with unlimited medical support and fitness resources, it is unlikely that they could ever regain anything like normal physical function and health. These individuals had wildly overshot their body's homeostatic set points; their chance of regaining health as slim as their odds of winning a jackpot. For many of these people, their clinical condition was, for all practical purposes, hopeless.

According to the strict definitions of modern medicine, the individuals that I observed may or may not have been suffering from any officially recognized pathology. But there is no question that they were sick. Even in the absence of some clinical finding of blocked arteries, diabetes or high blood pressure, they still must be classified as diseased. These were not normal, healthy human bodies by any stretch of the imagination. There was no joy in their tissue, no wildness, no exuberance. They were near death.

Please don't get the wrong idea. I am not a killjoy. On the contrary, I am an advocate of occasional, exuberant and passionate excess. But the scene I witnessed before me was not one of fun-loving people enjoying life. Rather, it was one of people in desperation, people whose only hope for authentic pleasure lay in the vanishingly slender hope of a monetary payoff. These people were not engaged in sedentary living, they were engaged in sedentary dying.

Whether or not these casino gamblers represent a true cross-section of American bodies is an open question. Perhaps things are different elsewhere. Perhaps my view of American health was skewed by a small sample size. Maybe these people were the exception to a generally healthy and vigorous population.

I think not. These casino patrons had come from every corner of America. Their bodies were in horrible condition, but they are not unusual. We can observe similar levels of physical degeneration in almost every community. Just go out in public and you'll see the evidence. Not only are a lot of people seriously overweight, but even more tragically, many—even those of normal weight—have no apparent interest in their bodies or in physical experience. What I observed in Vegas was not an isolated pocket of disease, but a widespread phenomenon, a genuine epidemic that now affects millions of people worldwide.

AT THIS VERY MOMENT...

It's one thing to watch people from a distance, but it's quite another to reflect on the actual physiological processes that are currently in motion across the planet. At this very moment, hundreds of thousands of coronary arteries are closing down to their minimum diameter, starving their owner's hearts of precious blood and oxygen. Billions of muscle fibers are shriveling into atrophy, no longer in use by their sedentary owners. Billions of pancreatic cells are giving up the ghost, exhausted after pumping gobs of insulin in a losing effort to process a continuous stream of high-fructose corn syrup. Thousands of pounds of bone minerals are being flushed into American toilets, lost to the lack of physical stimulation. Trillions of sensory and motor nerve cell connections are going dormant from abject disuse. Uncountable number of fat cells are swelling, their membranes stretched to the bursting point, scarcely able to contain an expanding surplus of unnatural nutrients. Human physiology is failing at a rate never before seen in human history.

SO HOW BAD IS IT?

The World Health Organization gives us these chilling figures:

"…more than 1 billion adults overweight–at least 300 million of them clinically obese."

"Physical inactivity is estimated to cause 2 million deaths worldwide annually."

In 2004, *The Archives of Internal Medicine* gave us this picture:

Obesity and sedentary lifestyle are escalating national and global epidemics that warrant increased attention by physicians and other health care professionals. These intricately linked conditions are responsible for an enormous burden of chronic disease, impaired physical function and quality of life, at least 300,000 premature deaths, and at least $90 billion in direct health care costs annually in the United States alone.

In March, 2005, *The New England Journal of Medicine* gave us this grim assessment:

From our analysis of the effect of obesity on longevity, we conclude that the steady rise in life expectancy during the past two centuries may soon come to an end.

A 9/11 EVERY WEEK

It's one thing to cite percentages and statistics for the prevalence of disease. Things come into even sharper focus when we compare our predicament to other, more spectacular events. This is precisely how Samuel Klein of the North American Association for the Study of Obesity framed it: "More lives are being lost to obesity than any war or terrorist attack."

To get an idea of just how bad the problem is, look at it this way: Each year, at least 250,000 deaths are premature due to physical inactivity. Do the math and you'll find that it works out to roughly a 9/11 every week. Because it happens in slow motion however, it fails to capture our attention.

Nevertheless, the overall picture is becoming increasingly clear. We are looking at an unprecedented, radical challenge to humanity and the human future. To paraphrase H.G. Wells, "we are now in a race between physical education and catastrophe."

REFERENCES

World Health Organization:
www.who.int/dietphysicalactivity/publications/facts/obesity/en/

The Archives of Internal Medicine: 164:249-258, 2004. Manson JE, Skerrett PJ, Greenland P, VanItallie TB.

The New England Journal of Medicine: A Potential Decline in Life Expectancy in the United States in the 21st Century, March 17, 2005

BROTHER, CAN YOU PARADIGM?

In March, 2004, the *Journal of the American Medical Association* reported on yet another study documenting the accelerating rise in American obesity. In the report, Dr. Julie Gerberding, director of the Centers for Disease Control and Prevention, summed up the findings this way: "The problem of obesity is really an epidemic, and we need to apply the same tools to combat it as if it were an infectious-disease epidemic."

This strikes me as an astonishing statement. Surely Dr. Gerberding knows the difference between bacteria and Big Macs. Surely she knows the difference between viruses and videos, between pathogens and potato chips. Surely she does not mean to put obesity in the same category as smallpox, malaria and AIDS. But if obesity is a different kind of disease, shouldn't we be using different kinds of tools to fight it?

Obviously, today's combination of obesity, diabetes and physical atrophy is an epidemic, but it is not infectious in the typical sense. Rather, it is an altogether different class of human affliction, something unique in human experience. If we are going to make any progress is treating this condition, we had best get our categories straight at the outset. Otherwise, we're going to waste a lot of time and energy.

A NEW ETIOLOGY

For the last thousand years, the single most deadly medical challenge facing humanity has been infectious disease. Plague, smallpox, tuberculosis, influenza, malaria, cholera, yellow fever–these diseases have killed hundreds of millions of people, many times more than have been killed in wars. Given the enormity of the death toll, it comes as no surprise to learn that the lion's share of our medical efforts and health care resources have gone directly into the diagnosis and treatment of infectious disease. When thousands of people are dying in the streets of your city, you aren't going to pay much attention to people who are suffering from obesity, coronary artery disease or arthritis. These afflictions are, by comparison, almost inconsequential.

Medical understanding of the role of infection has led to incredible advances in human health and lifespan. With a few notable exceptions, we know how to deal with infectious disease. Public sanitation, antibiotics and public education work wonders. We know what to do to prevent the spread of infection: wash your hands, keep the kitchen clean, wear a condom and get vaccinated before traveling to the tropics.

But now we're faced with something truly novel. From a medical standpoint, sedentary behavior and obesity are unique challenges. We are so accustomed to thinking in terms of microorganisms, environmental toxins and genetic defects that we are completely thrown when a health problem emerges that falls outside of these standard categories. If we're confused about how to classify it, we're likely to have an even greater problem in trying to treat it.

We know—in general—how to prevent and cure infectious disease, but what do we know about the prevention and treatment of lifestyle diseases? The answer is, not very much. For the first time in human history, we are afflicted by disease that comes, not from some external agent, but from our own habits of living.

WHERE IS THE ENEMY?

In one sense, infectious disease was an easy challenge for us because it fit right into our well-developed military mind-set. Bacteria and viruses are external agents and it's easy to cast them enemies. This made our challenge conceptually simple. We could either kill them outright, kill their hosts (mosquitoes for example) or harness our immune systems to do the killing for us. We could declare war on smallpox, war on malaria and war on AIDS.

But lifestyle disease is an entirely different challenge, one that will not yield to medical militarism. Outside of a few genuinely pathological corporations, there simply is no external agent that we can target. We are the ones who are responsible for our predicament. We built the cars that now confine us into a sedentary life of atrophy. We built the factories that pump our food full of trans-fats. We built the companies that drive employees to the limit of human endurance. As Pogo might have put it, "We have met the pathogen and it is us."

Yes, there are some individuals and corporations that ought to be treated with the same militaristic fervor that we apply to bacteria and viruses, but in general, most of us are co-conspirators in the atrophy and obesity epidemic. We are the ones who invented the internal combustion engine. We are the ones who buy millions of gallons of soft drinks every year. We are the ones who can't be bothered to go for a walk once in awhile. We are the ones who worship digitized images of physical perfection on magazine covers. For these reasons, medical militarism simply isn't going to work.

CONVENTIONAL APPROACHES

Some of us will turn to our familiar social and medical institutions for assistance, but is unlikely that we will get much genuine help from the Centers for Disease Control, the National Institutes of Health or the World Health Organization. These organizations are large, conservative and slow to respond to change. In general, they are still using disease and treatment models that were developed long before our modern epidemic. If influenza or avian flu breaks out into an epidemic, these institutions will know what to do, but they are helpless before the problems of modern lifestyle.

Some of us will turn to Eastern medicine for a solution, certain that it will give us the answers that we seek. But while there is value in the East, even this ancient philosophy is not up to the job. Eastern medicine came out of a historical context that was totally unlike what we face today. Asian physicians had no experience with the sedentary behavior, abstract stress and toxic food of the modern world. Shamans knew nothing about the 24/7 work environment, airline travel or instant messaging. It is tempting to look to Asian traditions in a search for guidance, but really, the ancients would be just as flummoxed by our predicament as we are.

NEW IDEAS FOR NEW EPIDEMICS

One thing is clear. We aren't going to solve this problem with conventional thinking or conventional models. Novel problems require novel solutions. We can rearrange the deck chairs all we like, but what we really have to do is change the direction that the ship is headed. Tinkering isn't going to help. Mandating thirty minutes of PE per week isn't going to make any real difference. Changing the shape of the food pyramid might be a good idea, but that isn't going to make much difference either.

What we really need to do is create a new kind of culture and a new kind of lifestyle—a culture that puts the body back into the center of attention where it belongs, a culture that honors movement, exuberance, play, health and broad-based physicality.

This is not something that can be legislated or implemented by policy makers and administrators. Rather, it will take the efforts of truly creative people who are willing to live in new ways, ways that are physically authentic, vigorous and vibrant. We need artists, writers, teachers, coaches and physicians in this effort, individuals who are willing to take some risks for the sake of health. If we wait around for big institutions to do it, we'll simply fall deeper into atrophy and apathy.

PRIMALISMS

It is possible to prevent most modern diseases. Strangely, this secret to health is not waiting to be unveiled by white-coated lab scientists. It has already been unearthed by dusty paleontologists. It is the lifestyle of our ancestors.

Noel Boaz
Evolving Health

It's about time

I elbowed my way down the sidewalk, hurrying to get across town. The streets were clogged with pedestrians and I was late for an appointment. My brain buzzed with a swarm of detail; my to-do list was five pages long and I had to get to get to the bank, download my e-mail and make a few calls before everything shut down on the east coast. I looked at my wrist to check the time and suddenly realized that I had left my watch back at the health club. "Damn!" I cursed. Now I was really up a creek.

I picked up my pace and looked around frantically for a clock. Unfortunately, there was no timepiece to be seen anywhere, but there was an old man sitting on a nearby bench. He didn't seem to be doing much of anything, so I stopped short and put the question to him.

"Excuse me, have you got the time?" I asked breathlessly.

"Yeah sure." He glanced down at his bare wrist briefly, then up again. "It's the late Cenozoic."

I hesitated, doing a double take. Furiously, I tried to process his reply, but I couldn't grasp it. At first I thought that he was insane, but his eyes were clear, steady and calm. He must have sensed my confusion and said, "You know, the age of mammals."

I blinked.

"Oh, doesn't that sound right?" He looked down at his wrist again.

"Yep," he said. "That's it. We're still in the Quaternary, although that could change. Probably will, actually."

The way he said it was so natural, so offhand, so perfectly true that I began to doubt my own sense of reality. I opened my mouth to speak, but my jaw just hung there. The man looked at me again with what seemed like pity.

"Oh, you're in a hurry? You need more precision? Well, yes, of course, I'm sorry, it's the Holocene, you know, the post-Pleistocene epoch."

Still staring, I blinked again. The man was so calm, so utterly rational. Suddenly I felt like a fool.

"You didn't think that it was the Cretaceous, did you?" He burst out laughing, slapping his legs in hysteria.

"Er, uh, well no," I finally stammered.

"A lot of people make that mistake, you know. Ever since *Jurassic Park* and all."

"Er, no, I mean, I thought that it was about two o'clock or so."

"Oh," the man said flatly, "that."

By now I had forgotten about my appointment and was engrossed in this most unusual conversation. Suddenly, I had a feeling that my to-do list really wasn't so important.

"Please sit down," the man said as he gestured to the bench. "You've got plenty of time."

SCULPTED BY CATS

The lion sleeps in the sun.
Its nose is on its paws.
It can kill a man.

> Wallace Stevens
> "Poetry is a Destructive Force"

Among the earliest forms of human self-awareness was the awareness of being meat.

> David Quammen
> *Monster of God*

Being a creature of intelligence and physicality, you've probably wondered about human origins and what your life might have been like in primal conditions. Perhaps you've imagined yourself as an intrepid hunter, chasing down hapless animals on the grassland and dragging them back to camp for a sunset barbecue.

If that's your vision of human ancestry, you may want to take another look because those animals out in the bush weren't all so hapless. In fact, many of them were cunning, hungry and exceptionally strong carnivores who liked nothing better than a quick hominid snack. While you were out there hunting, you were probably being hunted yourself. In this sense, the history of human beings has been not as hunter-gatherers, but as *hunted*-gatherers.

A SHARED HABITAT

Our coexistence with carnivores is revealed by the enormous number of carnivore bones found in the fossil record. Many digs have unearthed an incredibly rich assortment of carnivore fossils, especially lions and saber-toothed cats. This has led to a growing realization that our ancestral homeland was, as scientists like to put it, a "predator-rich environment."

This predator-rich predicament was not some unusual condition that held sway for an isolated part of human history or was peculiar to some remote bioregion. Rather, it was the norm. For the overwhelming majority of our time on earth, we have lived in intimate proximity to large, hungry predators that, in many instances, feasted directly upon us. We have been, for the vast majority of our time on this planet, cat food.

For modern humans growing up in predator-free environments, carnivore contact seems like a distant curiosity. When we think of lions, we think of remote regions of Africa, hardly supposing that we might ever have to face such creatures in the flesh. But in fact, big cats have been with us throughout our existence; they are our neighbors.

David Quammen drove this point home in his book *Monster of God*. As he tells it, lions have thrived not only in Africa, but across southwestern Asia, in Syria and Mesopotamia, along the bottomlands of the Tigris and Euphrates rivers. There were lions in Palestine and Egypt, in Turkey, Macedonia and Greece. There were lions in France and Germany and there is even evidence that lions ranged as far north as Great Britain, crossing over during a period of low sea level.

Our co-existence with predatory cats was further revealed in 1994 when amateur spelunkers discovered a major cave in southeastern France, *la Grotte Chauvet*. They found classic paintings of mammoth, bison, horses, reindeer and giant deer, but they also found seventy-three lion images, about 35,000 years old. If you lived in France at that time, lions were there too.

SCULPTING BODIES AND BRAINS

Our co-existence with carnivores has been so constant throughout human history that we can safely assume that our anatomy and physiology have been shaped in some measure by the experience. After all, carnivores are quite efficient at eliminating weak individuals from any pack of animals, whether they be zebras or hominids. We can assume that at least some of our physical traits have been preserved by virtue of the fact that they kept us one step ahead of claws and teeth.

Obviously, humans do not match up well against the average carnivore. Compared to the typical predatory cat, bipedal hominids are weak, slow and relatively defenseless. Even the strongest human is likely to be overwhelmed by the average carnivore. Given the relative weakness of our bodies, we had to develop other means to defend ourselves. The process began with our brains.

Conventional thinking holds that hunting was a primary stimulus for increased brain size. As hominids began to hunt, they entered into a positive feedback cycle that both rewarded and developed their intelligence. Successful hunting meant more protein, increased brain growth and even better hunting skills.

This all sounds plausible enough, but it seems equally likely that our intelligence was stimulated by being hunted. Our vulnerability was extreme; soft flesh is no match for feline weapons. The hominids knew their predicament and wracked their small brains to come up with strategies for avoiding such encounters.

Life on the mosaic grassland would have resembled a massive, three-dimensional chess game with all manner of creatures jockeying for position, gathering information, tracking one another and considering options. The hominids probably spent a good deal of time wondering "Where are the lions?" "What are the hyenas doing?" "How many are there?" "What about the leopards?" Such questions provoke intensive observation and further inquiry.

SCULPTING OUR SOCIAL BEHAVIOR

Not only did the big cats sculpt our brains, they also shaped our social behavior. Danger inspired tribal cohesion. By traveling in packs, we afforded ourselves a substantial degree of safety. A tribe of noisy, stone-throwing humans makes a pretty intimidating challenge for a predator. The carnivores surely picked off the weak, old and foolish, but most tribe members survived to reproductive age. Thus the Pleistocene motto for human survival became "Together we stand, divided we get eaten."

PHYSICAL FITNESS IN A PREDATOR-RICH ENVIRONMENT

Of course, living in a tribal gang isn't a guarantee of total safety. The vulnerable biped may still need to put his or her body on the line occasionally. So the question is, what kind of physical fitness would be appropriate for life in a predator-rich environment. Power? Speed? Endurance?

There is probably no right answer and we are free to speculate at will. Every feline encounter would be different. In all likelihood, survival was a combination of good locomotion, raw physical strength, keen senses and good luck.

Nevertheless, we can infer a few things from what we know about feline locomotion. We know from observation that most big cats will only chase prey animals for a few hundred yards before giving up. Their metabolism simply isn't structured for extended pursuit. In all probability, no lion has ever run more than a couple of miles. This suggests that for the vulnerable biped, powerful sprinting might be more important than long-distance endurance.

One thing is certain, however. Carnivores were unlikely to target hominid tribes directly. Rather, they'd go for stragglers, individuals who can't quite keep up with the group. Thus, the need for locomotor speed is relative; as long as you can keep up with your peers, you're fast enough. This brings some truth to the old joke that's popular in both Africa and Alaska: When faced with an imminent attack by a hungry carnivore, the man turns to his friend and declares, "I don't have to outrun the lion (bear, cougar, tiger…), I just have to outrun you." In this context, you don't need to be a champion, but you do need to be as fast as your tribe.

In any case, this discussion leads us to a surprising conclusion. That is, if observational acuity and tribal organization are really the most important factors in avoiding predation, it may actually be the case that physical fitness—as we think of it today—wasn't all that important. The ability to run fast and jump high, by itself, would be pretty meaningless. The smart and observant wimp would survive longer and leave more offspring than the studly but dim-witted jock.

BENEFITS OF A PREDATOR-RICH ENVIRONMENT

The drawbacks of life in a predator-rich environment are obvious—severe injury or grisly death spring to mind. And, even when the cats didn't attack us directly, they probably monopolized the easy prey opportunities. If there's a lame wildebeest limping through your neighborhood, the lions are almost certain to get to it before you do.

Nevertheless, there would have been substantial benefits. The constant presence of big cats would have concentrated our minds and focused our attention. This leads us to postulate a kind of "hominid Zen," a state of sustained concentration and readiness.

In the samurai era of Japan, master swordsmen often advised their students to "train as if you are facing a live blade." The presence of the blade brings one's attention into the present and mobilizes the body for action. But for our hominid ancestors, there was no need for imagination. Big cats are equipped with five sets of weapons and are faster than any samurai. Consequently, we can assume that the primal state of human consciousness was one of near-constant vigilance. As the tribal shaman might have put it, "always live as if you're facing a live cat."

In addition to the psychological effects of focus and concentration, we also would have enjoyed substantial biophilic benefits, the wonder of living in close proximity to such marvelous animals. In our modern world, people flock to zoos to see sleepy captive lions. How much more compelling to see them stalk, hunt and live right in your own neighborhood! The sheer awe of it would have been a constant source of amazement and joy, as well as fear.

LIFE IN A PREDATOR-POOR ENVIRONMENT

For better and for worse, our modern world is, for all practical purposes, a predator-free environment. It is only in the last few hundred years that we have managed to exterminate and isolate predator populations and remove this challenge to our daily existence. The fact that we are now free to walk around without being hunted is historically unprecedented.

The extermination of predators has increased our freedom and personal safety, but this has come at a significant cost. In the first place, our sensation has changed. We don't pay much attention to the natural environment anymore. Most of us could care less if we're walking upwind or downwind, except in as much as it might mess up our hair. We don't look out into the distance much either. Most of the action is right in front of our faces, an endless stream of symbols and images that pass before us at arm's length.

Not only is sensation altered, there are also social consequences to our carnivore-free lifestyle. When the predators disappear, some of the motivation for tribal cohesion goes with it. For the first time in history, we can wander away from the tribe without worrying about getting picked off. It is no surprise that tribal cohesion breaks down in the modern world; with no cats to drive us together, it's easier to drift apart. This reshuffles the social order with a cascade of consequences, some creative, some difficult and stressful.

Our "predator-poor" status also creates lazy habits of attention and awareness. The things that challenge us are now increasingly abstract: how to get through school, how to get a good job, make money and achieve recognition. True, some of us live in conditions in which we are exposed to physical attack, but this is different. Your neighbor may attack you with a knife and may even shoot at you, but it is extremely rare that he will try to eat you.

Consequently, we have less of a compelling interest in knowing our environment. Territories and terrain are far less relevant to survival than they once were. This leads to a severe dumbing-down of modern humans. Increasingly distant and abstracted from our immediate environment, we become environmental slackers, apathetic to the world around us.

THOUGHT EXPERIMENT

Romantics will suggest that we turn back the clock and reintroduce predatory cats into our suburban environments. Surely a few cougars roaming our neighborhoods would focus our attention and stimulate our bodies. Unfortunately perhaps, this sort of community enhancement program is unlikely to take hold. Most suburban dwellers can scarcely tolerate off-leash dogs these days, much less hungry megafauna.

Lacking actual animals, we'll have to make do with our imaginations. What we can do is keep our minds engaged. Next time you're walking down the street or going to the post office, look both ways and scan for felines. Taste the wind and keep your eyes open. The cats are hungry and they're watching you!

RESOURCES

Monster of God by David Quammen

Man the Hunted: Primates, Predators and Human Evolution by Donna Hart and Robert W. Sussman

Land of Lost Monsters: Man Against Beast–The Prehistoric Battle for the Planet by Ted Oakes

THE MOSAIC CURRICULUM

When our forebears pondered life's big questions, did they do so while contemplating an enveloping shroud of trees or an endless horizon?

Robert Sapolsky
"Are the Desert People Winning?"
Discover August 2005

As children, we all heard the myth about the stork. A new baby was due in the neighborhood and our parents told us the preposterous tale about a large bird that arrives with a human infant in its beak. But even for young children, the story didn't really seem to stick. Santa Claus maybe, but a stork? I don't think so, Mom. Birds don't work that way, anyone can see that.

By the time we're seven or eight, most of us have pretty well debunked the stork myth and started looking for the real source of babies. The bird story gets left behind, resigned to childhood's archive of dubious adult explanations. Years later, we assume that we've moved on to more sophisticated thinking, but in another sense, the stork never really went away. It still lives in the background of modern culture, most notably in our steadfast refusal to view the human body in a larger ecological context. Everywhere we look, the human body is presented as a stand-alone object, independent of the world and the environment.

Creationists are the worst offenders in this regard, the most notorious perpetrators of storkisms. As they tell it, the human body was simply called into being by a supreme organism. This storkish deity brought the human body to earth and now our species stands alone, independent from and superior to the rest of the biosphere. Those from the so-called "intelligent design" school tell an equally preposterous tale: "The natural world is astonishingly complex in its details; it is beyond our capacity to explain or understand it. Therefore, a stork created it."

But even among those who accept the reality of evolution, storkish thinking is also widespread. Popular health and fitness publications are among the most conspicuous purveyors of this mythology. As they present it, the human body simply appeared on the earth one day, out of shape and in desperate need of conditioning, cosmetics and fashion advice. No history, no environment. Magazine covers reinforce this mythology with every issue; an image of an impossibly gorgeous body, extracted from its background and Photoshopped to digital perfection suggests an independent, context-free organism. We are left with the stork as the only possible explanation.

SCULPTED BY THE ENVIRONMENT

Out in the real world, the stork is an actual bird that lives in an environmental context, a context that shapes its behaviors, its objectives and perhaps, to some extent, its thoughts. So too for human bodies and human ideas. We are products of our habitat. Our bodies and our culture have been shaped by thousands of generations of life and death in natural environments. Habitat and environment define our physical predicament and in the process, color our culture and our values. Religion, human relationship, morality and ideas about the body are all influenced by the land we inhabit.

This is precisely the point brought to light by Robert Sapolsky in the August 2005 issue of Discover magazine. In "Are the Desert People Winning?" Sapolsky cites a landmark study by anthropologist Robert Textor. In the 1960's, Textor gathered an enormous collection of data from some 400 different cultures and discovered powerful correlations between habitat and culture.

The most conspicuous example lies in the religions that we create. Exceptions abound of course, but in general, rain forest dwellers tend to be polytheistic, worshipping a diversity of spirits and gods. Desert dwellers on the other hand, tend to be monotheistic.

When we think in environmental terms, this comes as no surprise. The desert is simple, demanding and dogmatic, a land of unambiguous powers and harsh consequences. Faced with the elemental forces of aridity, burning heat and bitter cold, it makes sense that we'd conceive of a single god and a counter-acting Satan. As Sapolsky puts it, "Deserts teach large, singular lessons, like how tough, spare, and withholding the environment is; the world is reduced to simple, desiccated, furnace-blasted basics." Stark realities generate stark, often brutal explanations—fundamentalism is common in the desert and in desert-inspired cultures (such as our own).

Rain forests on the other hand, are places of multitudes, of quirky, jumpy, sometimes camouflaged surprises. Sunlight filters through the trees at peculiar angles, shadows shift by the minute, moisture comes each afternoon and food is everywhere. Colors and flowers abound; each tree is an ecosystem unto itself. What else could explain this exuberance other than a thousand deities? The gods may or may not be crazy, but they sure are diverse. Ponder this habitat for a few generations and you'll probably come up with a rich collection of stories and myths to explain what you see.

DESERT BODY, FOREST BODY

Just as the environment shapes our beliefs about gods and spirits, so too does it color our opinions about the health, training and aesthetics of the human body. If your culture evolved in the desert, you'll likely have very different ideas about physicality than your forest-dwelling counterparts. Specifically, you'll place a premium on bodies that can keep a steady pace for hours on end. Quite naturally, the desert is the ecological home of cardio and endurance training.

The source of this value system is easy to imagine: Your tribe is camped at a small stand of trees, surrounded by miles of forbidding, open landscape. You've eaten the dates off the local trees and managed to extract a small bit of water from a shallow creek bottom. But the sun is calling the shots now, forcing a journey. Tribal elders declare that you will make for a distant spot of color on the far horizon. The trek may take several days. It will be a dull, grinding journey, but there is no choice.

Under such circumstances, your tribe will come to value endurance, aerobic capacity, and the ability to sustain long periods of monotonous exertion. As your tribe matures and begins to create culture, this view will be integrated into a larger value system and will persist, even when the demands of the desert are obliterated by technology. So it is that today, desert cultures continue to value endurance of the body as the ideal quality, the pinnacle of health and fitness.

Over in the forest however, things are playing out in a completely different way. Here our predicament is defined by bushy terrain, abundant vegetation, moisture and mud. Travel is by faint game trails, bushwhacking and creek crossings. In most cases, it's hard to see where you're going, but the good news is that you usually don't have to go very far. Food is abundant and variety abounds. Don't like what you're eating? Move up the valley a few hundred meters and you can try again.

Under circumstances like these, the ability to travel long distances is not particularly relevant to survival. Instead, the ability to move quickly and powerfully would be held in high regard. Can you make your way through dense brush? Flee from a leopard? Climb a tree? Cross a creek on slippery rocks? Run to the next valley to rejoin the tribe after a thunderstorm? The forest athlete might be less endurant than his desert counterpart, but he'd be more powerful, more muscular and more agile. In short, he'd be a sprinter, a gymnast or a dancer.

DESERT SPORTS, FOREST SPORTS

With this habitat-based distinction in mind, we can classify our modern athletic enterprises into two rough categories: desert sports and forest sports.

Desert sports emphasize endurance and the ability to sustain long-distance suffering. Most obviously, we would point to marathons and ultra-marathons as the classic examples. But in essence, any endurance challenge qualifies as a desert sport. This includes triathlons, long-distance mountain bike events, the Tour de France, and the Race Across America. Even the swim across the English Channel is best described as a desert sport. By virtue of his sustained physical experience, the English channel swimmer actually has more in common with the marathoner than he does with the gymnast.

Similarly, Lance Armstrong is best described as a desert athlete. This has nothing to do with the specifics of bicycle racing, but with the nature of his physical exertion. That is, Armstrong is an endurance specialist. If you were stuck in the middle of a vast desert landscape, he'd be a good person to have on your team.

On the other hand, events that emphasize power, power-endurance and agility are best classified as "forest sports." Gymnastics, long jump, high jump, sport climbing, martial art, combative arts, dance; these are sports that would give us an edge in a bushy, arboreal environment. From this perspective, we would describe people like Michael Jordan and Jackie Chan as forest athletes. With their quick, fluid movements, multi-plane skills and short-range power, these athletes would have excelled in the forest.

WHO'S HEALTHIER?

This distinction between desert sports and forest sports makes for some great bar stool arguments. Everyone has their favorite sport and a thousand reasons why their athletes are the best. Naturally, the desert athletes will claim the fitness high ground, pointing to their superior endurance and ability to withstand prolonged, relentless suffering. The forest advocates will counter that their stars are the true athletes. By virtue of their diverse movement skills, they have the power, agility and grace to do anything that's worth doing.

These positions will get you through a few beers, but in a way, it's completely irrelevant to our modern predicament. That's because the body is supremely adaptable and incredibly responsive to movement of all varieties. The simple fact is that *all* forms of movement make us healthier. Desert sports and forest sports are both good for the human body.

This fact is revealed by a trick question. That is, who's healthier, Michael Jordan in his prime, or Lance Armstrong in his prime? This turns out to be a ridiculous comparison for both were outrageously healthy, in spite of the enormous differences in their physical adaptations.

Or, try this thought experiment: Take two identical twins. Put one on a desert training program with lots of mileage and endurance work. Put the other on a forest program with gobs of calisthenics, climbing and agility training. After a few months, compare results. Inevitably, each gets better at his specialty, but both get healthier. The salient ingredient is frequent, vigorous movement; the specifics are a sideshow.

THE MOSAIC BODY

Of course, it's over-simplistic to assume that human cultures arose exclusively in either desert or forest environments. Human tribes like to move, migrate and mingle. That's why so many cultures are hybrids of desert and forest philosophies. It's also the case that forest and desert are extremes on a spectrum of ancestral human habitats. Most of our ancestors would have sought out a middle ground; the semi-wooded mosaic grassland, the classic ancestral environment.

Neither desert nor forest, this habitat had–and continues to have– elements of both. It is a glorious place, a habitat that is friendly to the human body, mind and spirit. Patches of forest provide food, shade and shelter, but aren't dense enough to be oppressive. Open areas allow for visibility, walking and hunting. Together, this intricate landscape inspires curiosity and stimulates intelligence.

With this picture in mind, we're in a better position to reassess our physicality and create a training program that makes evolutionary sense. Instead of playing exclusively to the desert or the forest, let's develop a physical philosophy that gives us elements of each. This will give us a comprehensive set of capabilities, a hybrid of forest and desert skills that will keep our bodies happy and healthy.

If you're like me, you'll rev up your imagination and picture yourself standing in the semi-wooded mosaic grassland, wondering where the food and the predators are. You might even devise specific games and exercises that speak to the terrain challenges of sandy soil, mud, hills, ravines and trees.

This is all worth doing, but you don't really have to go the trouble. Just set up a rough alternation of desert exercise and forest exercise in your daily life. Do some cardio/endurance training one day, strength training the next, then add in some balance and agility training when you can manage it. A day off here and there for recovery and there you have it, a sensible program for health and fitness that's consistent with the human predicament in a natural environment.

The nice thing about this mosaic plan is that it's a lot more interesting than any abstracted, laboratory-based formulas for cardio and strength work. When you follow the mosaic fitness plan, you're not just logging boring miles or reps, you're putting your body back in touch with 6 million years of physical experience on the ground, in habitat.

It sure beats any stork-based program.

RESOURCES

"Are the Desert People Winning?" by Robert Sapolsky
Discover, August 2005

A Cross-Cultural Summary by Robert Textor

DON'T CALL ME A MONKEY

The question of whether we descended from apes, or split from apes, no longer arises, because it hasn't yet happened... We are apes.

Richard Leakey
The Hominid Gang by Delta Willis

O f the many psychic challenges that modern science has thrown our way, one of the most revolutionary has been the realization that humans are animals. Some people protest this categorization of course, but the anthropologists and biologists have made their case and it is a good one; like it or not, people are part of the animal kingdom.

Vertebrates, mammals, primates–most educated people now accept the reality of this classification. What remains confusing is the distinction between monkeys and apes and where we might fit in. Casual observers of the primate world use the terms *monkeys* and *apes* interchangeably but in fact, the difference between the two is profound. What's more, that difference tells us a lot about how we ought to conduct our physical training and education.

A QUESTION OF LOCOMOTION

The key difference between monkeys and apes lies in the nature of their locomotion. Apes enjoy a cluster of adaptations that allow movement by arm swinging or brachiation. This is a property exclusive to apes: gibbons, orangutans, gorillas, chimps, bonobo and humans. All apes brachiate when the need arises, but no monkey can.

Monkeys are best classified as arboreal (tree-loving) quadrupeds, not brachiators. While it's true that monkeys climb spectacularly, much of this has to do with the physics of their small, lightweight bodies, not the structure of their shoulders or torso. If monkeys were big, they would be poor climbers.

The locomotor difference between apes and monkeys is described most vividly by John Gribbin and Jeremy Cherfas in their book *The First Chimpanzee: In Search of Human Origins*:

> By contrast to monkeys, the collar bone of apes (and, of course, man) is longer and helps to keep the shoulder away from the chest. The shoulder is much freer and can move in all sorts of ways; it isn't much of an effort for you to scratch your right ear with your left hand from behind your head, but no monkey could do this... This cluster of adaptations that allows movement by arm-swinging, or brachiation as it is called, is a property only of the apes – gibbons, orangutans, gorillas, chimpanzees and men.

Researchers have even tested these locomotor differences in artificial settings. In one notable experiment, anthropologist Virginia Avis built a facility that included an ambiguous apparatus that could be climbed from below or walked on from above. She released various primates into the facility and observed their locomotor preferences. Her conclusion: "Apes brachiate, monkeys do not."

APES ON THE PLAYGROUND

Anthropologist Sherwood Washburn described the locomotor behavior of apes in a way that is particularly relevant to physical educators:

> "There is a profound similarity in the motions of the arms of man and apes, and on any playground one can see humans brachiating from bars, hanging from one hand, and exhibiting a variety of motions and postures which are similar to those of apes."

Recalling the experiments conducted by Virginia Avis, he writes: "Man is still a brachiator. He is simply the one who is least frequently in the situation which calls forth this behavior. Our legs are too heavy, and our arms are too weak for efficient brachiation but, when we climb, we climb like apes and not like monkeys." One implication of this understanding is that our playground equipment needs to be renamed. "Monkey bars" are out. The proper term should be "ape bars."

HUMANS: BRACHIATING BIPEDS

When we classify humans as apes, we are pleasantly surprised to realize that we are gifted with two forms of locomotion, bipedalism and brachiation. Of course, compared to other creatures, we are weak in both these modes. Compared to the carnivores and herbivores of the African grassland, we are slow. Compared to the chimpanzees of the forest, we are inefficient climbers. But while our specializations may be poor, our two-pronged abilities are comprehensively powerful. We are jacks of all terrain. We can go almost anywhere in the mosaic, semi-wooded grassland. This gift of hybrid locomotion probably played a big part in our ability to survive the harsh realities of East Africa. We are here today because we can climb *and* walk.

WHAT THIS MEANS FOR PHYSICAL EDUCATION

Once we understand that humans are brachiating bipeds—or bipedal apes—we are in a far better position to craft exercise and fitness programs that match the evolutionary reality of the human body.

Given our diverse locomotion skills, it makes sense to give students diverse locomotion challenges that include *both* brachiation and bipedalism. Sports specializations are out. Instead, we need a comprehensive two-pronged approach to address both our bipedalism and our brachiation.

No need to get overly sophisticated here. Run a mile, climb a tree. Do some field drills with cones and hurdles, then do some time on the local climbing wall. Work some cardio and agility for the legs, some power for the arms and some ab work to tie the hips and shoulders together. That's an ape workout.

When we look at primate locomotion, we also come to realize that the dual-arm pull-up in the President's Council physical fitness test is a poor way to train or test an ape's body. While an ape might pull up on occasion, he'd much rather swing. (When in Africa, I failed to witness a single chimp doing pull-ups.) Is it any wonder that human children hate pull ups, but love swinging on the bars? Our training and tests ought to take this into account.

Our status as apes also tells us a great deal about how to design our fitness and exercise facilities. Climbing walls are good, but the emphasis should be on easy, branch-like features, not extreme sport climbs on tiny edges. And of course, outdoor tracks should be uneven and littered with obstacles, just like real terrain. And they should allow us to run in multiple directions, not just make left turns like stock cars.

USE THE RIGHT WORDS

So, next time you ponder your physical training practices, keep your ape body in mind. And if you're looking to dish out some insults to those difficult people in your life, don't call them apes—that won't distinguish them from anyone else. Call them monkeys.

REFERENCES

The First Chimpanzee: In Search of Human Origins by John Gribbin and Jeremy Cherfas

Sherwood Washburn, "The evolution of man" Scientific American 239(3) 194-208 1978 p 204

Virginia Davis, "Brachiation: the crucial issue for man's ancestry" Southwestern Journal of Anthropology, 18: 119-48, 1962

GOING BONOBO: A PRIMATE FITNESS ALTERNATIVE

When we look at movement and exercise from an evolutionary perspective, it's inevitable that we'll eventually get around to comparing ourselves with our closest primate relatives. Most likely, we'd begin by comparing ourselves with the chimpanzee, the primate made famous by Jane Goodall and her work at Gombe Stream in Tanzania. This is a good place to start, but after some study, we're likely to turn our attention towards another, less famous primate cousin, the bonobo.

You may not be familiar with the bonobo. Originally mistaken as a variant of the chimpanzee, the bonobo (*Pan paniscus*) was only identified as a species in 1929. Even today, few people have heard of this animal, in spite of the fact that bonobo are, along with chimps, our closest relatives in the animal kingdom.

The bonobo inhabit a forested region of equatorial Africa. In appearance, they are remarkably human-like, with long limbs and occasional bipedal locomotion. They are endangered, as are most non-human primates.

Primate behaviors are highly variable and complex and many interpretations are possible. Nevertheless, there seem to be some very interesting differences between chimps and bonobo, differences that may shed some light on why humans behave the way they do, and maybe, just maybe, how they ought to behave.

Primatologists warn against making blanket generalizations about any primate species, but in the interest of brevity, that's exactly what I'm going to do. I'm going to make some rash generalizations, exaggerations and over-simplifications, condensing many thousands of hours of careful field observation into a few scientifically reckless conclusions. Here goes:

Chimps and bonobo have some distinctly different lifestyles and behaviors. For example, chimps are highly social primates with attitude problems. They tend to be patriarchal, highly political, territorial and xenophobic. Extremely rank conscious, they pay particular attention to social order and power structures. They hunt occasionally and males sometimes go on raiding parties, attacking and sometimes killing chimps in neighboring tribes. In terms of their defense policy, chimps are hawks.

The bonobo, on the other hand, are matriarchal, easy-going and laid-back. Social status and rank exist, but are not emphasized. Instead, bonobo seem to thrive on pleasure; they are the primate hedonists, the Epicureans. They enjoy their pleasures in all forms and have a notorious reputation as sexually-active lust masters. In the wild, bonobo spend most of their spare time having sex of all variations. In *Bonobo, the forgotten ape*, authors Frans de Waal and Frans Lanting call them "erotic champions." In short, bonobos are hippies.

We don't know why chimp and bonobo behaviors vary in these ways. Whatever it is, it lies in the tiny genetic difference that separates the two species from one another. There is probably a set of genes that codes for a neurotransmitter profile that lends a predisposition for one style of social behavior or another. As humans, we seem capable of going in either direction; a complex alchemy of individual physiology, environment and experience combine to lead us to become more chimp-like or more bonobo-like in our disposition.

Clearly, there are some unavoidable comparisons here and it is impossible to resist satire. You can probably classify the people you know as chimps or bonobo. Political hard-liners and neo-cons are distinctly chimp-like: aggressive, controlling and ambitious. Conservative talk show hosts are some of our most prominent chimps. Obsessed with rank, hierarchy and other people's behavior, they rant endlessly about liberal (bonobo) conspiracies. They run from issue to issue, trying desperately to keep everyone in their proper place.

Chimps read *The New York Times, Fortune* and *The Wall Street Journal*. Bonobos read *Penthouse, Calvin and Hobbes* and *The Far Side*. Chimps think that bonobos are wimps and pussies; bonobos think that chimps are nasty, brutish and stupid. Chimps are red; bonobos are blue.

Sports fanatics are highly chimpish. With their constant attention to the standings, scores and statistics, they reveal their interest in tribal hierarchy and their need to keep track of the alpha animal. We see the same thing in business rankings, where chimpish humans compile and update lists of Fortune 500 companies and the ten wealthiest Americans. Bonobos, on the other hand, could care less about the standings. They'd rather play the games than keep score.

PRIMATE FITNESS PROGRAMS

This discussion of chimps and bonobo naturally leads to speculation about how these creatures might design a physical fitness program. A few things become instantly clear:

If chimps designed a fitness program, it would be an intensive boot-camp experience, complete with sets and reps, competitions and rigorous eliminations. Fitness would be a grim business, with a lot of scowling, grimacing, character-building and throwing up. There would be pain and injury. The philosophy would be simple: Just Do It.

Discipline would be enforced by high-ranking males with big sticks. Bobby Knight and other macho-coaching zealots would fit right in to such a program. Authority structures and rank would be of vital importance. Program administration would be a strictly top-down process and students would be expected to comply without complaint. Competitors would use all manner of performance-enhancing substances to gain an edge over the competition and coaches would turn a blind eye.

This chimp program would get quick performance results, although the long-term viability of the participants would be an open question. Over-use syndromes and traumatic injuries would be common and careers would be short. Sportsmedicine chimps would be called in frequently to administer steroid injections. Because of rigorous competitive elimination, many members of the troop would be squeezed out of participation. This would eventually create two separate classes of chimps within the troop: the athletes and everyone else. Ultimately, the health of the entire troop would suffer; the athletes from over-use and the non-athletes from sedentary living and spectating.

If the bonobos designed a fitness program, we'd see an entirely different approach. They might use sex as a basis for creating their exercises, or they might just play. In any case, the emphasis would be on pleasure and process. They might play vigorous games, but no one would keep score or track the winners and the losers. They might do some sets and reps just for kicks, but they'd be just as likely to climb trees or do free-form gymnastics in the grass. There would be no head coach with a clipboard and a whistle, no yelling, screaming or head-butting. Participants would make up the movements that suited their particular styles. The matriarch would keep order as necessary, but there would be little pressure to conform or perform. The philosophy would be simple: Just Enjoy It.

Of course, the bonobo fitness program would probably not lead to Olympic-caliber athletic performances; chimpanzee athletes would probably beat the bonobo in head-to-head matches. (In actual encounters, chimps actually do beat up bonobos.) The bonobo fitness program would have other tangible benefits, however. In the first place, the process would be highly sustainable and participation would continue throughout life. Over-use syndromes would be rare and careers would be long. Plus, there would undoubtedly be vastly greater participation by all members of the troop. Instead of being eliminated by competition, participants would maintain membership in the process. While the chimps would produce the most awesome athletes, the bonobo troop would have a healthier profile overall.

GO BONOBO

When it comes to matters of health and fitness in modern culture, it's obvious who's running the show. Our chimps, as is their habit, seize power whenever possible and attempt to exercise control. They organize contests, playoffs, eliminations and championships. They give us advice on how to beat the competition and become winners. But their ways are growing tiresome and their results are far from ideal. The human body is in a state of atrophy and injury, due in no small measure to the overbearing, aggressive, and rank-obsessed ways of our chimps. Perhaps, given the tragic state of the modern human body and our many physical afflictions, we might take a few lessons from the bonobo.

RESOURCES

Bonobo: The Forgotten Ape by Frans de Waal and Frans Lanting University of California Press 1997

Our Inner Ape by Frans de Waal 2005 Riverhead Books

MIMIC THE RIGHT ANIMAL

In these days of chemically enhanced, superstar-approved, spread-sheet-managed workout regimens, we tend to forget that the history of exercise began in nature. Before the days of sets, reps and exercise machines, many people based their physical training programs on the movements of their favorite animals. Ancient tribes had their totems and later, martial artists designed movement disciplines that imitated tigers, birds and even dragons. Each school claimed that, by mimicking the nature of their chosen animal, they could draw upon its powers and defeat adversaries.

The idea of mimicking non-human animals has tremendous promise in the sense that it draws us into a world that is extremely vigorous and physical. Unfortunately, such mimicry tends to be awkward because it forces us to concentrate on animals that are dramatically different than ourselves. Tigers, after all, are carnivorous quadrupeds. We are bipedal primates. Different body plans, different locomotion, different physiology. If we're going to look to non-human animals as models for movement, we'll do better if we focus our attention on animals that are most like ourselves.

FORM FOLLOWS FOOD

One valuable way to study creatures in the animal kingdom is to compare food preferences. Animals that eat similar foods are likely to have similar bodies and similar metabolisms. What an animal eats determines how often it moves and how much rest it takes. If food is abundant and easy to obtain, we would expect an animal's movement habits and physiology to match that condition. If food is scattered widely, we would expect a different kind of physiology and movement behavior.

By looking at what a creature eats, we can learn something about its movement patterns and in turn, something about its muscular physiology. We can then draw some conclusions about what kinds of movement might be most effective in keeping it healthy.

HERBIVORES, CARNIVORES AND OPPORTUNISTS

While there is tremendous diversity within the animal world, there are only so many ways to eat. In fact, we can lump most creatures into three basic categories: herbivores, carnivores and opportunistic omnivores.

The herbivores are easy to understand. Grazers and browsers are serious munchers. Their food is not very rich, so they are compelled to keep at it. When your only food is grass or leaves, you've got to be diligent. Thus, for the herbivore, movement intensity and activity is pretty flat throughout the day. A little munching, a few steps, then more munching. Except for occasional play periods, matings or attacks by lions, your days are pretty simple. ("Long hours of boredom interrupted by moments of sheer terror.") Physical activity is generally minimal.

In contrast, carnivores have a completely different distribution of movement throughout the day. They live a high-contrast lifestyle with radical spikes in activity. Being meat eaters, these predators consume food that is enormously dense in nutrients; a typical meal is packed with calories and protein. Consequently, it's not necessary to eat so often. When you're eating super-rich food, you can go days between meals.

Therefore, an enormous percentage of the carnivore's day is spent just sleeping and lying around. When these creatures finally do get hungry, they become extremely active. They explore, stalk and move with explosive intensity. If successful, they enjoy a good meal, then settle in for another protracted nap.

The third major kind of animal is the opportunistic omnivore. Common opportunists include dogs, but our most compelling interest lies with the primates: the baboons, chimpanzees and of course, humans. These creatures can and do eat a wide variety of foods and thus use a wide range of movement behaviors to get what they need. On any given day, the opportunistic primate might gather plants, climb trees, nap, fend off invaders or hunt. Being intelligent and curious, these creatures also spend a substantial amount of time exploring and looking for opportunity.

The movement pattern of the opportunistic species is extremely flexible, but is not entirely random. Researchers at Gombe, Tanzania have suggested that chimpanzees tend to follow a "siesta model" of movement. That is, they are active in the morning, idle in the early afternoon and then active again later in the day. Likewise, many human cultures have grown up around this pattern, especially in hot climates where mid-day labor is particularly unpleasant.

WHERE DO HUMANS FIT INTO THIS PICTURE?

Like chimpanzees, we are opportunistic primates, adapted to eat a wide variety of foods. A diverse food supply leads to diverse locomotion demands and a physiology that is capable of all sorts of movement. Evolutionary logic would suggest that, for best health and fitness, we would adopt a movement pattern similar to other opportunistic primates, with movement distributed throughout the day.

Unfortunately, many of the exercise practices that we see in the modern world can be best described as "mimicking the wrong kind of animal." Frequently unaware of biology and animal behavior, many people devise exercise programs and sports that are arbitrary or completely inconsistent with our physiological heritage.

Of course, mimicking the wrong kind of animal is likely to have a host of physical and psychological consequences. If you train a cow like a lion, you're going to have a cow with some serious physical problems. If you train a lion like a cow, you're going to wind up with one very unhappy and rebellious lion.

THE HERBIVORE PROGRAM

When we look at the movement pattern of the sedentary American, we see that it closely resembles that of the common herbivore: get out of bed, graze, drive, talk, graze, talk, drive, graze, sit, sleep. Barring some unusual and demanding physical event, many of us are flat liners—herbivores in business suits. To make matters worse, many of us are grazing, not on nutrient-poor grass, but on nutrient-rich burgers or nutrient-displacing corn syrup. Inevitably, this combination leads to all sorts of physiological mayhem.

THE CARNIVORE PROGRAM

It's easy to recognize the folly of using herbivores as role models, but what about predators and carnivores? Would we do better to mimic the movement patterns of lions, leopards and other carnivorous megafauna? Would it make sense to live like a lion, resting for long periods and then exploding in a burst of hunt-like intensity?

Maybe so. Intense efforts with lots of rest in between allows for maximum recovery and the development of prodigious physical capabilities. Professional athletes appear to live this sort of high-contrast lifestyle, "hunting" intensely for several hours, then napping for long periods.

Of course, few of us have the luxury to live this way. But even if we did, the predatory movement pattern isn't really the optimal solution for maintaining human health. After all, you probably aren't going to consume one-quarter of your body weight in meat when you sit down at the dinner table. And you aren't going to lie in the grass for three days before your next meal. No, you're a primate and you like to eat a diversity of foods, gathered by a diversity of means. You'll eat a normal primate meal and then, after four or six hours you'll be hungry again and you'll be up and looking around.

ENDURANCE SPORTS

Some of today's sports are conspicuous examples of mimicking the wrong animal. For example, today's ultra-endurance sports are completely inconsistent with our animal heritage. Triathletes who train for 5 or 6 hours per day are doing something that is completely at odds with our primate nature. No self-respecting chimpanzee or baboon would ever move so consistently for so long. Not only is it risky, it is completely unnecessary for health. No human needs to run thousands of miles per year.

If endurance athletes are mimicking any creature, it is migratory birds. Running an ultra-marathon does not mimic normal primate behavior; it mimics normal bird behavior. Consequently, it comes as no surprise that so many endurance athletes are chronically injured. Human muscle and connective tissue is not adapted to constant hour-upon-hour locomotion; the pattern is alien to who we are. If you try to live like a migrating bird, you're probably going to get hurt.

TRAINING THE CHIMPS

To get a clearer picture of what kind of training program might work best for us humans, imagine that you are assigned the task of training a band of chimpanzees. (Remember, they're our closest living relatives.) Let's suppose that you're the director of a primate research facility at a major university. Unfortunately, your chimps are in sad shape. They've been lying around the compound for months, flipping through magazines, grooming one another and watching TV. They're putting on weight and they're starting to show some disturbing medical symptoms as well. Your job is to get them back into condition by whatever means necessary. How are you going to train them?

Obviously, you aren't going to choose the herbivore fitness program. And, it wouldn't make a whole lot of sense to use the predator program either; long periods of sloth interrupted by periods of intense activity just don't suit their bodies or their disposition. They might go along with the program for awhile, but eventually they're going to get surly and rebel.

Instead, you need to give them a movement program that's consistent with their heritage and their life in a wild environment. That is, you need to give them a diversity of activity, moderately vigorous, moderately frequent and moderately sustained. Enrich their environment with forest-like branches for climbing, toys that bounce and partners to play with. Give them some stimulation several times a day to keep their activity levels high and you'll get results.

PUBLIC HEALTH

This opportunistic fitness orientation is consistent with the advice that is now coming to us from major medical institutions. Desperate to stem the rising tide of diabetes, obesity and other inactivity-related health disorders, public health officials are looking for programs that are practical and effective. Increasingly, they are coming to the conclusion that physical activity works best when it is frequent, consistent and integrated into the lives of individuals. In the landmark report of 1996, the Surgeon General spoke of the need to "weave physical activity into the fabric of our daily lives."

When we look at physical fitness from a public health standpoint, evolutionary logic looks perfectly appropriate. As we now know, sedentary living has produced an epidemic of diabetes and insulin resistance, a condition that is highly manageable with regular movement. This approach works best when the movement is consistent and fairly regular. That is, it doesn't make sense to train a diabetic like a lion. It won't do him much good to give him a high-intensity workout every few days and let him spend the rest of his time on the couch. No, we've got to give him frequent movement challenges, just like a chimp.

VIRTUES OF THE OPPORTUNISTIC MODEL

The virtue of the opportunistic fitness program is that it gives us lots of flexibility for success. If you're an opportunistic primate living in a wild environment, it doesn't matter whether you do 3 sets of resistance 5 times a week or 5 sets 3 times a week. As long as you get some consistent, vigorous movement, your body is going to be happy.

Modern fitness and exercise science bludgeons us with an overwhelming flood of data, clinical studies and research results. From this perspective, fitness often seems like something that is almost impossible to do right. But if we look at it from the point of view of the opportunistic primate, we see that fitness is something that is almost impossible to do wrong. If we move consistently and vigorously, our bodies are going the remain substantially healthy.

The opportunistic program suits not only our bodies, but our temperament as well. Being generally sapient, we enjoy a diversity of challenges. We like movement of all varieties and we like to mix it up. The herbivore program bores us, as well it should. The predator program excites us, but the spikes come too far apart for our taste. Our bodies and our minds thrive on frequent movement of all kinds. Diversity contributes to sustainability which, in turn, contributes to psychophysical health.

TOWARDS AN OPPORTUNISTIC LIFESTYLE

If you're designing a fitness program for an opportunistic primate such as yourself, you'll have a lot of leeway. Don't get lost in the details of expert training practices. Instead, give yourself a diversity of physical challenges throughout the day. Do some strength work, a little endurance training, some balance and agility. Grab movement opportunities in the mundane activities of your life. Clean the house with primate vigor. Work your abs and shoulders by moving that pile of stuff out of the garage. Take the stairs. Park the car on the far side of the lot. Use a hand mower on the lawn.

As you'll discover, this opportunistic orientation leads us away from the idea of a discrete "workout" that we practice at a particular place and time. Instead, the entire environment becomes our gymnasium. Movement is not something to be concentrated in a specialized location at a particular hour of the day. Rather, movement is a way of life.

A DAY IN THE LIFE OF
HOMO SAPIENS

Imagine that we could hear the words and stories of our primal ancestors, living on the semi-wooded grasslands of East Africa, tens or hundreds of thousands of years ago. What would their lives be like? How would they make their living? What kind of challenges and pleasures would their bodies experience? Perhaps a typical ancestor would send us an account like this:

The darkness is palpable here, extending outwards in every direction, embracing my body and my senses. At first I see nothing, but then I realize that I am in a clearing, surrounded by low trees and an irregular patchwork of brush. I feel comforted by the earth below, but now I see bits of light, eyes flashing at the edge of the clearing, red-hot coals just visible in the gaps between the trees. Suddenly I'm aware of life all around me; creatures are jockeying for position in an intricate game of odor, threat, territory and opportunity. Some are making their way to the water hole, others lurk in the trees. A low, rumbling growl vibrates through the earth and a rush of bird wings cascades, then grows quiet. I stir. There is danger here, but my tribe mates are nearby and I feel comforted by their presence. The night deepens and now I'm standing in wide expanse of tall grass. A burning canopy of stars provides enough light to find my way, but there, a short distance ahead, I see sharp triangle shapes at the top of the grass and now I'm running, filled with fear and exhilaration. My limbs twitch in my sleep as I bound through the grass and my bare feet fly across the earth.

My eyes open and my body wakens. The familiar sights and scents of the hilltop camp return to me now as I sit up and scan my surroundings in the early light. Our position is both comfortable and exposed. On one side, a craggy pile of rocks offers some protection. On the other, a vast panorama opens up to a view that is both spectacular and forbidding. In one direction, a low range of hills, a smoldering volcano, a huge lake and a vast swampy marsh are the main features. In the other, a wide plain of open ground sprinkled with small groves of trees, brush and endless grass. In years past, this site has offered us protection and good pickings of roots and seasonal fruits, but this year has been different.

Our family has been sleeping together at the base of a large rock, partially protected by a thatched dome of branches and grass that we have woven together. The grassland is quiet and cool this morning, but the sun is already menacing, promising another day of intimidating heat. I crawl out from under cover, stand and stretch a bit, drawing deep breaths. The morning sun warms my bare body and feet. I am a young adult and strong, but not yet a hunter.

I walk a short distance to the perimeter of camp. As I survey the conditions, I wonder what this day will bring. Already my stomach has begun to rumble, as it has been days since my last meal. No one has eaten much at all since the bad day, four suns ago. My father and three of our best hunters ventured out in search of game that day, but never returned. We are now becoming desperate. Without our hunters to guide us, we are lost and leaderless.

As the sun rises, I greet my tribe mates as they awaken. Their movements are spare and some are obviously weak. There are about 50 individuals in our tribe, a loosely-knit band of family, friends and extended relations. Most are intelligent; all are highly physical and when well-fed, tremendously strong.

I join my brother and together we walk to the nearby pond for a drink and a wash. We squat in the mud and scoop up handfuls of water, scanning for predators as we drink. We talk little, but we're hoping for some easy game this day; maybe we'll have better luck as the season changes and the wildebeest migration begins. We wish that our elders were still with us.

On returning to the hilltop, we find that a heated discussion has broken out over the day's plan. Everyone seems to have a different idea of what we ought to do next. We need food now, but without our experienced hunters, we feel lost and uncertain. Some of the tribe wants to gather roots on the bushy slopes to the north. This is the conservative approach; there is likely to be some food there, but most of it will be coarse, tough and fibrous.

Others say that we must venture out to the far west, a place that is rumored to have more game. This is a riskier proposition; overland travel means the possibility of a kill, but it also carries significant exposure. The fresh memory of catastrophe makes this option particularly unappealing. Our hunters perished in this same area.

I am shocked when someone suggests that, as an elder son, I should assume leadership of the hunt, but I shake my head immediately. I have been out many times before, it is true, but always as a follower. I have seen the pursuit, the chase and the kill, but I am far from ready. This is something beyond my ability. I shrink back to the edge of the circle and try to disappear.

The debate continues as I wander off and sit down on a rock, trying to collect my thoughts. I feel myself sinking into despair, but I'm interrupted when our shaman limps over and squats down painfully in front of me. His face is wrinkled and dark as tree bark; an enormous scar runs across his chest and down his arm. His body limps, but his eyes penetrate. I want to look away, but I cannot.

Without a word, he places a shriveled hand upon my chest and looks into my face. As I stare back into his eyes, he says simply "The ancestors desire it." My mind tries to flee this declaration, but I understand. I am to lead the hunt this day. There can be no choice, no backing out. I nod my head, but as I do, fear grabs at my breath and my mouth goes dry.

Bowing to the inevitable, I return to the circle and declare myself ready. My first task is to assemble a party. I select my brother, four male friends of similar age and one scrappy girl who insists on joining us. We have hunted together before on occasion, but only under the guidance of the elders. I know from experience that going out in a party of fewer than 5 is too dangerous. On the other hand, big parties have problems of their own–more noise, more dissent and less mobility. A compromise seems to work best. With a group this size, we can stand down most carnivores and still hunt effectively.

We gather our tool kit and set out. Some carry simple bows and arrows, while my brother assembles a small collection of laboriously-crafted hand axes, wrapped in a leather satchel. I carry my favorite stick, carefully shaped and heat-hardened. Fully alert to the gravity of our mission, we say farewell to our mates and set out. We are terrified.

At first the going is easy. The territory is familiar and we follow a well-beaten path through tall grass and brush. As we leave our home ground, we tighten up our spacing. Instinctively, we know that it's crucial to stay together. Go too fast or too slow and we'll become isolated and vulnerable. A few arm lengths seems to be about right.

As we walk, we talk little and scan continuously for game and threats. Our eyes track in a fairly regular pattern, high to low, left to right. It's important to look for tracks in the dirt, but we try to keep our attention moving; there are threats and opportunities in all directions. This morning, we see a few birds and one of us gets off a shot, but the range is extreme and the arrow falls short.

It's late morning when we reach the river, a brown, muddy flow that marks the limit of our known territory. Some of us have been here before and we understand the challenge immediately. In order to reach the far ground, we'll have to make a crossing. There's a slender band of earth and logs that stretch most of the way across, but we all know the dangers. We can see enormous crocs lying on the river bank and we can be sure that others are lurking unseen beneath the surface. We've all heard stories about hapless people and animals being dragged under.

As we survey the scene, dissent breaks out. Some want to return to camp, others suggest an overland trek to an easier crossing. To my mind, such options are cowardly. I propose that we make this crossing straight away, but my voice goes nowhere. We argue and shout, but find no consensus. My mind races. The tribe is depending on us.

Frustrated and resolved, I decide that action is the only solution. I speak strong words, then turn and run. Within moments, I am crossing the spit and sprinting across the logs, slipping occasionally, but tracking true. My fear is intense, but my legs respond. I expect to be attacked and devoured at any instant, but somehow I make the opposite shore and with a mad yell, ascend the far bank. There, much to my great delight and amazement, I see my band following behind, running single file across the river and arriving without incident. Even the dissenters are yelling and laughing. They act as if it was their idea all along.

Invigorated by our success, we continue walking, picking our way through a lush mosaic of clustered trees and open meadows. It's early afternoon when we see the vultures circling in the distance. Without discussion or hesitation, we begin to run in their direction. The going gets tough when we're forced to cross a broad, swampy stretch of marsh. The mud is deep in spots and our legs burn with the effort, but we power through the muck and on to the other side. Our hearts are pounding and our breathing is furious, but we can't possibly stop. The promise of meat is too compelling to pass up.

As we get closer to the action, we slow to a walk and approach the scene with caution. Now we can see it, and yes, there are two young lions, ravenously ripping apart a fully-grown roan antelope. A ring of huge birds stands around them, darting in to grab a bit of flesh, only to be swatted away with vicious snarls.

There's no time to lose. We grab rocks and sticks, make eye contact with one another and sprint directly towards the action. Yelling with abandon, we start chucking rocks for all we're worth. The lions spin and snarl and our hearts fill with fear. At first they hold their ground, but we are persistent and close the gap. In the end, the sight of seven determined hominids is too much for the lions this day. Stinging from the impact of rocks and intimidated by our yells, they retreat, grudgingly, from the carcass.

Shaking with excitement and relief, we set upon the carcass and drag it towards the nearest refuge, a cluster of boulders and bushes. But the birds are on us straight away, and we have to split duties. Three drag, the rest walk the flanks to provide protection.

The work is tough. The carcass is heavy and the birds are persistent. We're sweating and struggling, but elated all the same. We keep dragging for all we're worth, praying that no competitors will arrive on the scene. Finally, we make it to the rocks and make a stand. We drive off the last of the birds and howl with success.

We start butchering immediately, quartering the carcass into more manageable pieces. My brother's hand axes are incredibly sharp and we make quick work of it. The lions have eaten a great deal, but there's still a fat hindquarter and a lot of good meat on the shoulders and neck. We eat some of the meat raw, but the real feast will have to wait until we get back to camp. This score deserves a fire and a celebration.

The walk back to camp is long and tense. We feel emboldened by our success, but there's always the chance that we'll be challenged. Once again, we are forced to slog through the muddy swamp that we passed on the way out and now the afternoon sky begins to darken with thunderclouds. We pick up the pace. There's a cluster of trees and boulders that we passed on the way out this morning and we make straight for it.

We're still exposed when the rain begins to fall–huge, luscious drops that cool our overheated skin. Before long, the shower turns to a down-pour, washing away the sweat and grime. Refreshed, we quicken our pace and make the trees just as the lightning begins to crash all around us. The scene is stunning. Darkness and light play across the grassland, illuminating distant hills, low cliffs and small lakes. We huddle beneath an overhanging rock as the rain turns to a torrent, then passes.

Rested and rejuvenated, we make straight for camp. The lightning has started a few small brush fires and we hope that our mates back at camp have captured some embers. We are tempted to scavenge some fire on our own, but I decide against it; there is simply no time.

The second river crossing turns out to be more difficult than any of us had anticipated. The rain has brought the river to a swollen torrent and the logs that we crossed so easily are now partially submerged. But this time there is no discussion and no hesitation. We share the load as best we can and plunge into the river straight away. We move with all possible speed, scrambling for the logs, sometimes getting our footing, sometimes sliding off into deeper water. Focused by a total commitment, our bod-ies respond with speed and power that would have been unthinkable just days before. A big croc slides off the far bank and into the river, but we're past the logs and onto dry ground before he closes the gap.

Finally, just as darkness begins to fall around us, we climb the hill back to camp and now we're running with joy. On seeing our big score, the tribe is elated. The pickings on the north slope have been predictably poor, but some of the children did grab some tender fruits and someone else found a nest with a clutch of large eggs. Together, this will make for a fine feast. The fire is already going and all that's necessary is to roast the meat.

As we squat around the fire, the stars begin to show and the smell of roasting meat fills the air. The scent is intoxicating and we're ravenous. We pass the prize around the circle and tell stories of the day's events. It's good to be alive.

THE WHOLE ANIMAL

There is profit to be gained, now and then, in viewing the structure and workings of the human body, not in isolation, but against this background of life and the universe…

Issac Asimov
The Human Body: Its Structure and Operation

THE TACTILE PATH TO FITNESS

Sentio ergo sum.

"I feel therefore I am."

Lord take me downtown, I'm just looking for some touch.

ZZ Top

Conventional thinking on today's obesity crisis holds that the whole problem can be boiled down to a simple formula: if we simply burn more calories than we consume, we'll lose weight and remain in good health.

This calculation makes sense, but it also sounds incomplete, like a caricature of an immensely complex problem. After all, there's a lot more to the human body than a simple calculus of intake and expenditure. Health is an intricate combination of diet, exercise, stress, culture and personality. It is also very much a product of sensation. The way that we absorb sensory information has a profound impact on our physical experience. My guess is that our appalling state of physical health can be traced in part to the way that we use our nervous systems. Specifically, we're using our sensory channels in new, unprecedented ways and in the process, changing the flow of information within our bodies.

ALTERED SENSIBILITIES

For the vast majority of our 6 million years on earth, human sensory experience has been comprehensive and integrative. Living in a dangerous grassland environment, we needed whatever information our bodies could provide. Obviously, vision must have been extremely important for survival; the ability to see animals, plants, terrain and weather would have been essential. Nevertheless, vision was heavily supplemented by touch, smell, taste and hearing. There was an active cross-referencing of the senses; vision may have been primary, but it was always backed up, verified and reinforced by data coming from the other senses.

In contrast, modern humans use their senses in a less comprehensive way. We now devote an overwhelming proportion of our sensory attention to vision. An enormous percentage of our civilization, culture and commerce depends directly on our ability to see and decipher symbols. Many of our occupations demand an enormous commitment to the visual channel and make little demand on any other sensibility.

Most significantly, our sense of touch has faded in importance. Fewer and fewer people depend on tactile discrimination for their ability to make a living. An increasing number of workplace duties depend primarily on the ability to push the right buttons in the right sequence, something that requires vision and cognitive understanding, but little else. We pay almost no penalty for poor tactile discrimination.

Using our senses in this way has very real consequences for our brains and bodies. The human brain actually remodels itself in response to the way that it is used. It is, as neuroscientists like to say, *plastic*. With use, some neural circuits become stronger while others go dormant with disuse. It is inevitable that this will have wide-ranging effects on the condition of our bodies. As tactile sensibility fades with disuse, we become disconnected from our physical experience and in turn, our health. Without touch, our experience begins to drift into abstracted, increasingly aphysical realms. Our lives become disembodied and disintegrated.

LIFE IN A HYPER-VISUAL, HYPO-TACTILE WORLD

It is clear that modern humans now live in a hyper-visual, hypo-tactile world. Just imagine a typical day-in-the-life example: The modern worker wakes up in the morning, swings his legs out of bed and places his feet on a smooth, friendly carpet. In the bathroom, he touches porcelain, plastic or tile and feels water at whatever temperature he chooses. In the kitchen, he touches synthetic counter tops, plastic food wrappers and polished metal utensils. On the drive to work, he sits in vinyl seats, surrounded by plastic. At work, he pumps his visual channel relentlessly as he works his computer, but his only touch sensation is via keypad, telephone, pen and paper. In the evening, he sits on a smooth couch and holds a smooth glass while he gets even more visual stimulation on the

TV. If he's lucky he has physical contact with another human body, but that's it.

Reading, watching, scanning, viewing—we go from one visually intense activity to another. Billboards, signs, brochures, books, movies, web pages and computer games; we now live in a sea of visually stimulating media. It is inevitable that the sheer proportion of time devoted to vision will make a profound difference in our physical experience. Just as junk food displaces authentically nutritious food, so too does visual stimulation displace tactile experience. Every hour spent in front of a screen or display is one less hour spent rubbing our bodies up against the world.

Many people have observed the fact that, by making widespread use of labor-saving machines, we have engineered physical activity out of our lives. Fewer people recognize the fact that we have also engineered a great deal of touch out of our lives. Labor-saving devices don't just eliminate muscular labor, they also tend to eliminate tactile sensation. If I use a fork lift to move a pile of building materials, I "save" the labor, but I also "save" the tactile sensation that I would have experienced in touching each of the boxes or bags on the pallet. All I feel are the levers and buttons on the machine. By constant use of such "sensation-saving devices," we become increasingly abstracted from the materials that we work with each day.

This trend away from touch has even infected the world of physical exercise. Many modern gyms do their best to eliminate tactile sensation from the movement experience. Every surface in today's facility is friendly and predictable. All the machines have padded grips, all the floors are level and perfectly regular. If you run on a shock-absorbing treadmill, you might increase your heart rate, but you won't be getting much in the way of tactile input. And, if there's a TV screen in your face and loud music in your ears, you'll be flooding your visual and auditory channels while depriving yourself of tactile experience. This combination of sensation is unprecedented in the history of human experience.

ATROPHY

Relentless use of the visual channel leads to visual hypertrophy and tactile atrophy. We don't use it, so we lose it. But more is lost than simply the ability to detect subtle gradations of texture or temperature. As our tactile sensibility goes dormant, we also lose some of the pleasure that comes with movement. If your sense of touch is diminished by constant visual domination, it becomes less likely that you'll find movement enjoyable. And, because you enjoy it less, you'll become increasingly sedentary.

Another consequence of our shift away from the tactile and is that we have also changed our sense of values. As we become increasingly devoted to vision, we simultaneously place increased emphasis on appearance. We care less about how a thing sounds, smells, tastes or feels. Instead, we evaluate almost exclusively on looks. Nowhere is this shift in values so blatant as in the fitness industry, where physical appearance is presented as the ultimate manifestation of health. The before-and-after photo spread has become an icon for physical success, with joyful movement fading to secondary importance.

TOUCH ME, HEAL ME

Massage therapists are famous for promoting the benefits of touch and are quick to point out the adverse consequences of touch-deprivation. The most dramatic example is the notorious Romanian orphanage event. During the reign of Nicolae Ceausescu, thousands of children were warehoused in orphanages and left in a state of profound touch-deprivation. When foreign doctors arrived in 1989, they discovered that the children displayed grossly delayed development of mental and motor skills and significantly stunted growth. The effects of touch-deprivation may not be as pronounced in adults as they are in children, but they are just as real. And, we can safely assume that if touch-deprivation has such negative effects on physical health, touch-promotion ought to have some positive benefits.

Whether it comes through massage, sports, labor or sex, touch is enormously powerful for health. A steady flow of tactile input keeps us in direct contact with the physical world; it keeps us grounded, anchored and integrated. By maintaining a tangible relationship with the physical world, we get a constant reminder of our somatic identity, of who we are. Tactile sensation brings focus and attention directly to the here and now.

No only does tactile stimulation give us information about the world around us, it also promotes movement. This is as old as life itself. Beginning with the most primitive life forms on earth, touch has motivated movement, either towards some pleasant stimulus or away from a noxious one. As touch promotes movement, movement promotes touch. But if we take away tactile sensation, the motivation to move goes with it. Because our modern world is so tactile-neutral, we have little motivation to move towards or away from anything. When everything around us is plastic, one place is as good as another. So why move?

TOWARDS A TACTILE-RICH LIFESTYLE

As we've seen, our modern physical discontent stems in part from the fact that we now live a hyper-visual, touch-deficient lifestyle. Consequently, it's safe to assume that most of us could benefit from a more balanced use of sensation and especially an increase in tactile experience.

The obvious solution is to engage in more tactile-intensive activities. Get yourself out of the polished, padded and tactile-poor environment that you normally inhabit and get some contact with a rough, dirty, textured, high-tactile world. It's no surprise that gardening, woodworking and home remodeling are popular choices, probably because their rich tactile qualities make our bodies feel better.

In particular, outdoor movement gives us the sensory rebalancing that we're looking for. Backpacking is a perfect activity in this respect because it is so intensely tactile. We get to feel the rocky trail, the dirt in our socks, the sweat on our brow and the straps of our pack as they dig into our shoulders. Then we get to feel the cold water of the creek as we wash up, the delight of the fresh socks that we pull onto our feet and later, the fabric of our sleeping bag. Even our blisters give us a boost of tactile sensation.

At the same time, the outdoor experience wakens other dormant sensations of hearing, taste and smell. We get to smell the trees and plants along the trail, the moldy, wet earth along the river, the smoke of the campfire and the aroma of the evening meal. Since we're authentically hungry after a day on the trail, we also get to promote our sense of taste.

At the same time, we give our exhausted auditory system a rest from the beating that it's been taking in the noisy urban environment.

So get out of the house and into the world. Scratch your back up against a tree and bushwhack your way up a hill. Climb some rough rocks and plunge your feet into the creek. Give your eyes a rest and massage your body with the biosphere. Your body will love it.

THE END OF RHYTHM AS WE KNOW IT

It don't mean a thing if it ain't got that swing,
It don't mean a thing, all you've got to do is sing,
It makes no difference if it's sweet or hot,
Just keep that rhythm, give it everything you've got!

Duke Ellington

All biological clocks are adaptations to life on a rotating world.

William Schwartz
Professor of Neurology
University of Massachusetts Medical School

If you think that you're overwhelmed with spam right now, just wait until modafinil is released into the wild. Your inbox is going to be overflowing with offers and special deals. Your friends are going to be taking it and your boss will be handing it out like candy. The media will be in a frenzy. Our already hyperactive culture will become even more frenetic.

In case you haven't heard about this developing craze, modafinil is a pharmaceutical product that allows users to go without sleep for up to 40 hours at a time. Apparently, the side effects are far less problematic than the anxiety and jitters that come with common amphetamines. Originally embraced by the military, this drug is poised to become a new "lifestyle-enhancer" along with the ever popular Viagra, Prozac and Zoloft. A generic version is due to hit the market in 2006.

Perhaps you find such a drug appealing. Maybe you'll rush out and buy yourself a year's supply. Maybe you're attracted by the prospect of finishing all those difficult projects, getting ahead of your sleepy competitors or partying for days on end. But before you sign up for a sleep-free lifestyle, think about what such a drug might mean for the human body and the human experience. This drug, even if it works as advertised, promises to obliterate one of the most fundamental physical rhythms in the animal world. This is not something to be taken lightly.

THE UNITED STATES OF ARRHYTHMIA

Modafinil is a dramatic example of the temporal transformation of modern living, but it's really just another symptom of a larger trend in human civilization and behavior. That is, we are engineering a culture that is detached from the natural rhythms of life. Through a combination of commerce, infrastructure, lighting and pharmaceuticals, we are creating a state of cultural arrhythmia.

In conventional usage, the word *arrhythmia* refers to disorders of the rhythmic beating of the heart. According to the American Heart Association, arrhythmia refers to any change from the normal sequence of electrical impulses, causing abnormal heart rhythms. Some arrhythmias are so brief that the overall heart rate or rhythm isn't greatly affected. But if arrhythmias are prolonged, they may cause the heart rhythm to become erratic and the heart to pump less effectively. Arrhythmias can produce a broad range of symptoms, from minor blips to cardiovascular collapse and death.

Cardiac arrhythmia is an interesting study in its own right, but the idea becomes even more fascinating when we broaden the definition to include the full scope of human physiology and experience. In this sense, we can use the word *arrhythmia* to describe any disordered rhythm in human and animal life. In this sense, we can also say that modern America is afflicted with a profound case of cultural arrhythmia.

ALWAYS ON, ALWAYS UP

Normal primates in wild conditions exhibit a profoundly rhythmic lifestyle. Like Taoist masters, they live in simple harmony with the waxing and waning of light, temperature, moisture and food; only in emergencies do they fight the rhythms of their environment. In contrast, the modern human primate is always on, consumed with non-stop work, non-stop activity and non-stop production. We are becoming 24/7 animals.

Not only are we always on, we are, in a sense, always up. One of our most notorious attempts to evade natural rhythmicity is the host of drugs we now use to promote erectile function in men. But as anyone who is familiar with the male penis knows, this natural function is a distinctly rhythmic affair. Not only does arousal vary with hour of the day and with the season, it also waxes and wanes over the lifespan. But now, with the advent of modern pharmaceuticals, we have no need to worry about the ups and downs of sexual potency. Just take the right drugs and it's up all the time, just like the rest of our culture.

Our constant state of arousal is best described as a cultural priapism. Named after Priapus, the Greek god of fertility, *priapism* is described in the medical literature as "a persistent erection of the penis." The condition is caused by certain medications and may be a side effect of other medical conditions such as sickle-cell anemia. While this condition may sound like a dream-come-true, it is actually a serious medical condition requiring treatment. Priapism is *not* something to be desired.

Nevertheless, our culture remains persistent in its quest to divorce itself from the natural rhythms of biological life. Locked into a constant state of excitation, our culture refuses to go flaccid.

GIMME THOSE OLD TIME RHYTHMS

For young people growing up in the modern world, our arrhythmic, always-up culture may seem normal, but it's not. Today's arrhythmia stands in stark contrast to the natural, primal rhythms that have held sway for many millions of years. In this respect, we are becoming biological deviants.

If we really take a serious look at the rhythms of life, we'll trace them all the way back to the warm, shallow pond, some 3 billion years ago, when life first got its act together. Even then, our planet rotated in space while diurnal and seasonal oscillations shaped the way that organisms dealt with the physical world and with one another; these were the ancient, pre-Cambrian rhythms. Any species that was insensitive to such rhythms would have been eliminated long ago. We can safely assume that all animal physiology on this planet is intimately linked not only with the day-night cycle, but also with other environmental cycles of temperature, moisture, plant growth and animal migration. All physiology is fundamentally rhythmic.

GOMBE: THE SIESTA MODEL

Another way to look at natural rhythms of primate living is to look at the lives of non-human primates, especially chimps, bonobo, gorillas and orangutans. The most familiar of course, are the intensively studied chimpanzees of Gombe. Clearly, these primates adhere to a strong diurnal or circadian lifestyle, always going to bed at dark and getting up at dawn. There's no wandering around in the forest in the dark, no late-night gigs with the neighbors. When the light gets low in the forest, it's time to go to bed.

On awakening, there's a pronounced ebb and flow of activity during the daylight hours. In the morning, there's a lot of feeding, frolicking and socializing. Things quiet down in the early afternoon and then pick up again later. Obviously, these primates are practicing a "siesta model." It comes as absolutely no surprise that many human cultures–ours excepted, of course–have evolved similar rhythms and afternoon down time.

THE ANTI-OSCILLANTS

If left alone in a state of nature, the human body would fall into a rhythmic pattern in harmony with environmental oscillations. Our physiologic rhythm would entrain with circadian cycles, temperature cycles, seasonal cycles and the waxing and waning of naturally occurring foods. Our hominid ancestors lived such a rhythm for millions of years. But over the course of modern history, our natural rhythms have been disrupted by a series of innovations, inventions that we might call the "anti-oscillants."

FIRE AND LIGHT

Strictly speaking, the disruption of natural human rhythm probably began about 2 million years ago, when *Homo erectus* first mastered the use of fire. For the first time in history, our ancestors had an incentive and a means to stay up late. Such a disruption in the normal sleep-wake cycle was modest and was surely a good trade-off. Warmth, roasted meat, predator protection and a dancing light show were real positives. And if we felt the need, we could just sleep in late the next day.

But things didn't stop there. Later, as people began to organize themselves into settled communities and live in dwellings, refinements to open fire led to the invention of wax candles and oil lamps. This extended human wakefulness into the night hours and disrupted the diurnal rhythm still further. In 1879, the disruption became more pronounced with Thomas Alva Edison's invention of electric lighting. Suddenly, we were free to disregard the normal diurnal cycle. Today, our lights can and often do stay on for 24 hours at a time.

ELECTRONIC ANTI-OSCILLANTS

Just as the electric light distorted our normal sleep-wake cycle, TV extended our wakefulness far beyond it's natural dimensions. But TV was just the beginning. Just when many of us were beginning to realize how disruptive TV was to human life, along came computers and video games. The addictive quality of these devices encourages us to extend wakefulness and attention even further beyond normal range. Wide-screen displays and ever more sophisticated technology promises to disrupt our natural rhythms even more completely.

24 HOUR FOOD

We also see the destruction of rhythm in human eating behavior. In the really old days, we were omnivores and opportunists; we ate whenever we could, but probably only during daylight hours. There were no late-night restaurants in the grassland, no 24-hour drive-ups on the Serengeti.

Our ancestral feeding behaviors were also linked to seasonal variations of plant and animal growth. Without a means to preserve food, we ate whatever was in season. This linkage between seasonal food and human physiology evolved in harmony over millions of years. It makes sense to assume that our bodies are well-adapted to this sort of seasonal variation.

Today however, these patterns are dissolving before our eyes. With 24-hour grocery stores and restaurants, we can keep eating without interruption. With regular and reliable jet transport, we can have our food delivered from distant hemispheres, freeing us from the local rhythms of the seasons. If you want fresh fruit in the middle of winter, you can have it. For the first time in animal history, we have a food supply and eating pattern that is completely independent from the natural world. Our eating has lost its swing.

24 HOUR LABOR

Another powerful anti-oscillant is our prevailing, over-arching commitment to labor. Only a few short decades ago "work" was a separate and discrete phase of an individual's life, something that took place for approximately eight hours on most days. Once quitting time came around, we could leave the cares and worries of the workplace behind.

But not anymore. Now our workplace anxieties come with us. A hyper-competitive marketplace puts extreme pressure on all parties: rewards go to those who are willing to push themselves out of their natural physical rhythms. In many settings, employers expect a 24/7 commitment. With modern communication technologies, work now follows us around wherever we go, weighing us down and killing our sense of rhythm.

JET AIRCRAFT

To some extent, all transportation technologies disrupt our natural rhythms. Beginning in the 19th century, long train rides tweaked travelers' sleep schedules and later, comfortable automobiles encouraged us to push on into the night. But none of these primitive technologies can compare with the profoundly disruptive effects of jet aircraft. These are among the worst of the anti-oscillants, especially when they take us from East to West or West to East.

Jet aircraft show complete disrespect for the rotation of the planet and in the process, disrupt our primal connection to sleep-wake cycles. Unfortunately, many of us have become completely dependant on these craft and are now forced to endure frequent disruptions to normal physiological oscillation. It is inevitable that such disruption will exact a toll on human health and fitness.

PHARMACEUTICALS

And then there are the chemical anti-oscillants, the drugs that speed us up and slow us down, keep us awake or put us to sleep. We all know the common culprits. The interesting thing about these drugs is that they are both a cause and a compensation. Some people take these drugs intentionally to disrupt normal cycles, but others take them in an attempt to correct the rhythm-destroying life that we now live.

Unfortunately, the number of substances that disrupt natural rhythms seems to be growing and many people take several in combination. Some are taken intentionally, but others are hidden inside popular food products. Consequently, we are creating a state of pharmacological anarchy, a situation in which substances combine in unpredictable ways. Only one thing is certain; this brew is bound to disrupt the normal oscillations of our bodies.

RHYTHM FOR HEALTH AND FITNESS

Unfortunately, the study of physiological rhythm is consistently underrated in both popular and professional circles. Most of us know that such rhythms exist, but we fail to appreciate their power in determining our health and fitness. We are so accustomed to training and treating the body in isolation that we fail to see the bigger picture. We are so locked into our various specializations that we fail to see large-scale relationships, especially those between the body and its environment.

Given the ancient and intimate relationship between human physiology and the rhythms of the natural world, it is reasonable to suppose that separation from those rhythms will cause stress and in turn, increase the likelihood of illness and disease.

Of course, some of us have a remarkable tolerance for arhythmic living; the body is flexible after all. Nevertheless, it seems inevitable that poorly synchronized lifestyles will continue to exact a significant toll. In fact, given the widespread disruption of the primal human rhythm and the resulting stress on the body, it seems perfectly reasonable to start talking about an epidemic of arhythmic stress disorders in the modern world.

BEAT THE DRUM

One way to get back into the rhythm of physical living is to think like a percussionist. When we start to think in terms of downbeats and time signatures, we begin to see rhythm all around us. The year, for example, is a four-count: 2 solstice counts and 2 equinox counts. If we mark these points with celebrations, we reinforce the rhythm.

The day can be counted out in several ways, but one thing is clear. That is, the morning wake-up is the "1." Your morning ritual is the first strong downbeat of the day. Breakfast is a crucial part of this beat; a good early meal gets your metabolism synchronized with the day-night cycle and makes everything run better. After that, you've got to find your own count. Work, play, exercise, school: whatever your activity, look for distinct markers and try to hit them in time. Then, make your bedtime another consistent, strong beat. If you hit the first and last beats of the day, you'll keep your physiology in time.

INTO THE SWING, OUT ON THE TRAIL

The hard-core solution to our dysfunctional rhythm is to reject the anti-oscillants whenever possible. Minimize electric lighting, minimize the use of clocks and alarms. Early to bed, early to rise. Build firewalls in your life and restrict labor to daylight hours. Resist the 24/7 lifestyle. Tune your life to the seasons. Lie low in the winter and get out in the summer. Eat the foods that grow in season.

Of course, these suggestions are somewhat naive; most of these pre-scriptions are completely impractical in today's world. Much as we might like to live in harmony with patterns of light and dark, for example, there is simply too much to be done now, too many distractions, demands and chronic emergencies. Most of us are just hanging on as it is.

A better solution may be to get out of the house altogether and get out on the trail. Of all possible ways to resynchronize our bodies with the natural rhythms of the environment, backpacking is surely one of the most promising. When we're out on the trail, everything that we do revolves around the natural rhythms of sky, sun, clouds and earth. Get up early because the ground is hard and you have to pee. Move around and try to get warm as the sky fills with light. Eat a big breakfast be-cause you're famished from yesterday's slog up the mountain. Take a morning walk up the nearby mountain to take in the view, then back for an afternoon nap. More activity in the late afternoon, another meal, some good cheer around the campfire then early to bed as the chill starts to descend. After a few days of this routine, your body is back in sync with the planet.

RESOURCES

The Silent Pulse by George Leonard
Breath Was the First Drummer by Dru Kristel

PERIPHERAL VISION STATEMENT

It is a terrible thing to see and have no vision.

Helen Keller

When I first started training in martial art, I used to get hit a lot. Our sensei would line us up in pairs and tell us to spar with one another. "Bow to your partner," he'd bark. "Ready, begin!" Being a raw beginner, I had no idea what to do so I foolishly chose the obvious— I looked at my opponent's hands and feet. I naively assumed that by watching these weapons, I'd be able to track their path and get out of the way. I might even be able to execute a clever block or parry.

Imagine my surprise when I was immediately pummeled. The more I looked at my opponent's hands and feet, the more completely I was defeated. After a few minutes, I began to feel like the slab of beef in Rocky Balboa's meat packing house.

This punishment continued for several weeks as I stubbornly returned to the dojo each evening. I tightened my focus on my opponent's hands and feet, only to suffer their impacts an instant later. I was completely flummoxed by this betrayal of my senses. What was wrong with me?

Fortunately, I was saved from permanent disfigurement by a friendly black belt who recognized the error of my method and took me aside. "Stop looking!" he said in a sort of mystical Chinese way. I prepared myself for an incomprehensible lecture on Zen philosophy, but he actually put it in terms I could understand. "Use your peripheral vision," he said. "It's much better at picking up movement. More rods, fewer cones. Relax your eyes and look a few degrees off target. You won't get hit so often."

I was skeptical, but amazingly, it worked. Over the course of the following weeks and months, I relaxed into the practice and found that I was spending far less time with ice bags on my face. Clearly, my sensei was on to something.

LOOKING AT VISION

As the years passed, I began to realize that peripheral vision is an important factor in all sorts of athletic and performance environments. Whether it's a running back weaving through tacklers or a pitcher trying to pick a runner off first base, peripheral vision often makes the difference between average performance and excellence.

Nevertheless, there's a lot more to peripheral vision than athletic performance. Wide-angle vision not only improves our physical function, it also provides some compelling metaphors for successful living. As highly visual creatures, the literal and the metaphorical are inextricably linked; when we talk about one, we invariably talk about the other. To a great extent, the way we see is the that way we live.

It's almost impossible to overstate the importance of vision in human experience. We are intensely visual creatures. Of all the sensory receptors in the body, 70% are in the eyes. A quarter billion photoreceptors line the neural retina and from there, a broadband connection carries information directly to the brain. This optic tract contains over a million nerve fibers. Only the spinal tracts that control voluntary muscles are larger.

While many people understand the basic facts of peripheral vision—its role in motion detection and low-light sensation for example—few appreciate how big a role it plays in our visual experience. A quick look at the structure of the eye bears this out. That is, each fovea or focusing point on the retina is only about the size of the head of a pin. Only about a thousandth of the entire visual field is in sharp focus at any given moment. The remainder is given over to motion detection and low-light vision. Obviously, peripheral vision must be important to our survival.

BIORAMA

It's easy to understand why peripheral vision would have been preserved in human evolution. As a prey species, humans have long had an urgent, compelling need to look around their world and monitor the periphery. Survival in a mosaic grassland would have required a comprehensive, wide-angle visual scan. Dangers can be anywhere: left or right, above or below, in front or behind. If you focus in one place for too long, you become vulnerable to attack from some other direction.

Given the demands of their environment, we can assume that primal humans used their vision in a comprehensive manner, a rough balance between peripheral and focused vision. They focused on objects of attention of course, but they also kept a broad scan going. They concentrated on food, friends and other curiosities, but they always maintained peripheral sensitivity. This is the default use of vision, the natural use of the human eye.

LIFE IN THE NARROWRAMA

Peripheral vision played a pivotal role in human survival for millions of years, but things began to change with the age of agriculture. As we gained an advantage over predators, our need to monitor the periphery became less urgent. At the same time, we created an increasing number of objects, tools and symbols that held our interest in center focus. Stone tools, then knives, writing implements, an alphabet, then books; all of these narrowed our vision and shrank our sense of periphery.

This might have been tolerable enough, but our visual field narrowed still further with the invention of television and computers in the 20th century. Now, many of us are committed to a single-point visual focus through most of our waking hours. As we spend our days reading, scrolling, focusing and clicking, our peripheral vision becomes increasingly irrelevant and atrophied.

We see this trend clearly in the devices we've created to eliminate peripheral sensation. The earliest was the library carrel. As students know, the carrel helps us to read more effectively by limiting outside distraction and cutting out the periphery. Later, we took the carrel to the next level with the invention of the cubicle, the notorious human pigeon-hole of the modern workplace.

Carrels and cubicles are profoundly double-edged; they succeed and fail by the same token. By eliminating our sense of periphery, they funnel our attention onto single points, allowing us to bring more of our intelligence to bear on the matter at hand, usually a set of symbols. This allows us to push our interests forward and to go deeper into study.

Unfortunately, this process is completely alien to our bodies. Carrels and cubicles create a narrowrama that shuts out everything that's more than a few degrees to either side. By eliminating the periphery from our experience, they introduce an artificial conflict into our sensibility.

Our primal bodies want to look around and scan the neighborhood for threats and opportunities, but the walls won't let us do it.

We can only wonder what effect this has on our bodies. What happens to our physicality when we tune out the periphery? Is this merely a benign loss of capability? Or is there something more destructive at work? What are the health consequences of chronically focused vision?

The answers to these questions are largely unknown. We haven't even mapped the neural connections between the peripheral retina and the deep brain, much less conducted large-scale research on peripheral deprivation. Nevertheless, there are some tantalizing speculations that we can draw, beginning with the experience of non-human animals.

THE WILDEBEEST SECURITY THREAT

Among animals who suffer predation (this includes humans), peripheral vision is an essential to survival. It stands to reason that if a vulnerable creature is deprived of this sense, it will suffer frustration and anxiety. Take away a creature's ability to monitor its surroundings and it will feel stress.

So let's speculate. If you're a wildebeest on the grasslands of East Africa and someone slaps a set of blinders on your head, you're going to start feeling pretty insecure about your predicament. You know the lions are out there, but you can't scan the neighborhood without whipping your head back and forth. You want to eat in peace and exercise some vigilance, but you can't concentrate on what you're doing. Under these conditions, life is going to be pretty nerve-wracking.

In the short term, this loss of peripheral vision may not have much impact on the wildebeest's body, but eventually, the deprivation will be expressed in cells, tissues and behavior. Reduced vision leads to anxiety which leads to an increase in stress hormones which leads to tissue degeneration and reduced performance. If this were to continue for long enough, our wildebeest might even become neurotic and dysfunctional. He might even come down with a case of wildebeest ADHD (attention deficit hyperactivity disorder).

Of course, it's not just wildebeest that would suffer from restricted peripheral vision. Humans would have a similar experience. We don't need much peripheral vision to survive in modern America, but our bodies don't know that. After all, we've been looking out for carnivores for the vast majority of our 6 million years history. Take away that capability, either by choice or by force, and we're going to get nervous, anxious, stressed and depressed.

This is basically what we're doing to students in today's classrooms. First we block out the periphery by eliminating panoramic studies such as evolution, outdoor education and art. Then we demand that students keep their focus on the standardized test of the day. Then we take away their recess because they might start looking around in an unproductive manner. And then we wonder why they get ADHD. But never fear, we keep them medicated to help them focus their concentration even more tightly, a "solution" that can only make the problem worse.

In the end, human children are little different than wildebeest. Their bodies are hard-wired to scan the neighborhood. Their brains need to look around, to reassure themselves that their habitat is safe. If they knew what was bothering them, they'd raise their hands in class and say "Teacher, how I am supposed to concentrate when you force us to use our central vision all day long? I need to scan my world. If I can't look around, I'm going to get nervous and jittery. If you want me to sit still, you had best give me a chance to look around occasionally."

VISUAL RHYTHM

The legacy of our evolutionary past remains with us in the way that we perform simple tasks in the modern world. That is, there appears to be a natural cycling that takes place in the way we use our vision. Take reading for example. In most reading sessions, it's likely that your attention and vision will oscillate between a wide and narrow focus. Read a paragraph, look out the window for a few moments, then read another paragraph and so on.

The pace will vary with mood and material, but in any case, there seems to be a natural swing to our vision and attention. When you shift your attention to the periphery, you're giving your brain a chance to absorb the ideas that you've just read. You're giving your eyes a bit of a rest, but you're also allowing your peripheral vision to do its work. An occasional peripheral scan (a quick check for predators) calms your body and allows you to return to your focused activity.

We observe the same sort of oscillating vision and attention in all sorts of tasks, from painting a picture to chopping the vegetables. Sure, if you're totally absorbed in your task, you won't look up so often, but there remains a certain visual rhythm that typifies our work and our hobbies. If we honor this process, we're likely to perform better. In other words, looking out the window may in fact be a vital part of reading, writing and creative work. Focus hard, scan the horizon, then return to your task. Looking out the window isn't wasted time; it's essential to the creative process.

THE ATROPHY OF PERIPHERAL VISION

As physical enthusiasts, we can think about our visual field in the same way that we think about biomechanical range of motion. As you know, modern athletic trainers make sure that their clients work their limbs and joints through complete ranges of flexion, extension and rotation. This makes sense. If you only use a small percentage of your range, the unused portion will begin to atrophy. Muscles may shorten, cartilage will go unlubricated and neurons will go into early retirement.

But what are the consequences of using a limited fraction of visual range? What if we go through life looking directly at objects, tightly focused on one thing at a time, never allowing sensation of the surrounding field? This is the rough equivalent of habitually limiting your hip joints to a 5 degree arc of movement. We would assume that such a restricted movement practice would ultimately lead to poor function, possibly even pain and disability. Can we assume similar consequences for a failure to use a full range of vision? I think that we can.

In fact, it is safe to assume that our visual capabilities follow the familiar "use it or lose it" pattern that we see so clearly in the musculoskeletal system. If we only use one part of our visual field, the rest of our visual circuitry will begin to go dormant.

INTELLIGENCE

It's not just our eyes that are at stake here. We can be sure that long-term overuse of hyper-focused vision, coupled with atrophy of peripheral sensation, will lead to extensive re-wiring of the brain. We can even speculate on a possible link between balanced vision and intelligence. Chronic, tightly focused vision can do amazing things, but it only taps a fraction of our visual-cognitive capability. Monotonous visual inputs may very well lead to static, stereotyped thinking.

In contrast, an oscillation between focused and peripheral vision keeps the stimulation moving and taps a far greater percentage of our processing power. Just as chronic overuse of center vision may limit intelligence, active stimulation of our panoramic vision may actually increase it.

FORESTS AND TREES

The atrophy of peripheral vision is sure to have consequence, not just in our ability to detect the movement of predators in our environment or players on the open field, but also in the subtle way that we think and respond to the world around us. As we focus in tighter and tighter on individual objects, we become progressively more ignorant of context and environment. We become adept at particulars but we become blind to relationship. Ultimately, this leads to a distortion of human sensibility and intelligence.

Peripheral vision gives us a sense of place and a means by which we can integrate our work into a larger whole. Focused vision can give us isolated ideas and payoffs, but peripheral vision serves as a counterweight, forcing us to connect to broader themes, landscapes and panoramas. Central vision can give us expertise, skill and execution, but peripheral vision can keep it all in proportion.

This leads us to the familiar metaphor of forests and trees. Our focused, central vision sees individual trees, but peripheral vision sees the larger forestscape. Quite obviously, this goes a long ways towards explaining our planetary predicament. Our bias towards focused centralized vision is enormously powerful at seeing individual objects and problems but is almost incapable of seeing larger interconnected systems. We can see individual elements, but the larger ecosystem remains invisible.

PANORAMIC ANTIDOTES

Given what we know about peripheral vision and its importance in our lives, we start looking for ways to bring our vision back into balance. How can we increase our peripheral sensitivity and compensate for chronically focused central attention?

The most obvious solution lies in our sports and games. Here we can stimulate our peripheral vision directly. Simply look for open field challenges that include peripheral challenges: open field running with the football, open court dribbling with the basketball and soccer are good examples. We can even adapt these games intentionally to promote peripheral awareness. Instead of giving this precious experience only to specialists such as running backs and point guards, give every player a chance to work the open field or court. You may also want to invent your own games that challenge awareness at the periphery. A simple game of tag is a good place to start.

The exercise of peripheral vision on the playing field is a good first step, but we can do more. Start by seeking out true panoramas. Get your body and your mind out of the cubicle. Climb up on rooftops, hilltops and mountain summits. Go up in light aircraft when you get the chance. Put a wide angle lens on your camera and shoot the big picture.

But don't stop there. You'll also want to seek out some intellectual panoramas. Give your favorite specialization a rest and turn instead to the broad view. Look for interdisciplinary studies and integrative approaches that knit the specializations together into a larger whole.

If we talked to the artists, they would encourage us to use our sensation in this new-old way: Get your eyes off of objects; don't look so directly at things. Allow peripheral input to flood your retina. Stop and sniff the periphery. Exercise your peripheral touch, peripheral hearing. Don't focus so intently on the object in question. Give it a glancing look and let the periphery come into its own. Pay closer attention to relationship, context and environment.

LOOK AROUND YOUR LIFE

So try opening up your panoramic vision. You may discover some expansive new quality or experience. Or, at the very least, you may find that you won't get hit in the face quite so often.

WHAT GOES AROUND

All of us have pet worries and chronic anxieties that we can never seem to get past. These days, my personal favorite is the problem of junk DNA. From what I have been able to gather, every cell in every animal body includes long stretches of nonsense code, base pairs in the double helix that don't add up to anything. They don't code for proteins, they don't switch genes on or off. They just sit there, taking up disk space and confounding our efforts to understand how the system works. Inexplicably, microbiologists don't seem at all concerned about this bizarre phenomenon; they just go about their business and concentrate on the parts of the code that make up coherent genes.

I, on the other hand, am completely flummoxed. From my perspective, it appears that the genetic code for animal life was written by the proverbial band of monkeys, banging away on 4-key typewriters, producing long strings of nonsense interspersed with occasional flashes of fluency. And so I lay awake at night, struggling to comprehend this apparent flaw in the system. Why would Nature—a famously efficient producer of elegant form and function—create such a wasteful, awkward and unlikely hack?

Unfortunately, this kind of befuddlement is not an isolated incident in my life. Rather, it is one in a long string of anxieties about the form and function of the human body. As I recall it, the whole thing began in 6th grade during a lesson on the circulatory system. Our teacher began by leading us through the fundamentals of the four-chambered heart, the lungs, the arteries and veins.

As I listened, I grokked the arterial system instantly. I understood that the heart was a pump and I could easily imagine it pushing gobs of blood down the arteries and out to the extremities. A nice, simple system, just like a pump in a car. The left ventricle pushes the juice, the arteries deliver, the capillaries distribute, and everyone's happy.

But at this point my comprehension turned to confusion and I asked my teacher, "So how does the blood get back to the heart?"

"Well," she told us, "It just sort of flows back through the veins."

This struck me as a completely unsatisfactory response. I tried to imagine the forces involved, but it didn't make any sense. Something had to be pushing that blood back. Shouldn't there be another pump in there somewhere?

"No," the teacher said again. "It just flows back."

Skeptical, I took another look at the diagram on the wall. It showed the classic cut-away view of an upright human form—the heart and arteries in red, the veins in blue. But the heart was obviously a long ways from the feet. And now I really started to get upset because I had also been learning about gravity. This I knew was a powerful force that pulled down on everything. And if it could keep the oceans from flying off into space, it sure as heck had the power to pull your blood down into your legs and keep it there.

Suddenly, the whole system began to seem fundamentally perverse. The heart was really on the wrong end of the cycle. Blood really didn't really need much help getting down to the legs, but it sure needed a boost to get back up into the trunk. Gravity was obviously the problem, but what was the solution?

In the days that followed, I began to have persistent, occasionally macabre visions of human physiology. Gallons of blood going one way, hardly any coming back. Why, it was a miracle that anyone could survive more than a few minutes of such an absurd plumbing job. All your blood would wind up in your legs, festering in bloated, swampy capillary beds. You'd become a sludge monster, a creature from the black and blue lagoon.

Convinced that just such a fate lay in store for me, I resolved to take action. I began to stand on my head at every opportunity and I took to hanging upside-down from tree branches and playground equipment. I even refused to sleep in a normal bed at night, terrified that I might—as my childhood friends put it—"wake up dead." I propped up my legs with folded blankets and even constructed an inclined ramp for my mattress that kept my feet higher than my head. Only when I was satisfied that gravity was on my side could I finally close my eyes. Naturally, my parents worried about my deviant behavior and even began to whisper about the possibility of medication.

Eventually, I managed to fight back my visions of physiology gone bad and came to accept the fact that my body would continue to function in spite of its absurd design. But years later, my anxieties returned in a high school physiology class. "Valves," my teacher told us. "There are one-way valves in the veins," he said, as if this was some sort of rational explanation. "They stop the blood from flowing backwards." I stared right back at him, slack-jawed at this lame bit of reasoning. Oh great, I thought. Now the blood can only flow one way. That's an improvement I suppose, but there's still no power to move it. There's still that giant sucking force in the center of the earth, pulling down on my blood and making a mockery of circulation. What good are valves when you've got nothing to move the juice? I was unconvinced and unsatisfied. Ultimately, my teacher grew tired of my persistent questioning and I barely passed the course. My grotesque images of human physiology returned and I began to imagine that I would be better off living like a bat, hanging upside down in the family garage for the rest of my life.

Somehow I managed to move on to other anxieties, but years later my problem resurfaced, this time in a college-level physiology course. By this time, I was a confirmed nihilist on the issue of human circulation, convinced that the physiologists and anatomists had somehow missed a key organ system in the lower legs or feet. My professor raced through the fundamentals of circulation and pointed out in passing that venous return was powered by muscular contractions. "Wait!" I cried out from the back row. "Are you serious? You mean to tell me that all those gallons of blood get pushed back to the heart, uphill against gravity, by contractions of the muscles? Are you sure? Why didn't someone tell me this years ago?"

The professor, momentarily taken aback by my curious outburst, assured me that this preposterous explanation was in fact true, that circulation depended upon muscular movement for its operation. Muscular contractions not only move our limbs, they also squeeze our veins and in the process, return our blood back to the heart and lungs for rejuvenation.

"So," I mused when class was over, "There *is* a return pump, only it doesn't look like a pump. It looks like, well, a set of legs." Suddenly, my anxiety and frustration turned to fascination. Ahhh, so that's it. The cycle does complete itself. The muscles are doing double duty. Not only are they moving us around in the world, they're also cycling the blood and keeping our physiology in order. Now that's an elegant solution. Maybe Nature isn't so perverse after all. There's no need for a secondary pump in our lower legs because our lower legs *are* the pump. In fact, our entire muscular system is a pump, a pump that's essential to healthy circulation and physiology.

That night I slept soundly but when I woke the next morning, I had a nagging feeling that something still wasn't right. As I walked to class, I could feel my calf muscles contracting and relaxing and I could imagine a vigorous venous return coursing up my legs. But all the way to my heart? How could it be that a simple squeeze of my calf muscle could propel blood all the way up my legs, through my torso and up my trunk?

It seemed implausible, so I checked my textbook and discovered the solution. As it turns out, the answer lies in something called the respiratory pump. When we inhale, the muscular diaphragm contracts and pushes down. In the process, abdominal pressure increases, squeezing the veins of the trunk. Since the valves prevent retro flow, blood is effectively pushed upwards. At the same time, pressure within the chest cavity decreases, allowing the thoracic veins to expand, which speeds blood entry into the right atrium of the heart.

At long last, I was happy. I could see that there are really two pumps for venous return. Not only that, I began to see why vigorous movement is so vital for health. Moving muscles and vigorous breathing complete the cycle. Not only does each recycling enrich the blood with fresh oxygen, it also gives the rest of our organs a chance to do their work. In this way, frequent recycling becomes a key to good health.

SEDENTARY CONVERSATIONS

My epiphany on venous return also explained the perils of sedentary behavior. For people who live inactive lives, circulatory turn-over is weak and infrequent. Venous pumps are operating at reduced capacity and the dreaded back-up really does begin, just like the nightmare visions from my youth. Tissues swamp, sludge builds up and the body starves for nutrients, especially oxygen.

If you're a muscle cell in a sedentary lower leg, you're not going to take this lying down. After a few hours of suffering in silence, you'll start getting hungry for oxygen. You'll also be getting annoyed by the fact that you're being swamped with the by-products of upstream metabolism; it's no fun sitting around in a pool of metabolic waste. So, you'll get on the neural Internet and send an n-mail to the head office...

"Hey brain, this is your gastrocnemius. Remember me? Yeah right, I'm a large muscle down here in the lower leg. I know that you're really busy and everything, but if you could just send down some motivation at some point, maybe some motor commands to the hips and legs, if it's not too much trouble, maybe I could get some movement going and some venous return, if you know what I mean?"

Now if you've got a good brain, it'll be responsive to such entreaties. "Sure, yes, sorry for not paying attention. Let's go for a walk." But if your brain is on sabbatical or is otherwise incapacitated, it will simply ignore the request and go on doing whatever it is that your brain likes to do. The ultimate result is that lots of blood is going to stay in your legs, pooling up while it stretches your veins to the limit. If your brain persists in its insensitive and sedentary ways, the valves in your veins will eventually break down and you'll lose your ability to squeeze blood back to your heart.

SOLDIERS FALL OVER

The most conspicuous example of inadequate venous return is the phenomenon of falling soldiers. As you've no doubt heard, soldiers who stand motionless at attention for hours at a time eventually pass out, their vascular systems having lost the battle for circulation to the head. This, of course, is the karmic payback for inactivity. When repeated requests for movement are ignored by the brain, fluid backs up, blood pressure plummets and the brain blacks out.

Clearly, the modern American resembles nothing so much as the soldier at parade rest, living on the verge of circulatory backup and impending loss of consciousness. Of course, the brain has only itself to blame in this drama. If your brain is too stupid to listen to your legs on occasion, it will eventually suffer a physiological payback in one form or another. What goes around is supposed to come around.

DVT: FLYING THE SEDENTARY SKIES

If we are stubborn in our sedentary ways, we may even develop pathological conditions and acute tissue damage. For example, deep vein thrombosis (DVT) is the formation of stationary blood clots in one or more deep veins of the leg. The calf veins are the most common sites of a thrombus (clot), but clots also occur in the femoral (thigh) and iliac (hip) veins behind the valves. Symptoms include pain, swelling and redness in the affected limb. Each year, an estimated 116,000 to 250,000 cases of acute DVT occur in the United States. Some are fatal.

Hard-core airline passengers are becoming increasingly familiar with the hazards of inadequate venous return and DVT. Imagine for example, a Singapore to New York flight (18 hours) and you'll get the picture. Long hours of stasis add up to pooling blood, ballooning veins, overstressed valves and a sense of creeping physical sludge.

Airlines have taken action against DVT, not by providing actual leg room for passengers, but by showing a grim in-flight video that instructs people in ways to move their legs. Whether or not such video instruction reduces the instances of DVT is an open question, but one thing is certain. That is, the very existence of such instruction is an indication of just how divorced we have become from our bodies. Just think of it: seven million years of human evolution, thousands of generations of walking, hunting and dancing on the grassland, only to arrive at a point at which we now require video instruction in how to move our limbs.

VOLITION AND MOVEMENT SNACKS

The symmetry of the vascular system now seems complete: a cardiac pump on one end and a movement-respiratory pump on the other. The whole system seems to balance out, but there is a key difference in terms of volition. That is, while the heart is primarily automatic, the venous pumping system is mostly voluntary. We can choose to run the venous return pump or we can leave it in idle. We can choose to move and breathe vigorously or we can stay on the couch and let the sludge build up.

Fortunately, it doesn't take heroic measures to keep the cycle in motion. Frequent movement "snacks" are quite effective in this respect. Public health researchers have even caught on to this fact and now advise that exercise doesn't have to come all in one large block. In fact, it works just as well if it's spread out throughout the day; 5 minutes here, 5 minutes there, take the stairs, get up from your desk every so often and so on. These short sessions don't build warrior muscle or Olympian power, but they do a lot for venous return and in turn, vitality. Practiced over a span of months and years, these frequent turnovers of circulation add up to some very real changes in physiology and health.

EPILOGUE

So goes the tale of my struggle with human circulation. At long last, I have finally come to peace with my anxieties about venous return. Now, if I could just get my over my issues with junk DNA, I'd be in for a good night's sleep.

CORE SMART

When neurologists write books about the human brain, they often begin with the observation that "the human brain is the most sophisticated structure in the known universe." This seems like a fair statement; we'd be hard-pressed to name any natural or human-made object that even comes close.

But if the brain wins top honors for the most sophisticated object in the universe, what comes in second? For this I nominate the human spine and its supporting neuromuscular system. This structure is exquisite in its form and astonishing in its capability. A stack of 26 bones separated by slippery, squishy disks, it not only manages to stay upright a large percentage of the time, it also coordinates a vast range of intricate and sometimes powerful movements. Three subtle curves conspire to flex, extend and rotate in combination. Not only can the spine move in three planes simultaneously, those movements can be fast or slow, subtle or powerful, all acting in concert with other bones, muscles and neurological feedback loops. It is a polymath of movement capability, simultaneously elastic yet solid, shock-absorbing, expressive and, when working properly, incredibly strong.

Of course, the mere possession of such a magnificent structure does not always inspire appreciation or functional development. Just as many of us fail to use our brains to full advantage, many of us also fail to use our backs to their potential. In fact, in our cortex-dominated culture, most of us actually do pretty well with our brains. But because of our sedentary habits, our spines fail to live up to their promise, languishing instead in a state of hypokinetic atrophy. This is not only a waste of potential, it also contributes to poor spinal health and in turn, deterioration of our physicality. Our spines desperately need a wake-up call; we need to develop a sense of spinal intelligence and spinal dexterity.

Modern trainers and coaches are well aware that spinal intelligence is essential to developing high-level athletic performance. Casual spectators are impressed by the movements of fast legs and strong arms, but all of this performance begins deep in the torso. Consequently, professional trainers now spend a lot of time on core conditioning. Core work has now become a staple in gyms and sport training programs across the country.

Of course it's not just for athletes. A sense of spinal dexterity is also valuable in the ordinary tasks of daily life. Obviously, the more intelligence you have in your torso, the more capable you'll be in any kind of functional movement. A smart core knows where its center of gravity is and can make precise adjustments to the movement of arms and legs. This adds up to a substantial increase in our ability to climb ladders, dig in the garden or carry furniture up stairs. If your core is working well, you might even be able to take some of the load off your injury-prone extremities.

CORE INTELLIGENCE

To say that someone has a "smart torso" or a "stupid torso" is not just metaphor. Rather, there is actual intelligence that exists in and around the spine. Reflexes that control the position and movement of the spine consist of intricate feedback loops that are capable of high-speed processing, immense adjustability and novel pattern generation, just like the highly regarded circuits inside our skulls. To say that the spine has a brain may not go far enough; we might do better to say that the spine *is* a brain.

It's easy to think of people with core body intelligence: belly dancers, gymnasts, figure skaters and martial artists come to mind. My favorite core masters include Bruce Lee, Mikhail Baryshnikov and Michael Jordan. Other cases are less obvious. Accomplished actors, for example, are likely to have developed their spinal dexterity to a remarkable degree. If your goal is to express emotion, you've got to get your spine involved in the process. A talented actor or actress knows the rotations, flexions and extensions that go into projecting an attitude. In fact, athletes and actors probably have a lot to learn from one another.

BACK PAIN: THE STUPID SPINE SYNDROME

Core intelligence offers us exciting possibilities for performance and joyful movement, but it also holds promise in the prevention and treatment of back pain. Intuitively, this makes sense. A spine that is sensitive to position and movement will be less likely to be overloaded in the first place and will be quicker to find ways to function in the presence of tissue injury. An intelligent spine is quick to find neurological work-arounds that put less pressure on bulging discs or inflamed facet joints.

Unfortunately, many back pain sufferers take a strictly structural approach to the problem. We feel pain and jump to the conclusion that a disc or ligament has a structural flaw of some sort—a bulge, a tear or a herniation. So we ask the doctor for a series of diagnostic images (X-rays, MRI, etc.) to give us a closer look at the offending tissue.

But in a sedentary population, back pain is unlikely to stem from any structural injury. After all, most Americans are scarcely using their bodies in the first place. Instead, common back pain is more likely to stem from poor use of the spine and reduced sensitivity to position and motion. Your physician wouldn't be so coarse as to put it this way, but here is what he'd like to say: "The reason your back hurts is because you never use it. Because you don't use it, your spine has grown dull and insensitive. You have a stupid spine and a stupid torso. It's time to wise up and get moving."

Of course, this is not a blanket explanation for all cases of back pain; some of us do have genuine structural flaws and we can be grateful that good physicians have their eye on that possibility. It is also true that some very accomplished athletes and dancers suffer occasional back pain that resists explanation and treatment. Nevertheless, it remains the case that, for a huge percentage of Americans, the "stupid spine syndrome" is a major obstacle to physical happiness.

HOW TO

So how do we go about developing a sense of spinal dexterity and intelligence? Many physical enthusiasts will suggest that we begin with something called a "core training program." This seems like a sensible place to begin, although many people are confused about the objectives. That is, many people believe that "core training" is simply a fancy new way to make your waist smaller; they think that it's a cosmetic, neo-weight loss program. Others confuse it with old-style ab training; we remember the thousands of sit-ups and crunches that were inflicted upon us in our youth.

In fact, a true core program is extremely sophisticated and is aimed not at appearance, but at functional movement capability. In a good core program, the primary objective is to strengthen spinal support mechanisms and provide a solid base for vigorous movement. Specifically, this training promotes intra-abdominal pressure and strengthening of the *transverse abdominus*, the wrap-around muscular belt that connects to a connective tissue envelope around your spine.

These strengthening activities are all valuable elements of core training and we do well to pursue them. Nevertheless, spinal support is only part of the picture. To complete it, we also need to think about the skill component, a person's ability to move their spine with precision and awareness; in other words, with dexterity. Strong is good, but strong and skillful is even better.

DIVERSIFY

There can be no single prescription for developing core intelligence because the challenge will be different for everyone. There is huge individual variation in spinal structure and function; Jackie Chan's spine is substantially different from Shaquille O'Neal's. Not only are we built differently, we also come to the clinic or class with entirely different histories of physical movement. Thus, there can be no universal prescription for proper form. If we want to increase the dexterity of our core and spine, we've got to do something different than what we already know how to do. In other words, we've got to diversify.

It also becomes obvious that chronic training in any one event or movement isn't going to do much for spinal intelligence. This is particularly the case for endurance specialists. If all you ever do is run or bike, your spine isn't going to get the varied stimulation it needs to remain awake and alert. Your heart and vascular system may be in great condition, but your spine needs more diversity of motion. For core body intelligence, you've got to mix things up.

ON THE PHYSIOBALL

The physioball offers a great opportunity to increase our core intelligence with diverse movements. The beauty of the ball is that it frees us up to perform movements with varying degrees of speed, angulation, rotation and emphasis; there are millions of possibilities.

The right way to use the ball is to abandon the notion that there is a single right way. Free yourself from form; forget expert knowledge. The movements that you've never done before are the ones that offer the most benefit. A trainer can give you some good ideas, but ultimately, you'll have to find out for yourself. You are in charge of your physical education.

Whatever you do, seek diversity. Do lots of free-form reaching and swimming on the ball, face down and face up. Look for diagonals, figure eights and spirals. Play with your torso in as many positions as you can; add dumbbells and medicine balls as desired. To use the physioball to its greatest advantage, let it destabilize you. Let it disrupt your movements, allow it to mess up your plans. Then, as you're losing control, try to wrest some new movement out of the instability.

IN STANDING

Many old-school exercisers assume that all abdominal work must be done lying on the floor, but in fact it is the standing position where the education really begins. Once you've done some exploration on the physioball, take the same spirit of exploration into the standing position. Seek diversity of movement, diversity of speed, diversity of sequence, diversity of expression. Try athletic movements with new twists, new speeds and new applications of power. Use stretch cords for resistance as you explore diagonal woodchops, snowshovel moves and lawnmower pulls. In every case, make your torso the main focus of your attention.

When you're done with those moves, try 'em all on the wobble board. And then, put on some music and go wild with free-form dancing, swinging, rocking and wiggling. Let your spine express itself in as many ways as you can think of. The more diversity you can generate, the smarter your core will become.

RELATED DEXTERITIES

It's all well and good to think about spinal dexterity and core intelligence, but the fact is that the spine rarely moves in isolation. In fact, the spine is deeply rooted in the structure of the pelvis and hips. Robust ligaments and powerful muscles connect the lumbar spine to the pelvis and the upper legs.

If we want to train the whole system, we also need to develop a sense of pelvic awareness and dexterity. And so the question becomes, "How smart are your hips?" Can you move 'em in all three planes? Can you tilt 'em and swing 'em just the way you want? Or are you a single-plane addict, constantly training your pelvis in a single dimension?

Of course, things don't stop with the pelvis. The legs are also intimately involved in the process and so now it appear that we're going to have to talk about dexterity in our legs and hips as well. After all, if our legs are dumb, our pelvis will be dumb too. And if our pelvis is dumb, our lumbar spines are going to be positively stupid.

This suggests we look for a comprehensive approach that involves all the links in the system. Agility, strength and intelligence over the whole chain will give us a sense of pelvic dexterity, lumbar intelligence and in turn, a happy back.

ALL YOU CAN EAT

We lived for days on nothing but food and water.

W.C. Fields

I hate health food.

Julia Child

To say that Americans have a problem with food is a gross under-statement. We consume thousands of diet books, articles and talk shows every year and we still crave more. We measure and analyze our food down to the last molecule and yet we still feel anxious. Our un-conscious minds are whip-sawed into a state of high anxiety, constantly under assault by food-marketing messages that tell us to eat and drink more of everything while we're simultaneously directed to lose weight. It is no wonder so many of us have dysfunctional eating habits.

It's tempting to approach our food conundrum on its own level, but I propose a philosophical solution. To get out of our food funk, we need to bump our discussion up to a higher level of abstraction. That is, we need to think less about food and more about nourishment, less about the stuff we put in our mouths and more about the things in life that really sustain us.

ONE SURGEON'S FOOD

Obviously, food is an essential part of nourishment, but the human animal does not live by food alone. A healthy diet is necessary, but it is far from sufficient. We feed off many things.

A few years ago I attended a sports medicine conference on functional training and rehabilitation. One presentation made a profound impres-sion on me: a prominent orthopedic surgeon spoke about his experience with knee reconstruction, especially the surgical repair of the anterior cruciate ligament (ACL). As I listened, I became fascinated not only with his detailed knowledge of anatomy, but also with his sheer enthusiasm for his practice. It was obvious that this man lived and breathed ACL repairs. Later, when I described this physician to my friends, I told them "This guy would rather do ACL's than eat."

At the time, I was simply working the language a bit, but now I realize the truth of the matter. This was no mere metaphor. Offer this doctor a choice between a plate of lobster and a new patient with a mangled knee and he'd go for the knee every time. He drew actual nourishment from his surgical practice, nourishment that sustained him in a substantive and meaningful fashion. For him, surgery was food.

So, instead of talking about food groups, let's talk about nourishment groups. I propose that we group human nourishment into 5 categories of roughly equal importance: edible, kinetic, social, experiential and biophilic.

These categories are somewhat fungible and will be subject to change and interpretation. Nevertheless, they will give us a simple way to look at nourishment. The idea here is that, for balanced sustenance, we need to pay attention to all these groups. It is not enough to simply eat good food. We need to nourish ourselves across a broader range of experience.

EDIBLE NOURISHMENT

Edible food is the tangible food that we eat every day; the stuff that we cook, chew and swallow. It's the stuff that we buy in grocery stores and eat in restaurants.

There is a lot that we can say about edible food of course, but most of it has already been said and there is little that needs to be added to the discussion. We know that it's smart to eat breakfast and consume lots of fruits and vegetables. We know that it's best to cut back on consumption of trans-fats and insulin-busting carbohydrates. We know that diets are usually counter-productive and that food marketers will say anything to get us to eat their stuff. There is little mystery left.

Primal diets are now in vogue, but here too we know most of what we need. Early hominids were purely vegetarian, but later hominids and early humans began to hunt and eat meat. Ultimately, we are versatile omnivores. As we migrated and settled in different bioregions, we fed on a wide variety of foods. Some indigenous tribes eat almost no meat, but the Inuit people of the arctic eat almost nothing but meat. Both remain generally healthy.

If we need additional guidance in edible food, we have only to turn to the Slow Food movement. Founded by a group of European culinary activists in 1989, the mission of Slow Food is to return to our nutritional roots by emphasizing quality ingredients, pleasure, community and sustainability. The Slow Food manifesto tells us most of what we need to know.

KINETIC NOURISHMENT

The second form of human nourishment is kinetic activity–movement and exercise. We now know that the tissues of our musculoskeletal system–our muscles, tendons, ligaments and bones–cannot thrive in a state of inactivity; they depend on gravitational and kinetic loads to maintain their integrity and health. When muscle tissue is challenged, it responds with growth and increased neural drive. When connective tissue fibers are challenged with repeated contractions, they supercompensate by growing thicker at crucial junctions. When bones are loaded repeatedly, they increase their mineral density.

In this sense, we can accurately speak of gravitational, kinetic and resistive stresses as nourishment. Our tissues need physical stress just as much as they need optimal amounts of proteins, fats and carbohydrates; in this sense, it is no exaggeration to say that vigorous physical movement is food.

SOCIAL NOURISHMENT

The third nourishment group is social food, the human need for contact, communication and recognition. On an intimate physical level, this means touch. There is no question on this score, human beings need to touch and be touched by others; tactile contact is food. This need is common to all primates. Take away touch and a large measure of health disappears with it.

Beyond touch, we also have a compelling need for social recognition. No one recognizes this better than Robert Fuller, author of *Somebodies and Nobodies: overcoming the abuse of rank.*

Recognition is to the psyche what nourishment is to the body. It's identity food. The sentient gaze of another human being confirms our very sense of being...Recognition is the meat and potatoes of our identity. It is as indispensable to mental health as food is to physical health.

Fuller even recognizes the problem in terms of dietary deficiencies:

Like nutritional deficiencies, recognition deficiencies can stunt growth and impair performance. As their hunger for recognition mounts, those who feel invisible become increasingly desperate. What begins as a deficiency congeals into full-blown pathology...Not surprisingly, people who go without the nourishment of recognition suffer serious consequences.

Fuller's appreciation of recognition as nourishment dovetails perfectly with recent studies on the relationship between social status and health. When we take a broad look at health in relationship to social rank, we see a consistent gradient. That is, individuals of higher status tend to be healthier than those at lower levels. Michael Marmot, professor of epidemiology and public health at University College, London, calls this phenomenon "the status syndrome."

The obvious explanation–that people of higher rank have more money and better access to medical care–is only a small part of the picture. Social disparities are not just about wealth, they are about participation, power, control and feelings of worth. These qualities are major contributors to health and disease. In this sense, people of higher rank are better nourished than their lower-ranking associates.

EXPERIENTIAL NOURISHMENT

The fourth category of human nourishment includes the mental, intellectual and psychological challenges that keep us engaged with the world around us. Just as we feed off protein, fats and carbohydrates, we also feed off of science, art and the humanities. The expressions "feeding your curiosity" and "food for thought" are more than just colorful language. In fact, ideas are essential human nutrients. We hunger for truth, philosophies, explanations and stories that shed light on our world and our predicament. Browsing a good bookstore is like going to a buffet.

Similarly, we also feed on risk, novelty and stress. We love to stick our necks out and expose ourselves to the world. Uncertainty, diversity and novelty stimulate us and keep us moving. Yes, stress can become chronic, overwhelming and physically destructive, but in proportion, it can be highly nourishing. Neuroscientists have confirmed this fact, discovering that learning is most effective when conducted under the influence of moderate levels of stress hormones.

BIOPHILIC NOURISHMENT

The fifth major nourishment group is contact with the natural world. This is our biophilic food source. As described by biologist E. O. Wilson, biophilia (literally "love of life") is our "innate tendency to affiliate with other living creatures and processes." Our bodies thrive on natural surroundings. Hospital studies show that patients with a window view of a natural setting had shorter post-operative stays, fewer complications and requested less pain medication than those without such a view. And we have all heard about the beneficial effects of pets on sick human patients.

Massage therapists frequently speak of the power of touch in human health, but we also have a wider need that goes beyond our species. Our bodies want contact with plants, animals, rolling terrain and open sky. We need to smell the land, touch the dirt with our bare feet, feel the textures of plants, see the movement of the animals, and feel the wind on our faces. In a sense, we need to be massaged by the natural world. Our bodies crave this contact.

THE WELL-BALANCED "DIET"

Intelligence suggests that the same principles that apply to healthy eating within the edible food group also apply to human nourishment as a whole. That is, we look for diversity, balance, proportion and harmony across all the categories. The ideal path to complete nourishment is to "eat" from all the groups, taking nourishment not only from edible food, but also from kinetic, social, experiential and biophilic groups.

Imbalance occurs when we attempt to get all of our nourishment from one or two groups; hyper-nourished in one area of life, starving in others. It's easy to think of examples. We all know people who derive the bulk of their nourishment from a single activity or a discipline while ignoring other parts of their experience: the intellectual who never moves his body, the athlete who never cracks a book or the video-addicted child who never goes outdoors.

Imbalances in nourishment also lead to compensations. That is, if we are deficient in one category, we may go looking for nourishment somewhere else. If we're not getting the social, biophilic, kinetic or experiential nourishment we need, we may compensate by "eating" more from some other group. These days of course, that somewhere else is usually edible food. Many of us overeat for the simple reason that we're not getting what we need in other areas of life. We're not really hungry for edible food, but we're starving in other ways and we feel the need to consume something.

And of course, when we talk about nourishment in the broad sense, it's inevitable that we'll look for analogues to the junk food that is such a notable feature of the edible food group. We wonder about junk exercise, junk sociality, junk ideas and junk biophilia. Like edible junk food, these things displace authentically valuable nourishment and leave us temporarily bloated but fundamentally unsatisfied. Naturally, there is plenty of room for interpretation on this one and I leave it to you to determine what is faux nourishment and what really satisfies.

THE MODERN AMERICAN IMBALANCE

Naturally, there are lots of ways to be nutritionally imbalanced, but we see a recurring pattern in American culture. In terms of edible food, our condition is obvious. We are over-fed, stuffed to bursting with all manner of substances, most notoriously trans-fats and high-fructose corn syrup.

At the same time, we are starving for movement. Professional athletes and dedicated amateurs get vigorous activity on most days, but millions of us are in chronic recline. Because of our sedentary behavior, we are missing a major form of nourishment. This leads directly to a host of predictable and easily preventable health problems.

In terms of social nourishment, we see radical disparities and deficiencies. A slim percentage of American celebrities receive the bulk of our attention, while almost everyone else languishes in obscurity. Some are fortunate to live within nourishing, active communities, but many others starve in isolation. Even our traditionally communal set-tings—schools and the workplace—provide diminishing social contact. As Robert Putnam has warned in *Bowling Alone*, we have become increas-ingly disconnected from family, friends and democratic structures.

For many, intellectual nourishment is also lacking. As TV tyrannizes our culture, many Americans show a decreasing interest in the world of ideas; many of us no longer read books or seek out new ideas. Media mergers squeeze out alternative voices and run independent bookstores out of business. Our post-9/11 emphasis on security drives many of us to chronic risk-avoidance. Paradoxically, our intellects are starving in the midst of plenty.

And of course, we also suffer from a deficiency of contact with the natural world. As we pave, fence and log the last wild places, we kill the nourishment that these places provide us. Pretty pictures and nature videos don't really give us what we need. Our bodies and senses are de-prived of contact and our primal need goes unmet.

It's obvious where our culture needs to go. We need more movement, more authentic social contact, more intellectual engagement and more contact with the natural world. The idea, as always, is to round out our diets, to nourish ourselves all across the spectrum.

Is it Food?

When I purchase a food item at the supermarket, I can be
confident that the label will state how much riboflavin is
in it. The United States government requires this, and for a
good reason, which is: I have no idea. I don't even know what
riboflavin is. I do know I eat a lot of it. For example, I often
start the day with a hearty Kellogg's strawberry Pop-Tart,
which has, according to the label, a riboflavin rating of 10
percent. I assume this means that 10 percent of the Pop-Tart
is riboflavin. Maybe it's the red stuff in the middle. Anyway,
I'm hoping riboflavin is a good thing; if it turns out that it's a
bad thing, like "riboflavin" is the Latin word for "cockroach
pus," then I am definitely in trouble.

Dave Barry

Look at it, sniff it, touch it, sniff it again. What is it? Is it edible? Will
it be tasty? Will it make my body happy or will it make me sick?
Animals ask these questions every day; the answer is fundamental to
their health and survival.

For humans, making the call on edibility has been a fairly straightforward task throughout most of our history. Sensation has usually been
a reliable guide. If a thing smelled and tasted good, it was probably good
for your body. If it smelled and tasted bad, it would probably make you
sick. Not much mystery here.

But now, as we plunge deeper into modernity, we find ourselves facing
a nutritional shell game in which the identification of edible, healthful
food has become an increasingly complex and difficult task. Faced with
a bewildering array of substances that may or may not be good for our
bodies, we find ourselves scratching our heads. Increasingly, the answer
to the question "Is it food?" is "I'm not sure."

This is something that parents from previous generations simply didn't have to worry about. Even the dullest child could recognize food. But today, the situation is far from simple. Are Pop-Tarts food? Is a PowerBar food? Is Captain Crunch food? What about the rest of those brightly-colored items on our supermarket shelves? A visitor from even a hundred years ago would be completely mystified.

FOOD FIRST!

This new predicament forces us to consider a new kind of nutritional orientation, a philosophy of eating that breaks with traditional assumptions and curriculums. We begin by shelving conventional wisdom: Forget the food pyramid. Forget vegetarianism and carnivory. Forget leptin, blood types, portion sizes and calories. Forget the glycemic index. Forget Oprah, Scarsdale, Beverly Hills, Pritikin, the Zone, South Beach, Atkins, Ornish, and the French.

The single most important thing we need to know about nutrition in the modern world is how to recognize the difference between food and food products. Once we've learned to make this distinction, our nutritional decision-making process will rest on a solid foundation. Simply follow this basic rule for healthy shopping and eating:

> Choose food over food products. Eat all the food you want, but avoid food products whenever possible.

That's it, the first rule for intelligent eating in the modern world. If we can manage this distinction with consistency, our health will improve and our anxieties about nutrition will diminish considerably. This may very well be the only rule for nutrition that we'll ever need.

EAT OLD

This Food First! nutritional program is based on the assumption that, when it comes to food, older is almost always better. Given the fact that humans co-evolved over millions of years with natural foods, it is safe to assume that our digestive system is well-tuned to ancestral food sources. Yes, there were probably toxic plants and poisonous meat in our primal homeland, but in general, most of what we ate was beneficial.

In contrast, today's food products are likely to be loaded with substances that are completely alien to our evolutionary heritage. The modern age has given us an impressive quantity of food, but we really haven't improved on its quality. We've found ways to keep food fresh for longer periods and in a few cases, we've added a few key ingredients that help to alleviate conspicuous nutritional deficiencies. But for the most part, food is no better now than it was a hundred or a million years ago. In most cases, this general rule holds true: older is better. Thus, an important restatement of the first rule: Eat old. Avoid new.

HISTORY OF FOOD PRODUCTS

When we set out on our Food First! diet plan, we're naturally inclined to question the origin of food products. This will be a matter of some debate, but in any case, we can have few complaints about early food preparation. That's because our first modifications to food were either benign or actually beneficial. Cook the meat and you kill the parasites. Cook the vegetables and you break down cell membranes to release more nutrients. Bake some bread and you've got a tasty snack that you can carry with you for a few days. Cheeses, wine, beer and other fermentations gave us culinary pleasure, sometimes with health benefits.

It wasn't until the 20th century that food production and processing became industrialized. Thousands of food products were created, but two pivotal events stand out: the invention of hydrogenation and the introduction of high-fructose corn syrup. These are the most notorious food product ingredients, the twin horsemen of our metabolic apocalypse.

HYDROGENATION/TRANS FATS

As you may already know, hydrogenation is the process by which hydrogen gas is combined with vegetable oil at high temperatures. Hydrogenated oils make food more pliable and act as a preservative, extending shelf life.

Unfortunately, hydrogenated and partially hydrogenated vegetable oils contain trans fatty acids, an ingredient that is quickly becoming infamous for its adverse health effects. Found in virtually every processed grocery item on the supermarket shelf, including commercial baked goods like crackers and cookies, trans fats lurk in our food products and ultimately wreak havoc on our tissues.

A comprehensive body of medical research has uncovered a connection between hydrogenated oils and health problems like heart disease, diabetes and Alzheimer's. In his Harvard School of Public Health Report, internationally recognized professor of medicine Dr. Walter Willett linked 30,000 premature American heart disease deaths each year to trans fats, calling the partial hydrogenation of oils one of the "biggest food-processing disasters in history." The U.S. Food and Drug Administration has recently taken the position that "intake of trans fats should be as low as possible." As Dave Barry would put it, trans-fats are the "cockroach pus" of the modern American food supply.

HIGH-FRUCTOSE DEATH SYRUP

The second disastrous innovation in the history of food products was the invention of high-fructose corn syrup, otherwise known as HFCS. In 1971, food scientists in Japan found a way to produce a cheaper sweetener from corn. Six times sweeter than sugar, HFCS soon began to appear in frozen foods to protect against freezer burn and in vending machine products to preserve taste. In the 1980's both Coke and Pepsi switched from a fifty-fifty blend of sugar and corn syrup to 100 percent high-fructose corn syrup, saving them 20 percent in sweetener costs.

Unfortunately, HFCS isn't simply a sweeter form of sugar. It's an entirely different chemical with entirely different metabolic effects. Unlike sucrose or dextrose, HFCS is selectively shunted to the liver, where it becomes a building block for triglycerides.

A series of well-documented studies now links high consumption of HFCS with obesity, insulin resistance (metabolic syndrome) and diabetes. Unfortunately, HFCS consumption now constitutes between 9 and 20 percent of the average American's caloric intake. Not only does HFCS wreak metabolic havoc on its own, it also displaces authentic nutrients that would normally come from food.

THE GRANDFATHER CLAUSE

When we think about this distinction between food and food products, it's sometimes difficult to pass judgment on any particular case. Is canned corn a food product? How about farmed salmon? What about pasteurized milk, coffee or tea? If we pursue this analysis to the limit, we eventually get bogged down in bickering and never come to a practical conclusion.

Fortunately, there is a better way to go about this. We begin by assuming that our modern age has done little to actually improve the nutritional quality of food. We've improved shelf life and added an occasional vitamin, but for the most part, we have failed to improve the actual nutritional content. At the same time, we've actually created many food products that are distinctly health-hostile.

This leads to the grandfather clause. Instead of arguing over specific cases, we simply assume a cut-off point. I suggest that we use 1903, the year in which the hydrogenation process was first patented. From this point forward, food products became an ever increasing feature of our nutritional landscape.

With this marker in mind, we can advance a corollary to our general rule: If it existed prior to the turn of the 20th century, it's probably beneficial or at worst, benign. Eat all you want and enjoy it heartily. If it was invented after the turn of the century, it's immediately suspect and probably a health-negative. Avoid these products whenever possible and if you do eat them, eat small amounts.

The date is somewhat arbitrary and remains open to discussion, but the concept is fundamentally sound. If you honor the grandfather clause, you'll be far more likely to make sound nutritional choices.

IDENTIFICATION

The grandfather clause is a good starting point, but it also helps to be able to recognize the difference between food and food products on the fly. Here's how to tell the difference:

FOOD:

- grown
- messy
- variable quality

- goes bad fast
- requires preparation
- vibrant colors, rich textures
- authentically flavorful
- strong connection to land, seasons and culture

FOOD PRODUCT:

- manufactured
- neat, convenient
- always the same
- keeps forever
- instant results
- dull, bland
- artificially flavorful
- no connection to land, seasons or culture

LABELS AND PACKAGING

If you read labels, you'll find some dead give-aways that tell you if something is a food product. If the ingredient list includes the words "shortening," "partially hydrogenated vegetable oil," or "hydrogenated vegetable oil," the item probably contains trans-fat. In other words, it's a food product.

Another way to make the call is to look at packaging. In general, food has little or no packaging. If it's sitting in a huge bin or stacked in a pile in the produce section of the supermarket, it's probably food. Food products, on the other hand, are wrapped in layers of plastic, foil and cardboard, all topped off with a digitally-perfect graphic-art layout. If your shopping cart contains lots of cardboard, plastic and synthetic wrappings, you've just bought yourself a pile of food products.

WHO PROFITS?

If in doubt, follow the money. Food may be expensive, but it rarely brings outrageous profits to those who produce it. Food products, on the other hand, bring enormous, occasionally obscene profit to manufacturers.

Quite naturally, food product manufacturers put their marketing dollars where they will bring the most financial return. That's why most of their advertising efforts go into food products, not food. We occasionally see an industry trade group that sponsors an ad campaign for say, California grapes, but in general, food is pretty much left to fend for itself in the marketplace. This gives us a another general rule: if it's advertised, it's probably a food product.

In turn, this leads us to adopt a new strategy of paradoxical consumption. That is, if we're intent on eating food and avoiding food products, we'll go against the flow of marketplace persuasion: the more intense the marketing, the less we purchase. Simply avoid anything that's advertised. Instead, buy and consume the invisible stuff –the vegetables, fruits and nuts that you find in the produce section of your market. If someone is promoting it, avoid it. If it's all sexed up, it's probably poisonous. If no one's yelling at you to buy it, it's probably safe to eat.

RESOURCES:

Fat Land: How Americans Became the Fattest People in the World
by Greg Critser, Houghton Mifflin 2003

Fast Food Nation: The Dark Side of the All-American Meal
by Eric Schlosser, Perennial 2002

JOINT EFFORTS

Of all the complaints we have about the state of our bodies, one of the most popular is to say that something feels "tight." Necks, backs, hamstrings, shoulders—we all feel a binding, locked-up sensation from time to time. Naturally, the most obvious solution is that we need to stretch the body part in question. If it feels tight, you need to stretch it–right?

These days, stretching is all the rage. Everyone tells us that stretching is an absolute necessity for physical fitness and injury prevention. We're told to stretch before and after exercise and that there are highly specific and proper ways to do it. Not only do trainers advocate stretching as a general practice, many promote it as a therapeutic method for treating injuries. Given the widespread adoption of this method, it's high time that we took a closer look.

IT'S NEUROMUSCLE

When we think about areas of our bodies that feel tight, many of us think about muscle tissue. If we've learned a little bit of anatomy, we might even point to specific muscles that seem to be the culprits. For example, "My shoulders feel tight; it must be my rhomboids." Or, "My legs feel tight, my hamstrings must be short." This analysis pins the blame on individual muscles, but in fact, the reality is far more complex. Muscles, after all, don't exist or function in isolation. The performance and perceived length of a particular muscle is a product of muscle tissue and the nervous system control circuits that regulate contractions. A muscle without nervous system wiring is just dumb, contractile tissue.

This complexity makes it difficult to diagnose our physical sensations. A nagging, unpleasant sensation might not be a short muscle at all, but rather some hot wiring or an overactive feedback loop. Normal muscle tissue that's coupled with a hyperactive control system may feel tight even though the muscle itself is of normal length. The problem is not that the muscle is short; the problem is that the nervous system is driving it too hard. In cases like this, stretching may not be the solution at all. In fact, if stretching aggravates an already over-excited nervous system reflex, it can even make your problem worse.

THINK LIKE A SKELETAL JOINT

At this point, it will help to turn our attention away from muscles and look instead at the characteristics of skeletal joints. As it turns out, joints are one of the most under-rated parts of the human body. We are so pre-occupied with muscle and adipose tissue that we miss the crucial role of these essential structures. Joints are not simply places where two bones come together; when we start looking closely, we find some incredibly sophisticated structure.

A quick look at an anatomy book shows us that skeletal joints are wrapped with layers of connective tissue and bathed with nourishing synovial fluid. This is pretty astounding in it's own right, but the most amazing thing about skeletal joints is the neurological component. If we look closely, we find that skeletal joints have a surprising amount of neurological wiring. Thousands of tiny mechanical receptors in and around each joint respond to physical pressure and in turn, monitor the position of the bones. These receptors are in constant communication with the spinal cord, giving nearly instantaneous reports on joint angles, speed and position.

The obvious question is, why would joints be so sophisticated? Why would they have so much neurological circuitry? Clearly, a lot of this capability exists to help us coordinate movement, but much of it has a protective function as well. That is, feedback loops help to maintain skeletal integrity—in other words, to prevent dislocation.

EVOLUTIONARY PERSPECTIVE

Once again, this all makes sense in terms of our animal history. For all vertebrates, skeletal integrity is an urgent priority. If a joint dislocates, movement is seriously compromised. If you live in a wild environment, this can be catastrophic. A dislocated knee, hip or shoulder makes you an easy mark for a predator.

In evolutionary terms, the most urgent priority for an organism is to make it to reproductive age. Skeletal integrity is essential in this process. If sloppy and lax joints allow dislocations, your movement will be enormously compromised and you will be vulnerable to the elements. From the body's point of view, skeletal integrity is far more important than degenerative complications that come with old age. In other words, the primal body doesn't much care about arthritis; what it really cares about is staying alive until tomorrow.

It makes sense that natural selection would have favored individuals with good skeletal wiring and joint integrity. Animals with fast skeletal feedback loops and dislocation resistance would be far more likely to make it to reproductive age and pass their genes on into the future. In contrast, animals with sloppy joints and slow skeletal feedback would be more likely to perish, either by the jaws of a carnivore or by the simple inability to keep up with the tribe.

So, for the skeletal joint, maintaining integrity is the first priority. Neurological control circuits will remind you of this imperative, stimulating muscles to contract whenever the joint is in a vulnerable position. It's safe to assume that this deep reflex is common to all vertebrates. If you've got an articulated skeleton, your default neuromuscular programming says "don't dislocate." Skeletal integrity is such an urgent priority that joints are given a hot line to the spinal cord and a powerful voice in orchestrating movement. In a very real sense, the joints are running the show.

From the joint's point of view, short muscles are not necessarily a bad thing, at least in the short-term. They may not allow for much in the way of nourishing movement or superior athletic performance, but they do keep the skeleton together. Short muscles aren't ideal for long-term pain-free movement, but they do prevent catastrophic loss of integrity.

COMPENSATING FOR WEAKNESS AND FATIGUE

Given the importance of skeletal integration, it seems likely that joints would have some neurological "knowledge" of the condition of their associated muscles. It seems reasonable to suppose that there is some sort of reciprocal signaling going on. That is, if muscle tone is low, the joint is likely to compensate by tightening things up. To personalize it, we might say that the joint doesn't trust weak muscles to protect it. This seems to be verified by our experience with prolonged inactivity; if you've been in bed for a couple of weeks, not only will your muscles have atrophied, your flexibility will be inhibited as well. The body is incredibly smart in this respect; the skeleton knows when it's vulnerable.

The same thing goes for muscles that are fatigued and overworked. A tired muscle is simply less capable of maintaining joint integrity than a well-rested muscle. It seems likely that neurological communication between muscles and joints would react to fatigue states and adjust the protective response. A smart body would detect tired muscles and tighten them up to preserve joint integrity. This speculation is verified by our athletic experience. Do a killer workout and then test your flexibility the next day. Chances are, you won't have the same range of motion that you're used to. It's not that your muscles got shorter; it's that your joints told them to tighten up for awhile. This makes perfect sense.

STRETCHING WITHOUT STRENGTHENING

Given the fact that joint integrity is one of the body's most urgent priorities, we need to take another look at stretch-only fitness programs and stretch-only therapeutic practices that are so popular today. For example, let's say that we're diligent about stretching a particular muscle that spans a particular joint. Over the course of a few weeks, we lengthen the muscle and the connective tissue around the joint, thus allowing a few extra degrees of movement. But are we any better off? The joint is looser now, but unless we have done some strengthening work, our ability to control that movement has not increased. In fact, the joint may now be *more* vulnerable to injury than it was before the stretching program. Long, weak muscles don't protect joint integrity. Joints are smart enough to know when they're vulnerable and may even tighten up in response to perceived vulnerability. This makes us skeptical of stretching as a stand-alone training method.

STRENGTH AS THE PATH TO FLEXIBILITY

In contrast, we can make a good case for strength training as an effective means of promoting flexibility. This may seem counter-intuitive, but when we think about the needs of skeletal joints, it becomes obvious that joints love strong, fast muscles. If the surrounding muscles are strong and fast, the joint can relax. It no longer needs to send urgent signals to the spinal cord; since the muscles are capable of powerful contractions, joint integrity is assured and all is well.

We also begin to wonder if the "tight" sensation that we're experiencing might be the result of something other than short muscle tissue. In fact, what we may really be experiencing is the body's response to weakness, overuse or inactivity.

To understand this fully, we need to correct the popular misconception that strong muscles are short and that weak muscles are long. Here we think of the bulked-up bodybuilder and tease him for being "muscle bound." But this kind of thinking is proving to be misguided. Modern athletic trainers and therapists are now beginning to understand that in many cases, weak muscles can be short and that strong muscles can be long. In fact, we're beginning to realize that increased strength can actually lead to an increase functional flexibility. We can get longer by getting stronger.

INTEGRATIVE EXERCISES

With this in mind, we'll look for exercises that challenge our muscles and nervous system circuits to work in harmony with one another. We'll look for movements that both stretch and strengthen. Instead of isolating particular segments and subjecting them to a sustained stretch, we look for integrated movements that stretch and strengthen at the same time. If we're going to be holistic about physical training we absolutely must practice strength training along with stretching.

There are lots of integrative possibilities. A lunge for example, challenges us to stretch and strengthen simultaneously, each exactly in the proper proportion to one another. Walking or sprinting with long strides is another long/strong physical challenge.

All of this is not to say that stretching is a bad thing or that we ought to avoid it. On the contrary, stretching is often beneficial, pleasurable and satisfying. Nevertheless, we need to respect the needs of our skeletal joints. If you stretch so often or so deeply that your joints feel threatened, you may be doing yourself a disservice. If you aren't getting results with what you're doing now, you might do better with some strength training.

THE GREATEST DISCOVERY YOU'VE NEVER HEARD OF

Next time you're down at the pub and someone asks you to name the greatest scientific discovery of modern times, you'll have to think fast. What will it be? Newton's laws of motion? Copernicus and the heliocentric solar system? Darwin's discovery of natural selection? Louis Pasteur's germ theory? Einstein's theories of relativity? Watson and Crick's discovery of DNA?

If you name any of these, you'll probably be able to bluff your way through the conversation, but if you really want to stir things up, you might want to see how well your colleagues know their neuroscience. Tell them that the most underrated scientific discovery of modern times is LTP. And to top it off, tell them that LTP is one of the most powerful concepts in health and physical education. This should get their attention.

WHAT IS LTP?

LTP is neurospeak for "long-term potentiation," the process in which the connection between two nerve cells is strengthened, or as they say in the business, potentiated. The phenomenon was first discovered in the 1960's when neuroscientists observed that a high-frequency train of electrical stimulation produced an unexpectedly high level of excitation in post-synaptic nerve cells. Prior to that time, neuroscientists speculated that people grew new neurons to store knowledge, but this idea has largely been abandoned. The consensus now is that LTP is the dominant process in learning and memory.

To appreciate LTP, it helps to remember that the nervous system is composed of billions of incredibly sophisticated nerve cells called neurons. These cells pass electrochemical messages to one another across synapses, the gaps between cells. Synapses are not just dumb gaps however; cell membranes at these sites are amazingly intricate structures, packed with thousands of receptors that respond and adapt to chemical influences of upstream or pre-synaptic neurons.

While the nervous system is often compared to a computer network, individual nerve cells are not static hardware elements. Rather, they are highly adaptable, constantly remodeling themselves in response to the way they are used. Specifically, repeated stimulation sets in motion a cascading set of changes in the post-synaptic membrane that make subsequent communication between the two neurons far more likely.

CAN'T YA HEAR ME KNOCKIN'?

The process by which a neural circuit is strengthened is non-linear. That is, repeated stimulation of a pathway leads to a sudden, dramatic rise in receptivity. To put it another way, the conversation between the presynaptic and post-synaptic neuron sounds like a neurological knock-knock joke...

Knock, knock...
no response

Knock, knock...
no response

Knock, knock...
no response

"COME ON IN! GLAD YOU COULD MAKE IT! WE REALLY SHOULD DO THIS MORE OFTEN! WHAT TOOK YOU SO LONG? LET'S DO THIS AGAIN REAL SOON!"

WHAT IT FEELS LIKE

Subjectively, the LTP experience feels like a breakthrough: the task in question is hard, hard, hard, hard, hard, then suddenly easy. You struggle to complete your reps and wonder if you'll ever grasp the concept or movement in question. Then, just when you think that you can't stand it anymore, the difficulties suddenly dissolve and you've got it.

LTP is most dramatic in young students who, after days or weeks of repetition, suddenly "get it." That difficult sequence of words, chords, ideas or movements suddenly becomes easy and automatic. Hand a child a musical instrument, persuade him to repeat a passage a few times each week and one morning he will wake up and know it instinctively. The process feels and looks magical.

CRACKING THE CODE

The discovery of LTP has the potential to improve our memory, our skills and our performance across a wide range of disciplines. In essence, we've cracked the code of learning. For the first time in human history, education can be conducted in a way that is consistent with the actual physical characteristics of the human body.

We now know that the basic formula for learning of any variety is exquisitely simple. That is, we learn by doing reps. Hammer away at the post-synaptic neuron with some concentrated repetition, then give it a rest. Hammer some more, then rest again. Repeat this cycle until the pattern locks in. That's it. You don't even have to know which neuron to stimulate. All you need to do is make the reps specific to the outcome that you're trying to achieve.

Now obviously, there's more to education than simply hammering away at post-synaptic neurons. There's a whole host of intangibles involved, things like emotion, curiosity, passion and sociality. These things are vital and we need to honor them. But without the repetitive stimulation that drives the physical transformation, learning will be weak and superficial.

ALL EDUCATION IS PHYSICAL

LTP not only suggests ideal methods of learning, it also leads us to conclusions that are deeply philosophical. For example, when we begin to appreciate that learning consists of actual, measurable changes to cell membranes, it begins to dawn on us that all education is fundamentally physical. In fact, the phrase "physical education" starts to sound redundant. Every time we learn some new fact or skill, we create a microscopic physical transformation in the body. In this respect, all teachers are physical educators, all coursework is PE.

HEALTH AND FITNESS

When we turn to the worlds of health and fitness, we find that the discovery of LTP is perfectly congruent with what we already know about physical training. That is, no matter what your physical game, success will always depend on how you organize your reps. Strength training, endurance, agility events, dance–all are built on a foundation of practiced repetition, learning and memory.

The important thing to remember here is that learning and memory are not just cognitive functions that take place in the brain; they are intimately involved in everything that we do with our bodies, from philosophy to strength training, from poetry to cardio. Just as LTP helps us remember the lyrics to a song or the password to a website, it also help us to remember the physical experience of being strong, fast or endurant. Indeed, more than one aging athlete has remarked that it's not so much that his tissue is weak but rather that he has forgotten the sensation of physical competence and vigor. Just as getting in shape is a process of learning new sensations and strengthening neural pathways, getting out of shape is a process of forgetting.

YOU CAN POTENTIATE ANYTHING

Neuroscientists sometimes describe LTP as "activity-driven synaptic plasticity." This is simply a way of saying that the nervous system is sculpted by activity, shaped and molded by the things that we repeatedly do. Use drives the transformation of the synapse which in turn makes learning possible. Repetition remodels our brains; activity becomes structure. The reps that we perform sculpt our nervous systems and in turn, all the other processes in our bodies.

Of course, the neurons themselves don't particularly care which circuits get strengthened and which go dormant. They simply respond to the way that they're used. This means that we can potentiate almost anything we want. Practice burning calories and you'll get better at burning calories. Practice building muscle or recovering from workouts and you'll get better at these skills as well. You can use LTP to sculpt strength, endurance, agility or any other physical performance quality that you're after. Or, you can do reps on the couch and use LTP to sculpt a life of apathy and atrophy. It's up to you.

BOTH A BLESSING AND A CURSE

LTP is an incredible phenomenon that inspires our curiosity and wonder. Nevertheless, it's important to remember that LTP does not always work in our favor. It's a blessing when the right circuits get potentiated and the right skills developed. But the reps that we do in life are not always the ones that will give us good performance, skill and grace. Bad teaching and bad reps can potentiate awkward, inefficient and injurious outcomes. Do some thing over and over again and eventually, you'll own it (or it will own you). As we know, the habits that LTP gives us can be incredibly strong and may require intensive counter-reps to break.

The lesson here is that it's crucial to begin educational processes with as much precision as possible. Whatever it is you're after, try to get it right at the outset. The first moments are crucial. If you begin the learning process with high quality experience, your nervous system will lock into place and you'll own the skill that you're after.

BACK TO THE PUB

So, next time you're down at the bar and your colleagues give you the same old stories about Newton, Copernicus or Einstein, you might want to mention the fact that without LTP, none of these heavyweights would have achieved anything of note. In fact, without LTP, they would have been mere dullards. This will give you the edge in the discussion and support your claim that LTP is really the greatest scientific discovery of modern times.

Oh, and by the way, you'll also want to make sure that your colleagues don't drink too much. Alcohol impairs LTP, and if your friends over-indulge, they aren't going to remember all the fascinating things you told them about how the nervous system works.

RESOURCES

Biology and Human Behavior: The Neurological Origins of Individuality DVD series by Robert Sapolsky, 2005 The Teaching Company

THE DIRT HYPOTHESIS

What do you think you have an immune system for?
It's for killing germs!
And it needs germs to practice on...

George Carlin

When we read popular health and fitness publications, we get all sorts of advice on how to improve our immunity. We learn that we should eat certain foods, drink certain drinks and practice certain stress-relieving disciplines. If we follow these practices, we'll increase our resistance to disease and live happily ever after.

One thing that we're never told, however, is to heed the advice of George Carlin. You probably never thought of Carlin as an immunologist, but as in so many things, George was ahead of his time. As comedy's most diligent scholar, Carlin was a performer who did his homework. Never content to simply rant and rave, George found a way to rant and rave with knowledge and intelligence.

In his 1999 performance, "You Are All Diseased," Carlin did a hysterical and visionary sketch called "Fear of Germs." He told the story of his childhood years in New Jersey and the wave of polio that threatened his community. His theory, subsequently validated by a growing body of medical research, was that the immune system is trainable by exposure to dirt.

THE STATE OF IMMUNITY

Immunity is a hot topic these days. We've all heard about auto-immune disorders, diseases in which the body attacks its own tissues. We also hear a lot about immune-deficiency, especially diseases such as AIDS in which the immune system itself becomes damaged and loses its ability to fight off infection. And we've even heard that the immune system might have a role in protecting us from some sorts of cancer; the "immune surveillance" theory holds that immune cells can identify and kill cells that are proliferating out of control.

Finally, we may also have heard about the twin epidemics of asthma and allergies that are now afflicting millions of people worldwide. According to a 2004 report by the Global Initiative for Asthma, 300 million people now suffer from asthma and that number is expected to rise by another 100 million over the next 20 years. At the same time, some 40 percent of American children have allergic rhinitis which includes hay fever and perennial allergies to substances such as dust mites and cat dander. By some accounts, food allergies also appear to be on the rise. Clearly, something is up with human immunity.

THE HYGIENE HYPOTHESIS

The epidemics of asthma and allergies present a mystery. Why would such diseases suddenly appear in such large numbers?

One of the original explanations was the "hygiene hypothesis," first proposed in 1989 by an epidemiologist at the London School Hygiene and Tropical medicine. The initial idea was that modern immune systems were under-primed because of the dramatic reductions in serious childhood infections. This seemed plausible, but now a revised version of the theory is emerging, this time focusing on our reduced exposure to common microbes, especially those found in soil.

The idea is simple. That is, exposure to the hordes of harmless microbes that children formerly came into contact with on a daily basis may have played a key role in teaching the developing immune system how to regulate itself and keep its aggressive responses under control. Without exposure to dirt and the alien organisms that it contains, the immune system never learns how to recognize the difference between "self" and "not self," the key judgment call in a functional immune response. An editorial in the April 16, 2005 edition of New Scientist summed up the modern view this way:

> "Today, researchers believe the innocuous microbes that
> children used to pick up from water, dirt and animals
> help to educate the immune system to identify threats and
> respond appropriately."

Epidemiological evidence supports this hygiene hypothesis. For example, allergies are far more common in Westernized countries than in the developing world. They are also more common in cities than in rural areas. Farm kids are significantly less likely to suffer from asthma than city kids.

Studies also show that allergies increase in immigrants who move to the Westernized countries. Asthma rates are extremely high among African Americans, but are low among Africans living in Africa. Taken together, these facts suggest that the hyper-cleanliness of American life may actually be the root of the problem.

SPECIFIC BIOLOGICAL MECHANISMS

We have even discovered some specific biological mechanisms that explain how exposure to soil might improve immune responses. Immunologist Dale Umetsu of Stanford University has advanced the idea that hepatitis A, a liver-infecting virus commonly associated with poor sanitation, may actually be protective against asthma and allergies.

Hepatitis A is an extremely common, non-fatal infection. Since the 1970s, the rate of hepatitis A infection has dropped from nearly 100 percent to less than 30 percent; meanwhile the rate of asthma has doubled. Umetsu discovered that a common immune-response gene, when combined with the hepatitis A infection, conveys strong protection against allergies, asthma and related diseases.

Of course, all of this makes perfect sense when we view it in an evolutionary context. The simple fact is that humans co-evolved with dirt. We have spent millions of years in intimate contact with the soil, walking on it, digging in it, sleeping on it and inadvertently eating it. It is safe to assume that our physiology is finely-tuned to these sorts of conditions. It is also safe to say that our modern isolation from soil, dirt and animals is a condition completely unique in human history.

MILITARY METAPHORS

To really understand the hygiene hypothesis, we need to appreciate the primary purpose of the immune system. As Dr. Carlin pointed out, the role of immunity is to defend the organism against pathogens and hostile microorganisms. That's why, when people attempt to explain the basic functions of immunity, they invariably turn to military metaphors.

As a first line of defense, the most important phrase uttered by the immune system is "Who goes there? Friend or foe?" This question is crucial because the microbial world is incredibly diverse. While some microorganisms are dangerous, many are highly beneficial to the human body, most notably those that contribute in digestion.

The human immune system is not born knowing how to discriminate between friend and foe. There is simply too much diversity in the microbial world. So, the immune system, like any military system, needs training. It needs to learn how to discriminate, not only between self and not-self, but between friendly others and hostile others. Given the immense variety and diversity of possible invaders or antigens, this is no small task.

As we all know, nothing is so frustrating as a military organization that is confused about the identity of the enemy. History is littered with cases of poorly trained military forces wreaking havoc and misery on all the wrong targets. There are few things more frightening than a poorly trained military force, especially when that force is guided by leaders who can't distinguish between self and other.

In fact, when we study immunity in military terms, we see that asthma, allergies and auto-immune disorders resemble nothing so much as "friendly fire incidents." The poorly educated military force becomes confused about its targets and winds up attacking its own tissues. Rheumatoid arthritis, lupus, multiple sclerosis, Type 1 diabetes—these are all cases of the body's military turned back on itself, attacking its own tissue.

THE DIRT CURRICULUM

This is where dirt comes into play. Frequent contact with the microbial world gives the growing immune system the opportunity to fine-tune its capabilities. Exposure leads to the formation of antibodies and highly specific cellular memory, memory that can persist for decades. Dirt, in other words, is educational.

Unfortunately, modernized Americans and Europeans carry a grudge against dirt of all kinds, believing it to be uniformly dangerous. This paranoia stems in part from our experience with the bubonic plague or Black Death of the middle ages. Back then, personal hygiene truly was a life-death issue. When the rats came to town, fleas ran amok and the bacterial population (*Pasteurella pestis*) exploded. Over the course of the 14th century, some three quarters of Europe's population perished.

Through excruciating and terrifying experience, we gradually came to the understanding that cleanliness offered protection against plague; cleaning up our act worked spectacularly well. Public sanitation and personal hygiene improved everyone's lives. But, as so often happens, we got carried away with the idea and went to extremes, this time in the form of a crusade against microbial life. Today, we continue to play out anti-plague strategies from the Middle Ages, long past the point of common sense.

To make matters worse, this quest for perfect hygiene is exacerbated by marketers who attempt to capitalize on our fear of germs. Advertisers warn us that, if we want to stay healthy, we have to buy their products and kill every possible microorganism. Some consumers take this message to heart and become obsessive-compulsive hygiene warriors, constantly on the hunt for every last bacterium. A sterilized environment is the ultimate goal.

WHERE'S THE DIRT?

And so, we create a lifestyle of hygienic insulation and hyper-cleanliness. Modern homes are pathologically clean; shampooed carpets, plastic desks and tables, an arsenal of antimicrobial cleaning solutions, easy laundry and daily showers erase every trace of dirt. On the way to school, well-scrubbed children sit in clean plastic cars, on clean plastic seats. At school, they play on plastic play structures. In class, they touch plastic keyboards. After school, they play sports in gyms and on artificial turf. At night, they sit on a clean couch and touch a clean remote control.

Only a generation ago, children had contact with dirt almost every day. Today, they can go weeks without such exposure. Well-intentioned parents celebrate such cleanliness, but this lifestyle is actually quite dangerous to all concerned. Without challenge, the young immune system drifts aimlessly, seeking a target to attack. Excessive cleanliness makes our immune systems stupid and dangerous.

THE DOSE MAKES THE POISON

Now obviously, it is not the case that we should simply abandon all hygiene. Clearly, the effect of dirt on human health is a classic dose-poison relationship. That is, occasional contact is likely to be highly medicinal while the extremes of hyper and hypo exposure carry some risk. As so often happens, pathology lies at both ends while health lies in the middle.

There are genuine dangers in the microbial world and there are sensible counter-measures that we should practice. If you cut your finger while digging a hole, it's still a good idea to wash up and bandage the cut. If you're going to remove someone's gall bladder, you really should scrub up before you begin. Clean food preparation facilities, clean restrooms, clean hospitals—these things will always be important. Nevertheless, we can and do go too far in our dirt avoidance.

HAVE A FIELD DAY

Right now, the hygiene hypothesis is making the rounds in the scientific journals and is even getting some exposure in the popular press. Momentum is gathering and the trend is clear. Within the next decade, dirt is going to get really big. We'll hear more and more physicians talking about dirt, and public health administrators will even begin to recommend daily "dirt time" for children.

Childhood is clearly the most important window of opportunity for immune system education, but we might also suppose that occasional contact with dirt would be beneficial for adults as well. The immune system, like every other system in the body, needs occasional reminders about its relationship with the physical world. Our bones need reminders about gravitation and kinetic forces, our muscles need occasional wake-up calls with vigorous movement, and our cognitive powers need refreshing stimulus in the form of new puzzles and conundrums.

Likewise, our immune memory needs to be refreshed from time to time. If you're living in a sanitized suburban bubble, your immune system will eventually get a case of atrophy and immuno-amnesia. We know that some vaccines wear off after a few decades; so too for garden variety immunity.

With this in mind, start looking for activities that offer dirt contact. Backpacking, climbing, mountain biking, rugby, gardening, landscaping and trail-building are all good candidates. Any game, sport or occupation that puts us in contact with the soil is likely to be good for immune education.

So go outside, get some dirt under your fingernails and leave it there for awhile. Take off your shoes and wiggle your toes in the mud. Leave your Handi-wipes at home and skip a few showers. Be a grub every now and then. It's all part of your education.

REFERENCES

Carlin, George: You Are All Diseased "Fear of Germs"
"Asthma and the Curse of Cleanliness" Discover January 2004
New Scientist April 16, 2005 "Love your bugs" editorial
New Scientist April 16, 2005 "Filthy friends" by Garry Hamilton

Mind, Body, Medicine

If we could give every individual the right amount of
nourishment and exercise, not too little and not too much,
we would have found the safest way to health.

Hippocrates

ABOVE THE BREASTBONE

When we talk about our bodies and how they work, we're bound to hear a story about someone with a case of hypochondria. Everyone seems to know at least one. These individuals have a curious preoccupation with disease and deformity. They complain about every physical sensation, convinced that the slightest unusual feeling signals the onset of a dreadful disease or disability. They constantly scan their tissue, always on the alert for impending and inevitable breakdown. Eventually, they become the butt of a thousand jokes. (Did you hear what the hypochondriac had engraved on his headstone? It said, "See, I told you so.")

In today's world we use the words "hypochondria" and "hypochondriac" to describe people with excessive, abnormal concern for their health. Sometimes this takes the form of a harmless neurosis; other times it is an expression of serious mental pathology that requires professional attention.

The word is actually something of a misnomer, however. It is a derivative of the Greek *hypo*, 'under' and *chondros*, 'cartilage of the breastbone.' This usage was originally based on the belief that dire humor and melancholy was caused by black bile, supposedly secreted by the spleen or kidneys. Apparently, an early physician associated the condition with pathology in the region below the breast bone and the label stuck. Today we use the term to describe people who complain about every ache and pain while predicting an imminent health catastrophe.

But if we can be hypochondriacs, can we not also be *hyper*chondriacs? Strictly speaking, this is not accurate terminology because the word would simply mean "above the breastbone." But for our purposes we can take it to mean the opposite of hypochondria, people who have below-normal or inadequate concerns about their health. We all know how hypochondriacs think and behave—a mortal illness embedded in every meal and a fatal prognosis in every sensation—but how would a hyperchondriac think and behave?

Just imagine the difference. Where the hypochondriac sees only threats and degeneration, the hyperchondriac sees only benefits and potential pleasures. Where the hypochondriac sees only danger, the hyperchondriac sees only opportunity. The hypochondriac is a psychosomatic pessimist, but the hyperchondriac is a psychosomatic optimist. Faced with identical health challenges, each will give an entirely different interpretation. The hypochondriac looks at the food on his plate and says, "The fat and toxins in this meat will give me cancer, heart disease and irritable bowel syndrome." The hyperchondriac says, "The protein in this meat will make me stronger, faster and smarter."

Even the most casual student of the human body now knows that outlook and perspective are pivotal factors in the creation of the health and fitness of our bodies. Attitude shapes the way we interpret the relationship between our bodies and the environment. The hypochondriac says "The environment is hostile and my body is fragile. If I relax my vigilance for a second, I'll be destroyed." The hyperchondriac will say just the opposite. "The environment is a playground and my body is wild, exuberant and resilient. If I relax my vigilance, I'll miss an opportunity for outrageous fun."

Einstein suggested that the most important question we can ask is "Is the universe friendly?" For the hypochondriac, the answer is a definitive no; injury and illness are constantly lurking, ready to pounce on every weakness. For the hyperchondriac, the answer is an enthusiastic yes. The glass is not only half full, it contains a magic elixir that quenches our thirst and nourishes our celebration. Who cares if it has a few noxious ingredients in the mix? We've got a life to live.

Obviously, we can go too far with hyperchondria. Intelligence demands that we pay some attention to the realities of physiology and keep an eye on potential diseases and injuries. We cannot simply ignore the forces of gravity, biochemistry and microbial infection. There are some authentic threats to our bodies that we would do well to avoid.

But by the same token, we can and do go too far with our hypochondria. Some comics have built entire routines around the popular observation that everything seems to cause cancer. Read enough newspapers and you will come to see an antibiotic-resistant bacteria on every food counter, a SARS virus on every stranger's breath, a debilitating back injury in every physical movement and a cardiac arrest on every plate. Whipsawed between actual health threats and a marketing industry that strives to maximize consumer anxiety, many Americans now inhabit a health culture that is distinctly paranoid.

The question now becomes "Who is healthier?"—the anxious fanatic who can't eat a meal without consulting his cardiologist or the wild exuberant who finds authentic pleasure and performance enhancement in the four food groups (saturated fat, alcohol, sugar and caffeine)? The former might have more years in his life, but the latter might have more life in his years.

Today we pride ourselves in being "health-conscious," but this now threatens to become "health-hyperconsciousness." We are becoming obsessed and this, like any extreme, is unhealthy. Clearly, there must be a middle ground.

THERAPEUTIC DECEPTIONS

He who can believe himself well, will be well.

Ovid
Roman classical poet

Like many writers, I enjoy a good cup of coffee in the morning, always on the lookout for inspiration in any possible form. And so it was that, during the course of writing this book, I stocked my kitchen with a generous supply of premium coffee, carefully selected from the bins at the local market. I enjoyed the brew and cooked up a steaming cup almost every morning. All was well in my kitchen; I was a happy, fulfilled and wide-awake java drinker.

But after a couple of weeks, my supply was getting low and so I ventured back to the market. As I looked at the bins to make my selection, I did a doubletake. The label on my favorite brand displayed familiar colors and images, but in the fine print at the bottom I noticed the word *decaffeinated*.

As you can imagine, I was horrified. Suddenly I realized that I had been drinking decaf for the last three weeks! All those zippy mornings of alert and focused concentration, all those creative ideas that coursed through my system had been stimulated, not by the actual properties of the bean itself, but by my imagination. It was belief, not chemistry, that woke me up and got my motor running. I was, depending on how you want to look at it, either a victim or a beneficiary of the placebo effect.

THEY'RE EVERYWHERE

When we talk about placebos, most of us think of those little white pills, for these are the classic placebos. But in fact, placebo effects are everywhere in our world and they are at work not just with sugar pills, but with every kind of medical and fitness program that we can name. Placebo effects are at work in surgery, chemotherapy, weight lifting, acupuncture, biofeedback, yoga, vitamin supplementation, psychotherapy, chiropractic, massage and a walk in the park. In fact, it is virtually impossible to escape the placebo effect in health and fitness; our minds are always at work evaluating the prospects for health and disease. If you believe that you are participating in a powerful therapeutic process, your condition will probably improve. (We might even say that this very book has placebo effects. Don't you feel more educated and empowered already?)

The universality of the placebo effect was vividly demonstrated at the 2001 meeting of the American Academy of Orthopedic Physicians when J. Bruce Moseley Jr., MD of Baylor University presented the results of his study comparing the efficacy of various treatments on knee osteoarthritis. Patients were divided into three groups: one received arthroscopic "debridement" (trimming and smoothing the internal surfaces of the joint), another received "lavage" (flushing or irrigation of the inside of the joint with saline) and the third received placebo arthroscopy (three stab wounds in the skin, but no actual arthroscopic procedure.)

Outcomes were similar for all groups, with the placebo group doing as well or better by some measures. "Patient expectation was the single best predictor of outcome," Moseley reported. "This study shows that the act of patients putting their faith in our hands carries a profound impact, and it can influence outcome as much or more than any treatment that we render."

There are more examples. In her New York Times Magazine article, "The Placebo Prescription" author Margaret Talbot cited several lesser-known cases of placebo effects. In one study, doctors successfully eliminated warts by painting them with a brightly colored, inert dye and promising patients the warts would be gone when the color wore off. In a study of asthmatics, researchers found that they could produce dilation of the airways by simply telling people they were inhaling a bronchiodilator, even when the device was a fake. Patients suffering pain after wisdom-tooth extraction got just as much relief from a fake application of ultrasound as from a real one.

A truly spectacular example of the placebo effect took place at the University of Kansas Medical Center in the late 1950's. Researchers conducted a trial of a procedure then commonly used for angina pectoris (chest pain caused by insufficient blood supply to the heart). Doctors made incisions in the chest and tied knots in two arteries in an attempt to increase blood flow to the heart. One set of patients received the authentic surgical procedure. Another set received only a chest incision, but no further surgery. Of the patients who received the actual surgery, 76 percent improved, while 100 percent of the placebo group got better. The procedure, known as internal mammary ligation, was soon abandoned.

Placebo effects are so universal in human experience that it would not be an exaggeration to say that, prior to the advent of authentically effective agents such as antiseptics and antibiotics, the entire history of medicine itself has been the story of the placebo effect. Did tribal shamans get results with seriously ill patients? Of course they did, but in most cases, those improvements were powered not by genuine therapeutic effects of rituals, herbs or spells, but by the patient's belief in the method and the practitioner. This effect is still at work in modern research hospitals, alternative clinics, and athletic training facilities.

(Just as we are influenced by placebos, we are also influenced by processes and substances that we believe to be harmful. These are called nocebos. If you live near an overhead power-line and believe that power lines cause cancer, that power-line will act as a nocebo, regardless of the actual physiological effects.)

PLANET OF PLACEBOS

In the popular press, the placebo effect is presented as an interesting but trivial quirk of human psychology. But it is not at all clear where the boundaries lie. After all, it's not as if the mind-body relationship stops working when we leave the doctor's office or the clinic. Our minds are always weighing the prospects of life and death, health and disease. Millions of years of evolution have given us an acute sensitivity to such issues.

Most people understand that a placebo is a fake substance that tricks us into healing our own bodies. But why just substances? Why not events? Why not words? Why not body language? Why not a wink? How about the weather? If a dummy sugar pill can have a placebo effect on my body, why not a song on the radio or a phone call from an old friend? Truth be told, almost anything can have a placebo or nocebo effect on the human organism. Everything that we see, touch and hear has the potential for medical meaning. Belief is always working in everything that we do. In this sense, the famous "sugar pill" becomes a metaphor for any experience that we believe is beneficial. We are deeply irrational beings, always looking for clues, suggestions and reassurance. Medical meaning is all around us. Omens are everywhere.

Consequently, it should not surprise us that placebo effects are at work, not just in matters of disease and illness, but in matters of physical fitness, training and conditioning. If a little white pill can have a body-altering placebo effect, so can a high-tech weight machine, a clever combination of sets and reps or an exotic method of mind-body integration. Every method works for someone. All physical training programs, from Pilates to bodybuilding to ultra-marathons to martial art, get some results. Even a program that is biomechanically or physiologically unsound, if administered with enough confidence (or con) will produce some improvements in strength, power, fitness or weight loss. Belief powers the body.

If you believe that your exercise program is the right one for you, it will be more effective than one you don't believe in (up to a point). This simple fact makes a mockery of any program or method that proclaims to be the "ultimate." Whether or not something is the "ultimate" depends on what we believe, and everyone has different beliefs.

CHALLENGES AND COMPLICATIONS

In both popular and professional culture, the placebo effect is consistently under-rated and under-appreciated. Most people, if they think about it at all, dismiss the placebo effect as a minor curiosity in medical philosophy, an odd glitch in our psychophysical system. You can listen to a thousand conversations about health and fitness and while you'll hear lots about diet, supplements and weight loss, you'll rarely hear any mention of the placebo effect. It just doesn't get the headlines.

But in truth, the placebo effect is tectonic in its implications. If we take this seriously, as we must, we find that we have to rearrange our entire health and fitness landscape, our assumptions, and our beliefs. The placebo effect is no minor irritant; it is cataclysmic.

In the first place, the placebo effect undermines our belief in the anecdotal "evidence" and testimonials we hear from one another. Suddenly, personal stories of health and fitness success become inherently suspect; when we factor in the power of human belief, the stories offered up by any one individual just don't carry much weight. Just because a substance or program helped your neighbor doesn't mean it actually works; he may be under placebo influence. Just because it "worked" for the sport star or actor means even less. This, of course, negates just about every health and fitness advertisement that we're exposed to. Even if health and fitness marketers were fundamentally honest, their claims would still be diluted by placebo realities.

In the second place, the placebo effect undermines our quest for certainty and reliable knowledge. Nowhere is this more evident than in health care, medicine and its little sister, fitness. We want doctors, therapists and trainers with rock-solid knowledge; if they start waffling or hedging their bets by talking about placebo exceptions, we'll go elsewhere.

Ultimately, the placebo effect complicates everything we do in health and fitness and makes it impossible to make blanket, black and white declarations about any substance, discipline, or method. There can be no health or fitness absolutism; there are just too many psychological variables. Just because a program "gets results" for some people does not mean that it is authentically effective. What works for one person may not work for someone else. Just as our bodies are different, our minds respond in their own unique ways. One man's placebo is another man's nocebo.

EVALUATING HEALTH CARE CLAIMS

As intelligent consumers of medical care and fitness methods, we would do well to keep placebo effects in mind when evaluating the merits of various health care practices and substances that we see advertised in health food stores and newspapers. Just because a practice produces occasional therapeutic results does not mean that it is authentically effective. In fact, in the world of health care and fitness, almost every method and substance gets some results.

The only way to measure the true effectiveness of a therapeutic method, substance or training practice is with a randomized, double-blind clinical trial, preferably many such trials. This is the gold standard for medical evaluation. Take the method or substance in question, "blind" the process so that neither the patient or the administrator knows who's getting the dummy treatment and record the results. As medical and fitness consumers, this is the first question we should be asking when considering a new treatment method or program: "Has it been studied in a double-blind clinical trial?"

Going further, we need to stay informed by reading whatever research results we can get our hands on. Find out what actually works. Ask questions. Do sit ups really make your back healthier? Does weight lifting really decrease your flexibility? Does massage really help recovery time? Does chiropractic provide any benefit? Does a high-protein diet really promote weight loss? Do supplements perform as advertised? Does craniosacral massage or homeopathy do anything at all?

Be skeptical, not just of anecdotal reports but of research itself. Don't base your opinions or beliefs on any single study. Health and medical research varies in quality, just like everything else. Thousands of studies are conducted every year. Some are poorly executed, some are too small to be significant. Just because a result was reported in a medical journal does not mean that it's the last word on the subject. The results, even if convincing, need to be repeated by others in the field.

THE ULTIMATE CHALLENGE: WHAT ABOUT ME?

Skepticism is a good general practice, but it's only the beginning. It's one thing to recognize placebo effects in other people's minds and to recognize the possibility that they might be deceived by belief. What makes the issue even more complicated is that our understanding of placebo effects forces us to doubt even our own personal experience in matters of fitness and health.

In the pre-placebo days, we could at least count on the reliability of the things that we saw, felt and experienced first hand. You've got an illness or a nagging injury and you start taking a new medication; a few days later you're feeling better. You know that the medication worked; there's no question in your mind because, after all, you experienced the event first hand. And now you feel confident in telling your friends that this pill, potion or program really does what it claims to do.

But you can't do it. If we're going to be intellectually honest, we've got to report therapeutic events this way: "Well I took the recommended dosage and I did get better, but it might have been a placebo effect." The same goes for all our fitness programs and techniques. "Yeah, I did the new training program and scored my personal best, but who knows?"

This is one of those difficult by-products of scientific advancement that many of us would just as soon do without. Things would have been a lot simpler if medical researchers hadn't discovered the nature of this mind-body conversation. But now, like it or not, we've got to acknowledge our capacity for self-deception and placebo-driven healing. Otherwise, we'll be forced into a truly absurd position, one that says "placebo effects influence everyone on the planet, except for me." In reality, no one is immune.

RESOURCES

Sports Medicine Digest, June 2001

"The Placebo Prescription" by Margaret Talbot, New York Times Magazine, January 9, 2000

The Powerful Placebo: From Ancient Priest to Modern Physician by Arthur K. Shapiro, MD and Elaine Shapiro, PhD 1990 Johns Hopkins University Press

"The Placebo Effect" Scientific American, January, 1998

TELL ME A STORY

Broken stories can be healed. Diseased stories can be replaced by healthy ones. We are free to change the stories by which we live.

Daniel Taylor
The Healing Power of Stories

The following story may or may not be true, but if it isn't, it should be:

A young, impressionable bicycle racer shows up for the big event and his manager tells him "Good news. The mechanic has inflated your tires with helium. You're going to go like a bat out of hell." The racer listens with rapt attention and his mind and body immediately go into action, anticipating the feel of his newly fortified bike. His brain, a massive endocrine gland, begins to secrete powerful hormones which surge through his body, preparing his tissue for the challenge ahead. The race begins and true to story, he goes off like a rocket.

Of course, a quick reality check would tell us that the actual lifting properties of such a small amount of helium would have no appreciable effect on a the weight of the racer's bike. A physicist would surely conclude that the helium would not give any advantage to the racer's performance.

But our bike racer doesn't care about physics, nor does he take the time to calculate the lifting properties of helium. Instead, he's thinking about possibility and potential. He's under the influence of an idea, a placebo. The idea of lightness filters down from cortex to quads and shaves a few seconds off his time. In actual practice, he really does go faster, just because of the story.

PNI: THE MIND-BODY CONVERSATION

Before we tell a story about storytelling, we need to step back a bit and do some homework. The operative word of the day is *psychoneuroimmunology* (PNI for short). Technically, this discipline is the study of the relationship between mind, nervous system and immunity. The details are complex, but the findings are pivotal to understanding who we are and how we work. Basically, PNI research is now beginning to show us that thoughts, belief, and emotion can have profound effects on physiology and in turn, health and performance.

The nuts and bolts of PNI are fascinating, but it's far too laborious to go into at the moment. Therefore, we're going to skip the entire discussion of cytokines, polypeptide hormones, interferon, transformational growth factor and interleukins. Not only that, we're going to bypass the research that tells us how a specific thought, attitude or emotion correlates with the rise or fall of a particular chemical agent in a subject's body. Suffice to say that PNI research has documented hundreds of instances in which subtle beliefs, attitudes and images can have real, measurable physiological results.

TALKING TO TISSUE

The power of language in this process is astonishing. Certain sounds and symbols, when arranged in a particular order, can trigger significant differences in hormone and neurotransmitter levels in the body. In turn, this can tip the scales in terms of health, injury and disease. The proximal cause is abstract and intangible, but the end results are real, concrete and measurable. Stories speak not just to our minds, but to our tissue.

It is no exaggeration to say that story-telling lies at the heart of the mind-body interface and when practiced intelligently, is an authentic form of mind-body medicine. The words that we hear and say don't just pass through our heads; they have a genuine effect on the health and fitness of tissues, organs and physical systems.

The power and influence over our health is substantial. We all tell stories, and we tell them over the course of most of our waking hours. Even when we're alone, we're always talking to ourselves, constantly spinning an explanatory narrative about our lives, our bodies, and the people and events around us. This nearly endless stream of language leads to real, sometimes profound physical consequences.

HEALTH AND FITNESS NARRATIVES

Everyone tells a story of their body and their physicality. We don't lay it out in long, coherent, Garrison Keillor-style narratives, but rather in short remarks, muses and quips about our physical experience. These micro-stories of our bodies are not just neutral descriptions; they contain the seeds of our future health and performance.

Obviously, there are as many kinds of health and fitness stories as there are human beings. Nevertheless, they seem to fall into some predictable, regular categories. Many are distinctly negative:

"I'm so out of shape."
"I'll get hurt if I try that."
"I'm no good at sports."
"I hate being fat."
"I'm too lazy."

This kind of nano-story is told millions of times every day across the world. In any given instance, the effect on the speaker's health is probably inconsequential, but when practiced as a regular narrative, as an explanatory style, this kind of language is bound to lead to poor results. When our stories go negative, they have a nocebo effect; our tissue eventually gets the message.

In contrast, imagine turning the narrative around. What if our micro-stories were not laments of physical inadequacy but instead were positive expressions of curiosity, passion and desire?

"My knee hurts, but I'm thinking I can still have some fun in the pool."
"I wonder if I can run across this park like one of those urban free runners."
"There's some hot dance music at the club. My body feels like moving."
"I haven't done any exercise for weeks, but once I get going, I'll be OK."
"I'm really sore from that last session, but I can adapt."

So what does your fitness narrative sound like? Do you tell a story of creeping inadequacy, sloth and lethargy? If so, you're simply pounding your nervous system into a self-fulfilling, low-performance network. Your words are making you slow, weak and injury-prone.

Perhaps a new story would be in order. No need to tell tall tales, but there's got to be some exuberance and passion that you can bring into the conversation. Change your language and see if your tissue doesn't start paying attention.

EXPRESSION IS VITAL

Stories are enormously powerful, but language is not the only way to have a voice. In fact, any form of expression can be immune-enhancing and health-promoting. We can tell our stories in thousands of ways, through sport, art, music, crafts, career and relationship.

Physical movement is of course one of our most fundamental forms of expression, but this fact has largely been lost in the world of pro-grammed, medicalized fitness. We have become conditioned to think of exercise as a means to lose weight and get in shape. In the process, we forget that for many people, movement is first and foremost a way to tell a story. For these individuals, physical movement says "This is who I am." Such an orientation has nothing to do with calories, METs, reps, anabolic thresholds or even a longer life span. Rather, movement is way to tell a story to the world.

This is especially true in the world of sports. For many participants, sport is an opportunity not simply to achieve victory, but to express one's personality. Sure, it's great to feel strong and maybe win some champi-onships, but the real motivator for many participants is the simple desire to tell the world "This is who I am." Unfortunately, our hyper-competi-tive sporting culture keeps a lot of this expression on the bench and off the field. When all your coach cares about is winning, the only players who get to have a voice are those with exceptional skills.

INHIBITION

Whatever the form, expression is vital to health and physical perfor-mance, just as vital as good food and vigorous movement. When our voices are heard, we feel validated, acknowledged and possibly even un-derstood. By telling our story, in words, pictures or movement, we lower our stress hormones and boost immunity.

In contrast, when expression is inhibited, we feel isolated and stressed. PNI has shown that the inability to express feelings, particularly about negatively charged subjects, is unhealthy for the immune system. This realization leads us to a fresh insight into how we ought to conduct our physical movement practices. Instead of focusing on strict programs of sets, reps, laps and mileage, maybe we ought to loosen up the process a bit and allow for more diverse forms of physical expression.

Remember, the people who visit our gyms, studios and practice fields are more than muscle tissue in need of resistance and aerobic pumping; they are also spiritual creatures in need of expression. This is why the spreadsheet-driven, clip-board-accountant model of physical education often misses the mark. It's obvious that we need lots of vigorous movement for cardiovascular health and muscle development, but if we deprive students of their voice, we also kill their love of the process. When data rules the day, expression disappears and so does participation.

"TELL IT!"

The moral to this story is simple: make expression a part of your life and fitness. Get your story out into the world. Say it, tell it, move it, sing it, paint it, play it. Let your voice out. Your body will love you for it.

And if you've got access to some helium, try putting it in your bicycle tires. You'll be amazed at how well it works.

RESOURCES

Feeling Good is Good for You
Carl J. Charnetski and Francis X. Brennan, Rodale 2001

MORE SIGNAL, LESS NOISE

Calling noise a nuisance is like calling smog an inconvenience. Noise must be considered a hazard to the health of people everywhere.

William H. Stewart
former U.S. Surgeon General

As **yo.u've pró~b"ably nôtIce<d, it"s h^arDd to FocuS yóuR c?once∞nTration w+hen thëre"s tOO mú¢h NoISe in~yo(ur eNvir©nmëntΔ. Yoùr miNd tri%es to stäy atttênt¬ive t0 the ta^sk at hAnd[, b•ut@ it's' cónsTA"ntly gettÎng> de##railêd by_stråy...+ senSatiòns, sensô=ry non-seqüiTurs thåt: hav€ nothInG to do w}ith y|our o.bJeCti√es. N.oisE d7egradês] oUR pErf®rma;nce, kom∑proMizez OuR héallth an.d ≥≥mak`es us Xtⲅeee^Mely IrrⲅΩittabLE¡

As I write this essay, my neighbors on both sides of my house are having their roofs replaced. The summer days in Seattle are long and the crews want to take advantage of every minute of daylight. So from sunup to sundown, I'm subjected to a stereophonic assault of circular saws, power vacs, sawzalls, power staplers, air compressors, portable generators and, to add insult to misery, talk radio. Overhead, a stream of floatplanes strafes my neighborhood at the lowest legal altitude. Across the street, my neighbor fires up his power mower, weed whacker and leaf blower for his Saturday chores. A few doors down, a woman sets her car alarm to hair-trigger sensitivity, which jumps to life with every passing gust of wind. A block away, the fire station sends out a stream of siren-blaring rescue rigs, rushing to the scene of another emergency. As you might imagine, I'm a little on edge at the moment.

DEATH BY DECIBELS

The problem is that my neighborhood isn't that much different from any other neighborhood in the modern world. Noise is everywhere now and it's not just acoustic. It's in our eyes, in our tissue and in our minds. We can close our doors and windows, but inexorably, the dissonance bulldozes its way in. Radio and TV commercials, bulk mail, pop-up ads and telephone pitches grate on our senses. Data smog, clutter and clatter: everywhere we go, noise assaults us.

Audio noise is simply the most obvious form, a subset of a much larger trend. Modern culture itself has become a distraction machine, an intrusive, obnoxious juggernaut of conflicting sounds, images and ideas, all competing for what's left of our attention. Some days it seems like every person on the planet is trying to get a piece of our awareness. Noise has now become a multi-channel problem and a genuine health issue.

Unfortunately, our experience of noise in the modern world is very much akin to the plight of the boiled frog. That is, the transformation has crept up on us gradually and so has gone largely unnoticed by most individuals. Any single generation is unlikely to notice the escalation, but all it takes is a simple thought experiment or trip to the outback to realize what's going on.

Just imagine the acoustic environment of pre-modern humans: no vehicles, no internal combustion engines, no electronics, no amplifiers, no cell phones. Even today, we can drive out into the Serengeti, shut off the engine and bask in the silence. No aircraft, no machinery, no distraction. Just the sound of wind on the grass, occasional animals, the afternoon thunderstorm and your companions. This is the norm, the auditory status quo for *Homo sapiens*.

It therefore comes as no surprise to learn that modern health researchers have discovered clear evidence of destructive effects of noise on the human body. Exposure to high levels of auditory noise raises blood pressure, increases stress hormones, disrupts sleep and probably contributes to attention-deficit disorders, in both children and adults. And of course, noise also impacts our athletic performance. Take a well-trained athlete, put him or her into a profoundly noisy environment for a week or so and then measure the difference in speed, strength or endurance. It's safe to assume that we'd see a decline.

Given the constant, escalating barrage of multi-channel noise in the modern world and its corrosive effects on our health and happiness, it's crucial that we take action to protect ourselves. As noise proliferates, defending ourselves becomes just as important as eating well and exercising. Unfortunately, no one is teaching us how to do this. We are awash in information about nutrition, weight-loss and medical care, but how do we protect ourselves from acoustic chaos and sensory mayhem?

ENVIRONMENTAL SOLUTIONS

The most obvious solution is to simply rework our environments to better insulate ourselves from annoying sensations. Better doors, windows and sound-proofing are a sensible place to start. Seal up the cracks, add some buffers. If we can trim just a few decibels off our daily acoustic load, we'll be a lot better off in the long run.

While we're at it, we can also do ourselves a favor by attending to the visual noise and clutter that distracts our eyes and causes us fatigue. This process begins with the tasks of throwing out the trash, cleaning up and restoring a sense of order. We can reshelve our books, organize our CD's, put the tools back where they belong and pick up the laundry. Form and function merge in this effort; when we make our places beautiful, we simultaneously quiet things down.

We can also look around for examples of clean, noise-free environments. One of the best models is the martial art training hall or dojo. In this environment, simplicity is taken seriously. Concentration is extremely important when you're swinging a sword, grappling with an opponent or doing expert calligraphy; we don't want noisy distractions interfering with delicate or high-risk work. Cleanliness promotes focus and eliminates wasted effort. We would do well to duplicate this style of quiet simplicity in our gyms, our training centers and our classrooms.

PHYSIOLOGICAL SOLUTIONS

After we've done some work on our homes and workplaces, we can turn our attention to our bodies. Clearly, the better our overall state of health, the better our ability to withstand the corrosive effects of noise. Any health-positive behavior will contribute to this effort. Eating well will probably help and getting lots of sleep is surely essential. And of course, any of our favorite stress control measures will help the cause. Relaxation, social support and touch all contribute to success.

Naturally, vigorous physical movement is vital. Like its twin brother stress, noise increases the production of toxic hormones in our bodies which, if allowed to fester, can make us feel even worse. The solution is to get some circulation going to flush out the offending molecules. Go out for a run, dance to some music or climb a tree. After a while, your body will return to homeostasis and you'll be in a better position to weather the sensory assaults.

PSYCHOLOGICAL SOLUTIONS

Environmental and health solutions are obviously important in our fight against noise, but we also need to consider the psychological elements.

The first issue has to do with our sense of control. The relationship is really quite simple. That is, if you can control it, it's not noise. My neighbor's construction projects are noise because I have no sense of control over how they proceed. If it was my roofing project, it wouldn't be noise; I could turn off the machines anytime I wanted. By the same token, my amplified music is sweet, vibrant and melodic, but your amplified music is annoying, loathsome and pathological. Control is the ingredient that makes the difference.

In this way, our experience of stress and noise are essentially identical. If you can control a situation, it's not stressful; if you can turn off an acoustic stimulus, it's not noise. If you want to reduce the noise and stress in your life, exercise more control.

This advice may seem powerful on its face, but is it really worth a damn? Not necessarily. At some level, we all know that control is the solution to noise and stress. That's why political power and money are so popular. If you've got power and money, you've got the means to make some of the stress and noise in your life go away. In fact, rich and powerful people tend to be healthier than the poor and helpless.

Of course, few of us are ever going to have enough power or money to get all the control that we'd like. After all, even rich people have to suffer the din of jet skis that assault their waterfront homes. The reality is that for most of us, control is only a partial solution. But even at that, we can still find success by adjusting our perspective. If we pay more attention to the things that we can control and less attention to things that are beyond us, we'll probably feel better about our predicament.

BOOST THE SIGNAL

Another way to adjust our attention is to concentrate less on the noise and more on the "signal." In the world of acoustic engineering, technicians often talk about the "signal to noise ratio." This term has a technical meaning that applies to things like radio waves and audio equipment, but we can broaden the definition to include the scope of human attention and performance. In this way, the "signal" is any message or quality that we are trying to sense or attend to. "Noise" is anything that interferes with that process. Obviously, a high signal-to-noise ratio will promote nervous system refinements and learning. If we can't turn down the noise, maybe we can boost the signal.

FOCUS ON OBJECTIVES

The most basic way to boost the signal is to focus on our objectives. Forget the distractions and the complications for the moment. What exactly are you trying to do in your life? What do you want out of this situation? What are you trying to create? These questions are standard fare in management and performance seminars, but they bear repeating in any environment. If we don't know what we're trying to do, we won't be able to sort out the sensations that come our way.

If in doubt, talk to your friends, or if you're really desperate, try writing down the things that really matter in your quest. Decide what you want to be doing and attend to that. Focus your powers of concentration on the objects of your desire and use that attention to power through the noise, distraction and clutter.

And of course, when it comes to objectives, the more specific the better. If you simply say, "I'm trying to get in shape" or "I'm trying to make a living," your attention will be easily weakened by distraction. Better to describe precisely what you're trying to do. The noisier your world, the more important this process becomes.

DON'T GET MAD, GET INTERESTED

Focusing on objectives is vital to survival and health, but we can do even better. As the world becomes ever noisier, we need to increase the motivation behind our objectives, the energy behind our chosen dreams. Passion is the key to this process. When we fall in love with a person, a process or a subject, distractions fade into the background.

As our curiosity deepens, the noise and clutter suddenly become less relevant. Passion becomes an antidote to noise.

In this way, we come to the inescapable conclusion that passion is vital to health, just as vital as good food and vigorous movement. You won't hear much about passion in boilerplate fitness prescriptions, but it's far more important to our well-being than nutritional supplements or any truckload of gadgets and gizmos. If we don't have some sense of passion in our lives, noise will overwhelm us and our bodies will suffer.

Not only does passion cut through the din of external noise, it also boosts our ability to function in the face of internal dissonance. As you have surely noticed, the human mind can be a powerful noise-generating device, churning out a staggering assortment of phrases, images, memories and ideas that weaken our concentration and obscure the signals that we are trying to track. This cognitive noise includes the voice of judgment, the authority figure, the internal editor (that loathsome beast), the nag and the cynic. These voices occasionally have something valuable to add to our internal conversations, but if left unchecked, they derail our attention and weaken our performance. This generates even more noise leading us into a spiral of distraction and chaos. Passion cuts through this din and clears the path to action.

THE PASSION CURRICULUM

In common conversation, we sometimes speak of passion as if it were a spontaneous gift or a fleeting inspiration that simply appears from time to time in our lives. But there's a lot more to it than dumb luck. Passion, like so many other human qualities, can be strengthened and enhanced.

Passion, like muscle tissue, thrives on use. Few of us would expect a muscle to grow stronger simply by hope; muscles just don't work that way. So too for our desire and curiosity. When we honor our passion, we give it life. Every committed artist knows this to be true. The more you feed your curiosity, the stronger it becomes.

Unfortunately, passion has been exiled from modern curriculums at almost every level. It doesn't appear in textbooks or on lesson plans, it's not on the state-mandated lists of educational goals and it's almost never included as a serious objective in classrooms or in gyms.

Everyone's afraid to talk about passion because it can't be measured, tracked and analyzed. The whole concept sounds vaporous, intangible and unprofessional—not rigorous enough for our serious, adultified efforts. And so we stick to hard-headed, pre-measured content that ultimately deadens our curiosity. No surprise here; by offering a passion-free curriculum, we ultimately get passion-free results.

I propose that we turn the whole thing around. Instead of relegating passion to the distant margins of human education, we need to move it back to the center. As educators and motivators, our role is to help people fall in love with the subject at hand, whatever it happens to be. Fall in love with movement, fall in love with physicality, fall in love with play. Fall in love with knowledge. Fall in love with health, vitality and pleasure.

If we can do this, even in some small measure, everything else will come into focus and the world will become a much quieter place.

ENQUIRING BODIES WANT TO KNOW

According to legend, reporters once asked Albert Einstein if there was a single crucial question that modern scientists needed to ask. Perhaps they expected a question about relativity or the unified theory of physics. If so, they must have been surprised when he answered "Yes, that question is, 'Is the universe friendly?'"

This question lives on as a koan for human existence on a small planet, a question that we might do well to ask on a regular basis. Amazingly, it also mirrors a similar question that the body asks continuously throughout life. When faced with the predicament of life in a dynamic and sometimes dangerous environment, the body wants to know "Is it safe?"

THE PRIMAL QUESTION

This question first occurs to the human animal at birth, but it really crystallizes when the child begins to walk and explore the world around her. The environment tantalizes and beckons, but doubts are ever-present, particularly when considering novel movements and body positions. Upright, bipedal postures are inherently precarious and falls are likely. It's no wonder that the body wonders about its safety. Creatures that failed to ask this question would have been eliminated from the gene pool long ago.

As the child develops, action provides an answer to the primal question. Vigorous movement convinces the body that little harm will come; action provides reassurance. Play, of course, is an essential part of this dialogue. The curious spirit wonders if a particular movement is possible and longs to attempt it, but the body is skeptical and reluctant. Through play, the young animal explores the edges of possibility. When she discovers a new movement, she repeats it over and over, enjoying the sensation and the growing sense of safety that comes with it. As the body becomes convinced, doubt fades and gives way to further wonder and renewed exploration.

ADULT CONDITIONING

By the time we reach adulthood, most of our doubts about the safety of basic movements have been largely eliminated or at least pushed into the background. But if we want to progress in athletics or fitness, the same basic issue confronts us. If we want to expand our movement repertoire, we need to convince the body that all will be well. In fact, we can view the entire athletic and fitness training enterprise in just these terms. Whether it's adding weight to the bar, running a little faster, stretching a little further or climbing something a little steeper, it's all a matter of making the case to a conservative and skeptical body.

For example, we hold this conversation between mind and movement when we do interval training and hill workouts. If you simply jog a few miles every so often, your body will adapt, but if you try to increase your performance, you'll trigger the body's natural skepticism. "Is it safe to run faster?" Pushing yourself by doing a few sprints or some hills will provide an answer. As the doubts are addressed, the body's mind is reassured and limitations begin to dissolve.

We see a similar process in the warm-up phase of exercise. Most fitness instructors explain the warm-up in physiological terms, but the body's psychology is at least as important. As you begin a set of easy movements, you're warming and liquefying your tissue, but you're also speaking to your body and convincing it that such movements are safe. After a few minutes, the body is convinced and ready to move more vigorously.

BACK PAIN AND BED REST

Our physical concern for safety appears not only in athletics, but also in the way we respond to injury. It is especially conspicuous in cases of back pain and rehabilitation. Back in the dark ages of the mid-to-late 20th century, physicians commonly prescribed bed rest for back pain. Doctors really had no clear idea of what actually caused back pain, but they assumed that the best course would be to treat it like other orthopedic problems such as fractures. If you break your leg, it makes sense to cast it and stay off of it for a few weeks.

Unfortunately, this approach proved to be spectacularly ineffective and often counter-productive. Study after study has now confirmed that bed rest is no more effective than simply getting on with life and moving as best you can. And, because bed rest also deconditions the muscles of the trunk, it can delay recovery even further. So, activity seems to be the best medicine. But why?

Advanced imaging technologies now allow us to look at the deep structure of the low back with incredible clarity and resolution, but no definitive answer has emerged. All our theories about pinched nerves, herniated disks and sprained ligaments have turned out to be inconclusive. Our ignorance has been further illuminated by the astonishing discovery that asymptomatic (pain-free) patients often have structural flaws in disks, joints, vertebrae and ligaments. They're "injured" but they report no pain.

We remain mystified about the ultimate causes of the pain, but we do know that activity works. It works because it answers the body's primal question, "Is it safe?"

Obviously, back pain creates doubt in the body. Safety of movement is called into question and the body begins to wonder what will happen in movement. But bed rest does nothing to address the issue. If you lie still for a few days or weeks, the pain may diminish slightly, but the memory remains and the primary question goes unanswered. In the end, bed rest proves nothing to the body. When you finally stand up and try to get back to life, you will still have to face your physical doubts.

In contrast, activity provides a convincing answer. By going about your normal routines of daily living, you convince your body that, even with pain, no harm will come, and that it really is safe to move. By moving, you provide evidence and build a case. By exercising, you convince the body's mind that it really is safe to move again. This reassurance is immensely powerful. Once the mind is convinced by action, doubts begin to fade and the pain diminishes. In this sense, activity really is medicine.

The same principle seems to hold true across many forms of common injury. Activity heals, not so much by what it does to tissue, but by what it does to the mind. Once safety is assured, the body has less interest in whatever pain messages are coming from the tissue. The tissue itself may still be torn or inflamed, but the brain's self-generated opiates moderate the sensation and our attention is free to turn elsewhere.

OFF THE COUCH

When we look at physical experience as a conversation between mind and movement, we see that sedentary living is an even bigger problem than we first thought. Without some regular movement experience, the body never develops a sense of safety in movement. We never learn that exuberant, vigorous movement is within our capability. The longer we remain sedentary, the greater our doubt and the more reassurance we will need if we ever do begin to move again. Obesity and diabetes get all the press, but the crux of the matter is really psychophysical.

The dialogue between the mind and movement is enormously important for people who are just beginning to exercise or who are coming back after a long layoff. Having nothing to go on, the body is skeptical of the entire enterprise and is leery of movement. If it's going to relax it's grip, the body needs ample evidence that movement really is safe.

Thus, the needs of the beginning or returning exerciser are heavily psychological and should be treated as such. At this point in the process, trainers, coaches and therapists are not really working with tissue at all and it makes little sense to think in terms of specific prescriptions. Rather, this is a time of tentative exploration and discovery. Early movements are probes into the unknown. Here the trainer may function best as a supportive guide and motivator, not as an authority.

EVERY BODY IS DIFFERENT

One fact that is often overlooked in standardized fitness and exercise prescriptions is that people's bodies have very different needs for physical reassurance. When it comes to answering the question "Is this movement safe?" everyone has their own standards and their own requirements for proof.

In the language of law, one person's body might find "a preponderance of the evidence" to be plenty adequate for further investigation. Another person's body may require evidence "beyond a reasonable doubt." One person's body might be convinced with one or two successful reps and be ready to move on. Another might need hundreds or thousands of reps to become convinced.

Physical history, stress and genetic factors all play a role here, so it's foolhardy to suggest that any particular level is 'normal.' Instead, we have to assume a dynamic dialogue, a shifting conversation between mind and movement. Our job is to listen to the conversation and adjust our movement challenges accordingly.

Unfortunately, this variability in human bodies is almost universally ignored in this era of institutional exercise prescription. In public schools and PE think tanks, administrators obsess over grade-level performance standards and objectives. They develop assessments and boilerplate lesson plans, always trying to determine who is keeping up and who is falling behind. Their standardized minds assume that all students have–or should have–standardized bodies.

But this pigeon-hole approach to the body totally misses the point. That is, physical education, especially in the early years, is primarily about a person's relationship with his or her own body. It is exploration. It is personal and experiential. It is profoundly intimate.

External standards are completely irrelevant to this process of physical self-discovery and knowledge. If I'm trying to work out my sense of safety with a particular physical movement, the last thing I need is a standardized administrator standing over me with a stop watch and a clip board. I need time, experience and freedom. A little encouragement and inspiration would be nice too.

In this process of physical self-discovery, it makes no sense whatsoever to compare my performance with others. What matters is the conversation between my body and my movement. If I can gain a sense of safety, I can move on to more powerful, more vigorous and more sustained forms of movement. This is something that needs to happen on my schedule, not on the timetable of an administrator.

THOUGHT EXPERIMENT

My guess is that even Einstein, a physical illiterate if there ever was one, would have understood the importance of this mind-movement dialogue. So let's conduct a thought experiment in his honor. Let's fire up the time machine, travel back to the patent office, drag him away from his desk and out to the local field for some vigorous movement. Once we explain our intentions, his first question is likely to be "Is this training process friendly?"

I suggest that we make it so.

MUSE IT OR LOSE IT

Your imagination, my dear fellow, is worth more than you imagine.

Louis Aragon

There comes a time in every young athlete's life when he begins to understand the potential of his sport and what it means for his body. He's practiced with the team for a season or two and has learned a few moves. With encouragement from his coach and parents, he's developing confidence and he begins to wonder what he's really capable of.

Each night, just as he falls asleep, he rehearses his favorite moves in his mind. Blissfully unaware of physics and the limitations of human movement, his imagination ranges over all sorts of possibility. He doesn't just run and jump; he leaps and soars. He doesn't just hit the ball into the outfield; he slams it over the wall, past the highway and over the horizon. He doesn't just complete a layup; he swishes from beyond the half-court line. He doesn't just lift big weights, he hoists cement trucks and boxcars.

If he ever shares such visions with the adults in his life, they are likely to laugh at his charmingly misguided ideas of what's possible. But really, the joke is on them because, accurate or not, the child's movement fantasies are powerful forces that will develop his body and shape his future.

THE POWER OF THE PHYSICAL IMAGINATION

Wonder and imagination pull our physiology in subtle, yet powerful ways. As soon as the mind conjures an image, the body begins to mobilize its resources in anticipation. Images stimulate the nervous system, promoting activity in certain circuits and the release of systemic hormones. Blood flow is adjusted, muscle tone shifts and cellular machinery goes into action.

In this way, the power of the physical imagination is closely related to the placebo effect, the process by which inert substances, when taken under the influence of belief, inspire actual physiological changes. When we think about placebos, we typically think of sugar pills, for these are the classic agents used in double-blind clinical trials. But if sugar pills can have a beneficial effect on a patient's condition, it is not at all unreasonable to suppose that a mental image can have beneficial effects to our fitness and performance as well. Our minds are always at work evaluating the prospects for health and disease.

SOMETHING FOR EVERYONE

The power of the physical imagination offers benefits all across the range of physical competence. When harnessed properly, creative wonder can turn average athletes into stars and sedentary people into activists. At the elite end of the spectrum, professional athletes spend an enormous percentage of their non-playing time thinking about their game and their movements. By coupling a vigorous imagination with intensive physical practice, they sculpt their physiology and bring their performance to higher levels.

But an active imagination is also extremely relevant to the routine physical experience of normal people. Imagination will even have a profound effect on whether we do movement at all. For people who are worried about not getting enough exercise, imagination can transform a sedentary lifestyle into one of action and movement. A vivid, movement-oriented imagination can literally draw us off the couch and out of our sedentary habits. If you're balanced on the cusp of action and sloth, a simple physical muse can make the difference, tugging at your mind and tipping the scales in favor of movement.

With this in mind, it's not necessary to imagine ourselves turning in epic, world-class performances. Instead, we imagine the simple actions involved in the movement activity of our choice—blocking out time on the calendar, putting on the proper clothes, lacing up the footwear, driving to the location, doing the warm-up and participating. These images are not spectacular in the least, but they still provide a subconscious pull that can make the difference between participation and sloth. By visualizing participation, we make participation more likely. Practiced over the course of years and decades, this can make a substantial, even spectacular difference in health and fitness.

PRACTICAL BENEFITS

To some people, working with the physical imagination may sound like a fringe pursuit, a mushy New Age mysticism. In fact, imagination offers an extremely practical, sensible and straightforward approach to all sorts of body-intensive activities. In particular, imaginative previewing gives our bodies a sense of sequence and quality that makes physical movement far easier than it might otherwise be.

This effect is particularly obvious in the world of sport rock climbing. Prior to roping up at the base of a route, the experienced climber examines the climb in detail and looks for the sequence of movement that seems most plausible. He maps the entire route in this fashion, imagining every reach and step. By previewing his movement, he solidifies neurological connections and clears away psychological distraction. Then, when he actually climbs the route, he moves with far greater confidence and authority.

This imaginative rehearsal gives climbers enormous advantage, but it also works in disciplines as varied as carpentry, cooking or cleaning out the garage. If you can get your mind out ahead of your body, you'll move with greater power, endurance and effectiveness. If your mind has already been there, your body will know what to do.

SUSTAINABILITY

Another powerful quality of the physical imagination is that it offers intrinsic motivation. When we craft a joyful, playful and powerful physical muse, we draw ourselves deeper into a meaningful experience. We go towards movement, not away from disease or obesity.

By allowing the imagination to play with our physical experience, we make the entire training process immensely more interesting. Instead of simply logging sets and reps, we engage our minds and bodies in an interactive dance of wonder, influence and persuasion. No longer is exercise simply a matter of logging a certain required number of miles or laps. Rather, it becomes a fascinating interplay of tissue and imagination. This makes our quest far more sustainable.

IMAGINATION IS A MUSCLE

We will do well to think about imagination in the same way that we think about muscle. Like living tissue, the physical imagination is capable of growth or atrophy in response to stress/rest cycles. If challenged on a fairly regular basis, it grows more capable. If left unchallenged in a state of sedentary inertia, it begins to atrophy. If you don't muse it, you'll lose it.

Naturally, an active body and a robust physical imagination tend to stimulate one another in a positive feedback loop. If you're moving frequently and vigorously, you're probably also wondering about new possibilities for movement. No matter whether you're running cross country, building houses or playing music, you'll probably spend some of your off-hours wondering how to make your movements more powerful, endurant and effective. The more you use your physical imagination, the more powerful it becomes.

Of course, like muscle, the imagination atrophies when its activity is dampened by cultural or technological forces. Particularly noteworthy is the widespread use of "imagination-saving devices" such as TV, movies and computers. Like labor-saving devices, these technologies give us incredible new capabilities, but at a substantial long-term cost. Increasingly realistic media pump images directly into our brains where they are absorbed without effort. There is no mental effort involved in using these devices, no challenge to our creative capacity. As political scientist Benjamin Barber put it, "The abstraction of language is superseded by the literalness of pictures—at a yet to be determined cost to imagination, which languishes as its work is done for it." The more we use such "wonder-saving devices," the less capable of innovation and wonder we become. We don't use it, so we lose it.

CRAFTING AN APPROPRIATE MUSE

So, the question before us is "How can we go about crafting physical images that will improve our health and fitness?" In the first place, it's important to make our musings intentional. Given the fact that we are under constant bombardment by images of all varieties, it is easy to simply absorb visions that are crafted by others. Our minds become littered with images, many of which are totally inappropriate for our personal lives and bodies. Therefore, we need to take charge of the process by making our own personal creations, physical muses that are relevant to our own lives.

Second, we need to concentrate our attention on images based on movement, not appearance. Imagining yourself as a slender, muscular cover model may be worth doing, but it won't pull your body as effectively as an active, dynamic muse. Our bodies are physiologically predisposed towards movement and are far more responsive to movement-based images. And, if we concentrate on movement, we'll eventually improve our appearance as well.

It's important that we fine-tune our imagination to fit the reality of our bodies and objectives. For adults, the dream has to fall within a certain range of plausibility. If the dream is too outrageous, the adult mind instantly rejects it as impossible and moves on to the next passing thought. What we're looking for here are physical dreams that lie just outside the limit of what we think we are currently capable of, something with a little stretch to it. Can you make your movement just a little bit faster, a little more powerful, more graceful, a little more enjoyable? A modest vision may turn out to be far more powerful than something outrageous.

DREAM FORWARD

For the child, the physical imagination is a projection into the future; children dream forward, always wondering what feats their bodies might be able to perform one day. This forward dreaming pulls their bodies into reality and assists in the development of their physical performance.

For adults, the physical imagination often works in reverse. Instead of projecting their physical imagination into the future, adults long for the way their bodies used to be—strong, resilient, slender and attractive. While children are futurists, adults are historians and romantics, students of their long-lost physicality.

In small measure, the retro dreams of adults are natural and harmless. But beyond a certain point, they become exercises in futility. If we spend too much time dreaming about our past physical glories, the imagination becomes an outright drag on physical progress and development. Retro dreams don't pull the body into new movement, they add friction and resistance. In excess, they suck us down into sedentary resignation and apathy.

As the body ages, our physical dreams may become more modest. Yet, even in the face of tissue aging and inevitable performance decline, there's no reason to give up on forward muses. You may not fall asleep imagining that tomorrow, you'll fly over the playground like a bird, or jump over 10 foot fences like a kangaroo, but you can still get your mind out in front. Maybe your plan for the weekend is simply working in the garden; if you've got an idle moment, you can still imagine yourself digging, squatting and piloting the wheelbarrow with skill and ease. You can imagine yourself climbing a ladder with power and control. No, this won't spontaneously transform you into a gardening and home improvement superhero, but you may very well enjoy an edge in the process. Do this routinely over the course of several years and it could add up to a huge difference.

FOR OCCASIONAL USE ONLY

Stress is basically a disconnection from the earth, a forgetting of the breath. Stress is an ignorant state. It believes that everything is an emergency. Nothing is that important. Just lie down.

Natalie Goldberg

Stress is when you wake up screaming and you realize you haven't fallen asleep yet.

unknown

Word on the street is that there's a major stress epidemic in our land. We're hearing increasingly dire warnings about the way that stress leads to a host of nasty and expensive physical disorders: heart disease, diabetes, obesity, osteoporosis, stomach ulcers, reduced memory capacity and cognitive decline. Stress has been described as a "silent killer" but it won't be long before the whole situation becomes positively deafening. In the years to come, stress is going to start yelling its head off.

Not only are we increasingly aware of stress and its links to serious disease, we're also beginning to understand how stress can sabotage our efforts to get physically fit. We now know that stress can interfere with the quality of our training and derail our recoveries. If you're trying to excel in a sport or just stay healthy, you've got to have an understanding of what stress is and how it works.

STRESS ME OUT

The story of stress is usually told like this: The regulation of the human body is controlled by the autonomic nervous system. This system has two branches: the *sympathetic* and the *parasympathetic*. In pop talk, the sympathetic branch is known for its "fight and flight" action, while the parasympathetic branch is known for its "feed and breed" effects.

Unfortunately, these standard labels don't really tell the story. In fact, the terms *sympathetic* and *parasympathetic* are completely outdated and useless. For our purposes, it's better to think about these branches as "short-term" and "long-term" drivers. The short-term branch generates hormones and neurotransmitters that drive the body for immediate physical action, while the long-term branch coordinates tissue repair and rejuvenation. One system for running away from carnivores, another system for rebuilding the body back at camp.

This is all well and good, but it's important to remember that, at any given moment, the action of these two systems tends to be mutually exclusive; in most cases, we don't turn them both on at the same time. That is, we can't mobilize for physical action and rebuild our tissue simultaneously. We don't make the heart beat faster and slower simultaneously. We don't inhibit and stimulate digestion at the same time. It's basically an either-or proposition.

Thus, the whole enterprise begins to resemble a simple accounting exercise of credits and debits. The more time we spend pumping our short-term physiology, the less time we spend doing our vitally important anabolic, rebuilding projects. In other words, if you're chronically stressed, your workouts are wasted. You may be putting in the mileage, but you're not rebuilding tissue. You might be better off reading a book.

ELIXIRS AND POISONS

We can get a better understanding of the dynamics of stress by backing up and looking at substances that lie outside the body—things like foods and drugs. As our modern understanding of substances has become more sophisticated, most of us have come to accept the idea that substances can have paradoxical effects, depending on the amount or duration of exposure. We see it in everything from coffee to aspirin, from red meat to red wine. In all these cases, the story is the same: small amount OK or beneficial, large amount bad. This principle holds true even for seemingly innocuous substances such as water.

Similarly, we're OK with the idea of an inverse U-shaped curve that describes this effect. It would be easy to sketch out such a curve for red wine consumption for example, showing a rising benefit as we go from 0 to 2 or 3 glasses per week. Then we'd see the curve flatten out and cross a tipping point after which further increase in consumption would lead to increasing physical, mental and social distress.

So, when it comes to exogenous substances (foods and compounds that are "out there") most of us are pretty comfortable with the inverse-U paradigm. But when it comes to substances produced by the body itself, we're not so sure. In all likelihood, we haven't even thought about it in these terms.

But as it turns out, the same principle often holds true, especially in the world of hormone concentrations and effects. In this sense, stress hormones are just like red meat and red wine; they follow the same inverted U-shaped curve of benefit and damage.

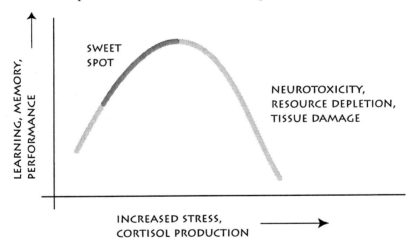

Here's how it works: The stress response acts in large measure by stimulating the secretion of glucocorticoids, especially cortisol, by the adrenal glands. In the short term, cortisol is an endogenous elixir. It makes us strong, fast and smart. It increases heart rate, blood pressure and dumps all sorts of good nutrients into the bloodstream so we're ready for physical action. It sharpens cognition, sensation, learning and memory. It's a great feeling, especially if you're in a position to move your body with the action.

But in the long term, cortisol acts as an endogenous poison. It shuts off long-term physiological rebuilding projects, dampens digestion and damages blood vessels. It contributes to a wide range of afflictions including heart disease, obesity, high blood pressure, diabetes and osteoporosis. And to make matters even worse, it also contributes to premature cognitive decline. It shrinks brain centers responsible for memory and learning. And, to complete its vicious cycle, it actually dampens the regulatory centers of the brain that control bloodstream cortisol levels. In other words, the more stressed you get, the more stressed you get. This is bad juju.

"FOR OCCASIONAL USE ONLY"

"Don't write checks that your body can't cash."

Prince

If you visit your local pharmacy you'll find a an entire row of over-the-counter drugs with the warning label "for occasional use only." In other words, these products have paradoxical effects of their own. Small, infrequent doses of these substances might very well relive your symptoms and improve the quality of your life. But large doses or chronic, long-term use will wreak havoc with your body. In other words, don't make a habit out of it; if you do, you'll find yourself at the wrong end of the inverted U.

By the same reasoning, a similar label ought to appear on the human nervous system, especially our stress-responsive glands and tissues. Somehow, we need a reminder that the stress response is "for occasional use only." It's for acute, episodic physical emergencies like predator attacks, championship matches and big presentations. It's not intended for chronic day-in and day-out use. Spikes of cortisol can be highly beneficial, but sustained concentrations are bad news. Flat-line cortisol levels spell trouble.

So maybe we need tattoos on our bodies to remind us. Or better yet, maybe we need personal podcasts or implanted audio with the message

"Don't get frightened or frustrated unless you really need to. Don't obsess over abstract threats. Don't dip into your reserve unless you really need it. Don't go "fight or flight" unless it's an actual emergency. Stick with your "feed and breed" behavior as long as you can. Reserve your cortisol boost for authentic, real-world, real-time stressors."

"USE AS DIRECTED"

While we're at it, we might also give some thought to the other tag line that we see on so many over-the counter medications. The voice of authority booms at us from the TV screen: "USE AS DIRECTED." This means, of course, "read all the fine print inside the box." It might also mean "go see your doctor and find out what he thinks."

But what might this mean for our case at hand, the human stress response? We're not talking about a medication in a box, we're talking about a wet-ware system inside our body that behaves in paradoxical ways. So what about it? What about our adrenal glands? How are we going to "use as directed?" Who is the authority here? And where are the directions?

You might be tempted to visit your doctor at this point. Surely he's an authority on this issue. Someone must have given him the directions back in med school and he'll just tell us what to do. In fact, I would encourage you to do this, just for the field work if nothing else. Unfortunately, it's probably not going to work.

In the first place, doctors are busy doing triage and they don't really have time to teach us about how to live in this modern world. In general, doctors are postemptive medical providers. They're trained to work on sick and injured people after the fact; preemption is simply not part of their world view. If you're not currently sick or injured, they're generally not interested.

So who 'ya gonna call? Is there an expert in the house? Who can tell us how to use our stress response in a way that won't kill us after a few years? There must be some stress-medicine specialists out there. In fact, we'd do well to read the work of Robert Sapolsky, author of *Why Zebras Don't Get Ulcers*. Another good source is Bruce McEwen, author of *The End of Stress as We Know It*. Also try Richard O'Conner and his *Undoing Perpetual Stress: The Missing Connection Between Depression, Anxiety, and 21st Century Illness*. We can also seek out yoga teachers, cognitive therapists and comedians who know how to reinterpret the world and turn stress into laughter.

HIGH CONTRAST LIVING

These sources are all worth a try, but fortunately, many of us have a superior expert and role-model on hand. For this we turn, as we often do, to the dog on the porch. His baseline norm is relaxation; unless otherwise stimulated, he'll stay in his long-term, anabolic, tissue-rebuilding phase as long as possible. His norm is feed and breed physiology. He's content in this phase and will stay there until further notice.

But now suppose there's an unfamiliar sound or odor at the front gate. Alert! An intruder! Our friend's short-term physiology kicks in instantly. His amygdala sparks a danger response and a hormonal cascade that generates barking and a threat posture. Within a second, he's up and ready for action. Heart rate up, blood pressure up, glucose levels up, digestion down. Cortisol surges, doing its powerful work.

If the intruder turns out to actually be a hostile invader, our faithful friend is ready to leap, snarl and repel. But when the intruder turns out to be a friendly neighbor who's been visiting your house every week for the last 10 years, the whole system changes polarity in an instant. Short-term physiology immediately shuts down, adrenals relax, blood pressure drops, vessels dilate and our friend returns to the serious work of napping and rebuilding his body. There's no obsessing over the encounter, no second-guessing his decision to "go-short-term." There's no moment-by-moment review of the encounter. No lingering rationalizations. No, it's all very simple. Threat over, turn off the stress response. Forget it; it's done.

This is how it's supposed to work. And this is how it does work for the overwhelming majority of animals on this planet. It's time we took some lessons from the creatures around us; high contrast living is the way to go.

So go ahead, turn on your fear response when you need it. Get stressed and activated—when you need it. Enjoy the pumped up blood pressure, heart rate, glucose surge and sharpened cognition. Milk those adrenal glands for all the glucocorticoids you can get. And then once the challenge has passed, give up the whole thing. Lay down on the porch and forget it.

RESOURCES

Why Zebras Don't Get Ulcers by Robert Sapolsky 2004 Third Edition Owl Books

The End of Stress as We Know It by Bruce McEwen 2002 Joseph Henry Press

Undoing Perpetual Stress: The Missing Connection Between Depression, Anxiety, and 21st Century Illness by Richard O'Conner 2005 Berkley Books

LIFE ON THE LEFT

Meet the first beginnings; look to the budding mischief
before it has time to ripen to maturity.

Shakespeare

Tension is who you think you should be.
Relaxation is who you are.

Chinese Proverb

By now, sophisticated observers of the human body are familiar with the idea that stress and stress hormones have paradoxical effects, depending on dose and duration. A small amount of stress sharpens intelligence, memory and performance, but a large amount over a long duration not only degrades performance, it can actually damage key brain structures.

This effect is often described as a "classic inverse U-shaped curve." Inverse-U curves are everywhere in physiology, spanning the range from hypo to hyper. We see rising benefit on the left, up to a point of reversal and then a decline, ultimately ending with pathology on the right side of the curve. This curve reflects the fact that there's two types of stress: good stress, also known as *eustress*, and bad stress, otherwise known *pathological stress.*

This inverse U is destined to play an increasingly important role in human life and we'd do well to make ourselves familiar with it. As our world becomes more stressful, we need to not only insulate ourselves against stress, but learn how to recognize when stress effects change from good to bad.

This kind of understanding is crucial for athletes and non-athletes alike. As athletes push the envelope, they are increasingly at risk for over-training, which is simply another form of chronic, damaging stress. But even for the sedentary office worker, the challenge is similar. Being alert to changes that signal the onset of dangerous stress is fast becoming an essential life skill.

Ultimately, the objective for all humans—athletes and non-athletes—is to stay in the sweet spot of stress and try to stay out of the pathological stress zone. Occasional bouts of high stress aren't going to kill you; your body is highly plastic and will usually rebound. Nevertheless, it's best to avoid spending too much time in the high-stress zone. Camping out on the right side of the curve is bad for your body, your mind and your life.

WHY WE NEED STRESS EDUCATION

In coming years, diagnostic tests will probably be available to measure stress hormone levels and pinpoint exactly when stress becomes pathological. A drop of blood will tell the story—maybe. In the meantime, we will have to rely on subtle cues, observation and awareness.

The thing we need to remember is that there is no benefit in going beyond the reversal point. You can work longer hours, train harder, stress yourself deeper, but you aren't going to gain any physical or performance benefit. In fact, just the opposite. You might manage your short-term situation, but at a significant long-term cost to body and brain.

Recognizing our stress status is also important in the context of public health and medical care. In general, modern medicine is post-emptive. In other words, our system waits for people to get stress-related diseases and then attempts to apply some sort of heroic treatment. Consequently, we need to take matters into our own hands. If we want protection against the destructive effects of stress, we're going to have to learn how to do it ourselves.

Another reason we need stress education is that many of us are largely unconscious of our stress status. Stress creeps up on us gradually and never trips our conscious alarms. Long-duration events trick us by moving slowly. You can handle the stress load for a month or a year, but reserves drain away, completely outside of awareness. Education can help us spot these trends earlier.

WHAT IT FEELS LIKE

So let's begin with experience. What's life like in the sweet spot? What does the left side of the curve feel like? If you've ever been an athlete or a musician, you know the answer. There's stress, absolutely. But that stress feels about right for what you're capable of. It's just a little bit beyond your capability. You're stretching to reach the objective, but it's not out of the question. It tantalizes and pulls you. It challenges and fatigues you, but it exhilarates as well. You focus and strive, but there's an end point on the horizon, a haven, a rest stop that you can aim for. Your sense of stress might be acute, but it's buffered by the knowledge that your predicament is temporary.

In contrast, the right side feels heavy, dull and oppressive. There may be breaks in the action, but it doesn't feel like it because the pressure lingers even into your rest periods. The challenge weighs on every moment and even sleep doesn't feel like much of a break. Your entire predicament feels chronic and relentless. There's no swing, no cycle, no oscillation, no rhythm. Ultimately, the right side is a dead zone.

RECOGNIZING THE REVERSAL POINT

These descriptions are a start, but we can do more. Our goal is to recognize the point of diminishing returns and prevent ourselves from falling into the right-side abyss. So, how do we recognize the reversal point? Is there a warning sign? A set of symptoms?

Clearly, there are some general patterns and typical responses. Let's start with the obvious signs of severe, crippling stress. You don't have to be a clinical psychologist, neurobiologist or athletic trainer to recognize when someone has been suffering chronic exposure to stress hormones. We typically see some combination of:

- severe and/or chronic depression
- insomnia
- substance abuse
- overt hostility and chronic anger
- wildly distorted social relationships
- major loss of vitality and severe fatigue
- frequent injury and illness
- severe declines in performance

If you or someone you know has these symptoms, they're probably well past the reversal point and deep into the right side of the curve. They need help.

THE SUBTLETIES

The obvious signs are clear to most of us, but the real challenge is to recognize the subtle clues, the early changes in a person's body and behavior that mark the shift from good stress to bad stress. If we're alert, we can pick up on these signs when the problem is still manageable. If our sensitivity is finely tuned, we can make a big difference in our own lives and the lives of the people around us.

Of course, there will be lots of speculation here and plenty of room for error. It's important to remember that there are enormous individual variations and that it's not always possible to generalize. Everyone has their own stress-response profile and everyone responds differently.

We can suppose that a person who's approaching the reversal point might behave in a particular way, but there's no guarantee. Many of these things could be matters of personal style and perception. Many could be transient and temporary. No matter what, it's going to be a judgment call. In any case, here are some possibilities to consider:

ATTITUDE AND PHILOSOPHY

When stress escalates, the most subtle changes will be those of attitude and philosophy. Where does a person find meaning? What does he relate to? Has he become more cynical? How does he interpret complex events and relationships? Obviously, this is slippery stuff, but if you notice a change from optimism to cynicism, it might signal a shift to the right.

LANGUAGE

Philosophy and attitude are of course revealed in our language; we can assume that language will change as a person comes under increasing stress. Do you hear more blanket generalizations and all-or-nothing statements? Do you hear more hostile tones, more blame? Do you hear a shrinking vocabulary? Unusual cursing?

POSTURE, BODY LANGUAGE

We might also suppose that a person who's suffering under a chronic stress load might express it in the way he holds his body. Has there been a change? Are the eyes down? Shoulders hunched in a protective posture? And what about gait? Does it shuffle and drag?

AHEDONIA

Another subtle sign of pathological stress is ahedonia, the failure to take pleasure in normally enjoyable things. Does someone you know take less interest in pleasure? Does he avoid things that he normally enjoyed and take refuge in labor or punishing work-outs?

NEOPHOBIA

Closely related to ahedonia is neophobia, the fear and avoidance of new things. Do you find yourself avoiding novelty? Do you see someone in your life or your workplace who's clinging to a single way of existence, locked into rigid habit patterns? Someone who insists on eating at the same restaurant and ordering the same meal every time out?

REDUCED AMBIGUITY TOLERANCE

As stress increases, the organism becomes less tolerant of diversity and variety. In an attempt to protect its dwindling capacity for attention, the human mind tries to eliminate complications. It begins an unconscious practice of triage and attempts to protect itself from everything but the most crucial activity and decisions. This may help short-term survivability, but it ultimately backfires into reduced creativity and small-picture thinking.

DECREASED PLAY BEHAVIORS

Does the person enjoy the same kind of playful games that he once did? Is there a diminished sense of curiosity and wonder? A decrease in playful language? As stress increases, we shut down our peripheral sensations and restrict ourselves to the immediate threats. We forget to bounce and swing. We stop exploring.

DIMINISHED SENSE OF HUMOR

We might also notice a diminished sense of humor, or a change in the kind of humor that the person finds appealing. A person may become humorless, or his humor may turn dark. Humor may become biting, sarcastic and aggressive.

IRRITABILITY

As stress becomes chronic, irritability rises. The organism is constantly on high alert for any additional threat. This irritability is psychological, but it is also physical. When the organism is under chronic threat, normal aches and pains are felt more intensely. They may not make it all the way to consciousness, but they still have an abrasive, irritating effect.

DECREASED POWERS OF FOCUS AND CONCENTRATION

We may also see a break down in powers of attention, a sort of sub-clinical ADD. Increasing stress erodes our concentration and leaves us vulnerable to a wider range of distractions. We multi-task more feverishly, but get less accomplished.

SOCIAL WITHDRAWAL OR ISOLATION

Social contact is a powerful stress antidote, but for the person who's already under threat, social contact can also be an unwelcome stressor. Meeting new people or dealing with relationships may be perceived as an unacceptable burden. One "solution" is to withdraw.

QUICK "DECISIONS" AND SMALL-PICTURE "THINKING"

For people under increasing stress, quick "decisions" are not really decisions, as in "made with deliberation." Rather, they are impulsive acts, made out of an unconscious desire to make stress and ambiguity go away. People under increasing stress also limit the range of their attention and in so doing lapse into small-picture thinking. They fail to see context. They are content to deal with microscopic problems while ignoring a wider range of relationship.

SO NOW WHAT?

So now that we have a list of possible warning signs to work with, let's suppose you see a trend towards pathological stress. You or someone you know is nearing the reversal point or is drifting over to the right side of the curve. What to do?

The short answer is that you may not have to do a whole lot. The simple act of recognition may be extremely powerful in its own right. By paying attention to subtle signs, you can catch the problem while it's still small. And small problems only require small solutions.

Once you've seen the problem, you can devise adjustments and turn to the popular stress antidotes: vigorous movement, rest, community, revised interpretations of events and so on. These are all important, but if you see things clearly, half the battle is won. If you're nearing the reversal point, all you need to do is back off a few degrees and you'll be back in the sweet spot.

CLIMBING THE LADDER TO HEALTH AND FITNESS

The experts are full of advice about what we should do for our health and fitness. Swallow this pill, they say; it will raise the level of an essential hormone. Do this workout; it will give you stronger muscular contractions. Follow this diet; it will increase your metabolic rate and burn more fat. In the world of health and fitness, we're always looking for methods and substances that produce specific physical results. So we study nutrition, biochemistry and biomechanics, always trying to tease out physiological causes and effects. We feel certain that if we study hard enough, we will eventually arrive at the truth of health and fitness.

THE PLACEBO EFFECT

Unfortunately, it turns out that our quest to understand physical causality is a lot more complicated than we first thought. The first blow to certainty was the discovery of the placebo effect. Beginning in the 1940's, medical researchers began to realize that patients' beliefs were a major complication in the effort to evaluate the true effectiveness of various drugs. Patients who believe that they are participating in an authentically therapeutic process actually do better than would otherwise be expected.

This effect has been demonstrated, not just with pills, but across a wide spectrum of medical methods. Judging from what we've seen in clinical trials, we can safely assume that placebo effects are at work in every health care method and process, whether Eastern or Western, traditional or alternative, complementary or integrative. In fact, it is almost impossible to escape the placebo effect in health and fitness; our minds are always at work evaluating the prospects for health and disease. Belief always has a hand in physiology.

THE STATUS SYNDROME

The placebo effect has been a real distraction for proponents of deterministic medicine and fitness, but things really started to unravel with the 2004 publication of *The Status Syndrome* by epidemiologist Michael Marmot. Marmot has compiled thirty years of evidence demonstrating the crucial importance of social rank in our health and well-being. His conclusion is that "health follows a social gradient."

In reviewing hundreds of studies from around the world, Marmot found that social inequalities are powerful determinants of human health. "Wherever we are in the social hierarchy, our health is likely to be better than those below us and worse than those above us." This holds true, not just for one particular kind of illness, but for all forms of human affliction. "Being low in the hierarchy means a greater susceptibility to just about every disease that's going."

Marmot spent almost three decades studying the health of British civil servants in two studies known as the Whitehall studies. His team followed thousands of individuals, all classified according to their rank in the occupational hierarchy. The findings showed a dramatic social gradient in mortality for most major causes of death: disease of the cardiovascular, renal, gastrointestinal, and respiratory systems, most cancers, accidental deaths and violent deaths. His conclusion was that "subtle differences in social ranking can lead to dramatic differences in health."

A WORLD OF VIPS AND VUPS

The discovery of the status syndrome leads us to suppose that there are two main characters in our health gradient drama, the Vips and the Vups. The Vips are the Very Important People, the ones that we celebrate and honor. We shower them with money, attention and recognition. We honor them on magazine covers, listen to their speeches and award them honorary degrees. Consequently, the Vips enjoy good health, superior physical fitness and long life.

The Vups, on the other hand, are the Very Unrecognized People. These are the people that we ignore. We keep them out of our clubs and our consciousness. We give them minimal pay and minimal recognition. Because of this social rejection and isolation, the Vups suffer more frequent and more serious illness than the Vips. They become frequent visitors to hospitals and clinics. They have low levels of physical fitness and high levels of obesity and diabetes. Not surprisingly, this drags them deeper into a downward spiral. Low status leads to ill health, but ill health also leads to a demotion in status. It sucks to be a Vup.

ROCKING THE HEALTH CARE WORLD

The discovery of the status syndrome is profoundly threatening to many of our assumptions about how the body works. Biochemistry, biomechanics, and physiology are shown to be probabilistic, not definitive. The popular belief that certain procedures and substances have consistently predictable physical outcomes is shown to be unfounded. The idea that medical experts have absolute knowledge of health and disease is also undermined.

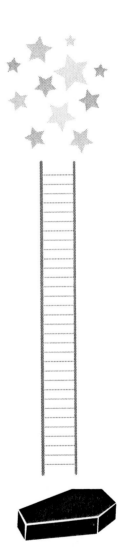

Not only that, we also begin to realize that medical effectiveness is not uniform across society. If health varies with social standing, then it must also be the case that the success of any given medical substance or treatment will also vary with status. To put it bluntly, medicine simply works better on rich, famous people than it does on the poor and invisible; medicine works better on Vips than it does on Vups.

People of higher status respond better because they expect things to work out in their favor; their past history of success in life predisposes them to believe in a positive outcome. In other words, they are already under the influence of a placebo effect even before they set foot in the doctor's office. In contrast, those below society's middle rung are predisposed to a negative outcome. Their life experience has been one of frequent rejection, struggle and disappointment. When Vups enter the doctor's office, they don't expect to be cured. They expect to be disrespected, rejected or ignored. Obviously, this decreases the likelihood of a successful outcome.

And that's not all. The status syndrome even forces us to broaden our understanding of *medicine* itself. Traditionally, we tend to think of medicines as substances that are swallowed or injected into the body, but in light of what we now know about the health effects of social position, we may now say that anything that promotes a person up the social ladder is medicinal, just as anything that demotes us is toxic.

In this light, we come to the conclusion that social attention and recognition are at least as powerful as many of the herbs, potions and pills that we consume in such prodigious quantities. Attention makes us feel wanted and important; as our sense of status improves, so does our outlook. As our outlook improves, so does our health.

All the positive and negative strokes that we give to one another have social and, in turn, medical consequences. Perks, promotions and pats on the back act as medicine while insults, slights and verbal digs act as poisons. Love, of course, is medicine, just as indifference is poison. Hiring is medicine, firing is toxic. Good grades, gold stars and glowing performance reviews are therapeutic. Bad grades, black marks and bad reviews inflict pain and eventually, disease.

And of course, we also come to the disturbing conclusion that, in some real sense, money can also be medicinal. A fat bank account not only gives us more options in life, it also gives us more respect. Like it or not, people bow down to wealth and heap recognition on those who have it. Money may or may not buy happiness, but it apparently buys some degree of health and probably fitness as well.

ROCKING THE FITNESS WORLD

Just as *The Status Syndrome* wreaks havoc with our traditional ideas about health care and medicine, it also disrupts our thinking about physical fitness and training. Professor Marmot's work concentrated primarily on health and disease, but we can be sure that similar principles apply to matters of hyper-health or fitness. That is, if a social promotion can decrease your risk of heart disease, it's not unlikely that it would also propel you to a personal best in your favorite athletic event. This is precisely what we see in the careers of great athletes. Good performance is rewarded with higher social standing, which leads to better performance and so on. In this sense, adoring fans make great athletes better.

The more praise and reward we heaped on Michael Jordan, the better he got.

The same principle also holds true with common fitness prescriptions from weight training to yoga, Pilates, cardio or martial art. None of these practices have strictly causal results; all of them are more likely to succeed with people of high status. Physical training simply works better on Vips than it does on Vups. Sad, but apparently true.

The status syndrome explains a lot, maybe even more than we'd like it to explain. We've known for a long time now that obesity, like health in general, follows a social gradient; the poor are far more likely to be obese than the rich. We generate all sorts of explanations on this score–good food is more expensive, rich people receive better nutritional education and so on. But there is clearly something else going on here besides calories and exercise. It sounds absurd, but it may actually be true–if you want to lose weight, try exercise and diet, but if that doesn't work, get yourself some recognition, a promotion or a raise. Win a Nobel Prize and watch the pounds melt away.

THE RANK-BODY LINK

Given the evidence demonstrating a social health gradient, the obvious question becomes Why should social rank have such a profound effect on our health and performance? What is the nature of the rank-body link?

The knee-jerk explanation is to say that the rich have access to superior medical care and fitness resources, so of course they would enjoy better health, fitness and longevity. In fact, the health gradient goes far deeper than access to resources. As Marmot points out, it's the psychological experience of inequality that lies at the root.

Because we are intensely social animals, our standing in the social hierarchy has a powerful influence on our sense of identity. This in turn shapes our interpretation of events and drives placebo and nocebo events in our bodies.

HYPER-SENSITIVE HOMINIDS

If we look at the status syndrome in the context of human evolution, the origins of the rank-body connection become clear. The story begins with primates, especially big-brained, bipedal hominids with narrow hips that are necessary for bipedal locomotion. The combination of big heads and a small birth canal mean that children are born–in effect–prematurely, unable to meet the challenges of life. This means a prolonged state of immaturity and dependency. For humans, social support in childhood is vital for survival.

This was especially the case in our ancestral environment, where bipedal hominids lived in close proximity to a wide assortment of hungry predators. In this environment, social cohesion was an urgent and compelling necessity. This predicament favored individuals and tribes with a high sensitivity to social cues, especially matters of rank. When tribal cohesion and social support are essential to survival, everyone has a powerful interest in knowing where they stand.

In this environment, acceptance and rejection are not just matters of hurt feelings or self-esteem, they are matters of life or death. Banishment from the tribe would be a death sentence. You might be able to survive on your own for a few days or weeks, but the odds would be slim; a solo hominid on the primal grassland is best described as cat food. Conversely, high rank in the tribe offers greater safety, better food and reproductive perks.

This is why our bodies react so strongly to acceptance and rejection events in our modern lives. Our brains are wired for social sensitivity; we continue to respond as if tribal membership is a matter of immediate survival. In today's world, most instances of social acceptance and rejection are not matters of life and death, but we continue to react to them as if they were. You probably won't die if you get fired from your job, but your body doesn't believe that for an instant.

TRUE PAIN

In recent years, neuroscientists have discovered some of the actual physical mechanisms involved in the rank-body link. Specifically, researchers have discovered that physical and social pain share a substantial amount of neural circuitry.

In a study published in the journal *Science*, Naomi Eisenberger, a neuroscientist at UCLA, found a physiological basis for the pain of social rejection. She exposed test subjects to artificial social exclusion and measured their brain activity with MRI. She found that test subjects registered rejection in the same part of the brain that also responds to physical pain, the anterior cingulate cortex.

In other words, rejection doesn't just hurt in some literary or metaphoric sense. No, from the body's point of view, the pain is real. Ostracism hurts just as much as any insult to our tissue. And so, the status syndrome makes even more sense. Over time, frequent social rejection becomes a sort of chronic pain syndrome. Chronic pain stresses the body, weakens the immune system and compromises our disease resistance. It is no wonder that people of lower rank suffer more affliction and disease.

POWER, CONTROL AND STRESS

Ultimately, the social health gradient comes down to a question of power, control and stress. If you're above the middle rung of the social ladder, you'll have access to resources that will insulate you from the crush of unpredictable events. A car crash, a layoff, a death in the family—you can probably weather these things and get on with your life. If things get really bad, you can call for help from your friends (who, in all likelihood, also live above the middle rung).

But if you're on the lower half of the ladder, your buffer is weak and you know it. The unknown is a constant worry. Your mind races, trying to find some sense of security and calm, but things remain precarious. Much of your worry may be abstract and symbolic, but your body knows that something dangerous is nearby. Catastrophe looms like a carnivore at the perimeter of camp.

Obviously, the higher you are in the hierarchy, the more power and control you will have over your situation. This sense of control means more options; more options mean less stress. Lower rank means fewer choices, reduced power and greater stress. Powerful mind-body effects are at work here. Reduce an animal's control and stress hormones increase. In turn, disease resistance falls.

A PERENNIAL PRIMATE PREDICAMENT?

The dilemma of social standing is one of the oldest, not only in human history, but in the history of all social animals. Every social animal wants to know the secret to advancement and promotion. In all likelihood, the status syndrome is something that afflicts all primates. Neurobiologist Robert Sapolsky has documented clear differences in baboon stress hormones based on status. The same thing probably occurs to a greater or lesser extent in all of us.

Social animals being what they are, some degree of ranking, hierarchy and inequity seems unavoidable. In all likelihood, the Vips will always enjoy better health than the Vups, regardless of whatever miracle treatments might we invent. As Marmot himself puts it, "health gradients are inevitable."

Nevertheless, it would be foolhardy to ignore the status syndrome and its implications. If we really want to thrive as individuals and as a culture, we are going to have to face the reality of the socially-based health inequality. Just as the discovery of the placebo effect transformed medical care and led to astonishing advances, so too might a recognition of the status syndrome lead to some real progress, if we are willing to look it in the face.

RESOURCES

The Status Syndrome: How Social Standing Affects Our Health and Longevity Michael Marmot 2004 Times Books

The Placebo Effect: An Interdisciplinary Exploration Edited by Anne Harrington 1997 Harvard University Press

Why rejection hurts: a common neural alarm system for physical and social pain: TRENDS in Cognitive Sciences Vol. 8 No. 7 July 2004 Naomi I. Eisenberger and Matthew D. Lieberman, Department of Psychology, UCLA

Primate's Memoir: Robert M. Sapolsky

BOUNCING, JUMPING AND GLIDING

We play because we have an exuberance of spirits and
energy, but we are also exuberant because we play.

Kay Redfield Jamison

A BRIEF HISTORY OF PLAY

One of the exuberant animal's core beliefs is that play is an essential component of physical education and healthy living. This seems self-evident and scarcely worth arguing about, but at the same time we're led to wonder about the natural history of play. Where did it come from anyway and how long has it been around?

Some scholars hold that the entire history of the universe itself, from the big bang forward, has had a playful quality to it. From the dances of light and electromagnetic radiation to the swirling of galaxies, we can see a kind of physical play on a grand scale. This perspective has its appeal, but others hold that play is something of a purely animal nature.

So, let's look at the history of life and see if we can identify the point at which play first appeared. The main events in life's history are now well known. The earth is roughly 5 billion years old. Simple life appeared sometime thereafter and remained simple for a very long time.

We can seriously doubt whether much play was going on in those very early days. Life was just too simple. Creatures lacked sophistication, not to mention the ability to jump, hop or skip. We find it hard to imagine viruses or bacteria doing much in the way of bouncing, wrestling or frolicking.

CAMBRIAN EXPLOSION

Things didn't really get hopping until about 500 million years ago. After a long period of simplicity, a sudden burst of diversification occurred, with the appearance of the lineages of almost all animals living today. This stunning and unique evolutionary flowering is called the "Cambrian explosion" and is unmatched in biological history. As Stephen Jay Gould described it, "The Cambrian explosion was the most extraordinary event in the history of life."

If we think of the Cambrian explosion as the birth of animals, we may very well think of it as the birth of play as well. We have no way of knowing if these early animals actually played with one another, but it does seem possible. Play does not fossilize of course, so we can't really tell how much play was going at the time. Can we imagine a trilobite at play? Early vertebrates? A squid perhaps, but who knows? The popular view is to imagine early life as a period of intense violence, with ravenous creatures eating one another in a primal feeding frenzy. But even these creatures must have become sated at some point, and what else would you do when your brothers and sisters are heckling you with their proto-noses?

MESOZOIC PLAY

Fast-forward now to the Mesozoic period, commonly referred to as "the age of dinosaurs." The obvious question that we have to ask at this point is "Did dinosaurs play?" The obvious answer is, "It depends on who you ask." Our knowledge of dinosaurs is, shall we say, skeletal. Most of us tend to think of them simply as ponderous, vicious beasts, mindlessly ripping each other to shreds in the shallow, fetid swamps of the Jurassic era.

Recent fossil finds suggests other interpretations however, and some paleontologists now say that dinosaurs had a more nurturing side to their personality and that they may have even cared for their young.

At least one paleontologist believes that dinosaurs played. Robert T. Bakker, most famous for his proposal that dinosaurs were active social animals, argues for social bonds, care of the young, and in the process, play. In his book *Raptor Red*, Bakker speculates about the lives of dinosaurs by describing the life of his *Utahraptor* protagonist:

> Raptor Red was the most successfully selfish chick in her brood. She snatched the most food. She grew faster than her sibs. She was first out of the nest, first to join mother and father on a hunt. A sister was next. Once they were out of the nest, much of the chick-chick rivalry evaporated. She played with her sister, and the two bossed the male chicks around.

Of course, Bakker could be wrong. But if he's right, the origins of play might just go all the way back to the beginnings of the Triassic, 245 million years ago.

But whatever the child-rearing behaviors of dinosaurs, we can be sure that they did a substantial amount of hunting and fleeing from one another. As we know from observing today's hunting animals, such movements are highly sophisticated and complex. These movements require practice and this practice often comes in the form of play. Any dinosaur that played would have enjoyed a survival advantage over his less exuberant competitors.

CENOZOIC PLAY

Whatever the dinosaurs were doing, it all came to an nasty end when an enormous asteroid fell from the sky some 65 million years ago, bringing the Mesozoic to a close and opening up the dawn of the Cenozoic.

In popular accounts, the Cenozoic is usually referred to as "The Age of Mammals." This is partly correct; mammals really did begin to flourish after the demise of the dinosaurs. But in fact, mammals had already been around for a very long time. Scientists have traced mammalian heritage as far back as 210 million years ago, smack in the middle of the Mesozoic

In the Hall of Mammals at the American Museum of Natural History in Washington D.C., one display features a replica of a small, rodent-like animal. It sits on a pedestal in a prominent location, surrounded by huge, stuffed mammals of all description.

The scientific name for this creature is *Morganucodon oehleri*, but we'll call him Morgan for short. Morgan represents the first of his kind, a founding partner in our mammalian lineage. Our question of course is, "Did Morgan play?"

A common take on this is "no." If you're living in the brush with dinosaurs tromping and screaming all around you, your predominant emotion is going to be fear, not playfulness. I don't know about you, but if I've got a massive beast looming over me all day long, I'm going to be cowering and quivering, not frolicking.

But that's just the standard-issue picture. Morgan's life may have been difficult, but we can also assume that he had some dinosaur-free time to enjoy with his brothers and sisters. Modern day rodents and shrews play with one another, so why not Morgan? If you buy this story, then play is some 200 million years old.

JURASSIC BEAVER

In any case, our assumptions about early mammalian life were called into question in early 2006 with the discovery of a fossilized "beaver" that lived 164 million years ago, smack in the middle of the Jurassic period. This creature, *Castorocauda lutrasimilis,* looked like a cross between a platypus, river otter and beaver, almost half a meter long from nose to tail.

We know nothing about the behavior of this so-called "Jurassic beaver," but it's pretty hard to believe that such an animal didn't play. Any animal that looks like an otter has to be playful, right? Unless we are willing to imagine a serious, dour and playless otter, we have to suppose that there was play in those primordial creeks, rivers and lakes.

MAMMALIAN LIBERATION?

When the asteroid fell to earth, the dinosaurs fell too and for the first time the mammals could come out of the bushes and have a look around. Naturally, they were enormously relieved that their oppressors had been eliminated. In fact, if we were writing a *Far Side* cartoon, we might even say that the mammalian play impulse originated in this wild celebration: "When the asteroid appeared in the sky, all the mammals stood up on their back legs, let out a wild cheer and began to frolic." If the *T. rex* suddenly left my neighborhood, I'd be celebrating and playing too.

Maybe, maybe not. But in any case, the mammals had some easy sailing ahead. Big wide open habitats lay all around them and all that they needed to do was eat and reproduce. Of course, there were still some problems in the form of large predatory birds and reptiles, but the playground was now open.

PRIMATE PLAY

As the mammals diversified and radiated into open habitats, they became exuberant, evolving into a host of fascinating and furry forms. Before long, one branch adapted to life in the trees; these became the primates.

Mammals are famous for play, but it's primates that really excel. Show me a primate and I'll show you an animal that's looking for some bounce and some swing. In fact, we would find it very difficult to image a primate that didn't have a strong interest in play. With 233 species in 13 families, the primate lineage is 60 to 70 million years old. As *Homo sapiens*, a primate in good standing, our play heritage goes back at least this far.

So, we are left to speculate to our heart's content. Maybe play goes all the way back to the warm, shallow pond. Maybe the dinosaurs. Certainly the mammals. If we're looking to explore the limits, we are free to do so, but we can say with confidence that play is at least 60 million years old, with roots much deeper in the past.

However we frame it, there can be no question that play has been around for many millions of years. It constitutes a status quo for mammals and primates. It is a default behavior, a given, a normal, natural behavior for human animals. We ignore it at our peril.

OUR SACRED CREEK

Back before the silicon hit the fan, California's Santa Clara valley was a paradise on earth. An exceptionally friendly climate for *Homo sapiens*, it was rich in fruits and vegetables, with beaches, mountains and wetlands just down the road. My brother and I grew up in the twilight days of this paradise—back when you could still go a little bit wild on the outskirts of San Jose, Sunnyvale and Palo Alto.

Every day was an adventure back then. Our neighborhood in Mountain View was bordered on one side by a green belt of sorts, the last of the raw land, and a creek that fed into the San Francisco Bay. Naturally, the creek was a major attraction for my brother and I; whenever Mom would give the OK, we'd make straight for it.

Off we'd go, racing out the back door, over the back fence and across our neighbor's yard. The journey was just as important as the destination back then; there were intriguing obstacles and opportunities every inch of the way. We ran past houses with strange people and unsolved mysteries, then cut through another neighbor's yard and into an orchard. Beyond that, we faced the dreaded greenhouses. Rumor had it that they were patrolled by a giant dog that hated kids. We'd take a quick look and run at top speed as if our lives depended on it.

Once we cleared the greenhouses, we raced down the embankment to the creek. Here we felt safe and before long, the wonders began to unfold. We discovered small animals, strange plants and an assortment of discarded junk that, with a little imagination, could easily be transformed into space ships, forts, trucks and animals. To the adult eye, there was nothing particularly noteworthy about this creek, but for us, it was a place where our bodies and imaginations could run wild. The creek was our art studio and gymnasium, our theatre, our laboratory and our wild kingdom; it was whatever we wanted it to be. Look! Here's a hubcap, here's a stick. Here's an old tire and a barbecue grill. Trash became treasure, rocks became toys, sticks became tools.

We played there for hours, entirely without the benefit of mass-produced toys, guidebooks, rules or self-help manuals. No one told us how to play or laid down any rules for proper form. There were no standards for performance, no eliminations, no judges and no test scores. We learned with our whole bodies—mind, muscle and sensation working together in synchrony. We were performance artists on the loose, our imaginations reaching out, exploring the world around us. We were livin' large.

THE VIRTUES OF WILD PLAY

Our creek experience would make perfect sense to Betty Beach, a professor of early childhood education at the University of Maine at Farmington. Professor Beach has a particular fascination with the play memories of mature adults and has done some intriguing field research. In extensive interviews with adults in rural communities, professor Beach noticed that early play memories, especially in outdoor settings, hold a special status for many people. She was struck by "the tenacity and clarity of these play memories even after half a century into adulthood" and suggested that the "commonality of such memory evidences a widely shared bond of human experience."

As we take a closer look at this wild, unsupervised play, we begin to understand why such memories are so powerful and enduring. Aside from the obvious benefits such as fresh air and exercise, wild play offers children and adults a host of qualities that are profoundly meaningful.

In the first place, wild play is authentic personal creation. Because it is spontaneous and self-directed, wild play is also highly engaging. The experience is not imposed by some large creature with a deep voice. Rather, it is self-generated and personally meaningful.

Children who practice wild play learn with their bodies and their minds simultaneously. This is no fragmented or prepackaged curriculum. It is integrative and multi-sensory; the player learns by exercising his body and imagination in tandem.

Wild play is closely allied with the spirit of exploration. The free child follows his curiosity wherever it leads, looking into corners, around obstacles and under rocks. Adults tend to forget the intensity and depth of the experience, but the child's exploration of the local neighborhood is just as powerful, engaging and immediate as any adult journey into the wild. Our little creek was as impressive to us as the Columbia River was to Lewis and Clark.

Since it is free, wild play also gives players the opportunity to express themselves as they choose; this is their chance to have a voice. Temporarily liberated from a world of adult words and ideas, they can speak their minds and express their emotions freely. Their audience may consist of animals, trees, rocks and clouds, but this hardly matters.

Wild play also gives us a chance to practice divergent, lateral thinking skills. Those curious objects we found down at the creek could be whatever we wanted them to be, no matter how outlandish. By conjuring up a wide range of possible explanations, we generate hypotheses that we can test for validity or simply enjoy on their own merits. This practice is not only exciting, it is also immensely valuable in later life.

As wild play gives us an opportunity for authentic engagement with the world, it also deepens our appreciation of nature and develops our primal inclination towards biophilia. Outdoor play teaches us not only that the wild earth is generally safe, but that it is incredibly rich and fascinating as well.

THE DISAPPEARANCE OF WILD PLAY

Unfortunately, wild play–like most wild things in today's world–is endangered. As natural habitats disappear, there are fewer places that children or adults can play freely. Professor Beach and other play researchers worry that

> as children are increasingly cut off from the opportunity to roam, confined instead to adult-designed and constructed play areas that are barren of natural materials so vital to their development, fewer occasions for productive childhood will exist. Such constriction would be disastrous not only for individual children but also for our collective ecological well-being…

She predicts that we can "expect to see fewer examples of children at play in the natural environment, fewer future memories of sacred places, time and objects, and presumably fewer corresponding benefits to healthy human development." Tragically, our current generation of children may be the first in human history to grow up without memories of sacred, natural play experience.

FORCES ACTING AGAINST WILD PLAY

The forces acting against wild play are powerful, relentless and well-funded. The most obvious threat is the juggernaut of suburban development. Every new building project that destroys a vacant lot also destroys an opportunity for wild play. Every new strip mall takes away some child's secret hiding place, some child's cherished short cut. New roads are built for cars, not people, so it's increasingly dangerous and unpleasant to walk anywhere. Thirty years ago more than 66% of children walked to school; recent surveys indicate that only 18% of children walk or bike to school today. Development not only destroys natural habitat, farmland, forests, biodiversity and wildlife corridors, it also takes away those places where people can be extravagantly and joyously alive.

Another powerful agent acting against wild play is the professionalization of youth sport. In today's world, children are channeled into organized leagues almost as soon as they can walk and are taught to mimic the movement specialties of professional athletes. Many Americans now assume that athletic experience is essential to personal development, but the fact remains that youth sports have a substantial cost. Practice time has to come from somewhere and the easiest place to take it from is unsupervised, unstructured play. In this way, sports displace wild play; every hour on the practice field is one less hour spent at the creek.

Another force that displaces wild play is the overwhelming onslaught of gee-whiz products and toys that are marketed directly at children. Flashing lights and bright colors capture our attention and keep us indoors, scrolling through menus and pushing buttons. While some of these toys and games have authentic value, they still keep us away from the creek. Even when they have educational merit, digital devices still tend to displace wild play.

Other forces acting against wild play are psychological. In this post-9/11 world, fear and insecurity keep many of us pinned down in our homes as if they were bunkers. We are increasingly reluctant to face the wider world, especially the untamed outdoors. Our normal sense of nature-loving biophilia gives way to biophobia; we imagine all sorts of evils lurking in outdoor places–bird flu, SARS and terrorists are just outside. The more time we spend inside, the more paranoid and xenophobic we become. The outdoor world–our natural habitat– becomes alien.

The final force that puts the squeeze on wild play is adult imperialism, the over-active and over-bearing supervision of children's play by adults. As professor Beach put it, "…prominent play observers bemoan the encroachment of adults on children's imaginative play. They see play as increasingly regimented, dominated and 'domesticated' by adults." Obviously, the vast majority of this adult supervision is well-intentioned, but all the same, supervision changes the nature of childhood play dramatically. Supervised play is really no play at all.

CONSEQUENCES

The disappearance of wild play is not just a children's issue. Rather, it is a cultural problem of immense significance. For the overwhelming majority of human life on earth, play has been wild, unsupervised, unstructured and free. In essence, we have been going down to the creek for 6 million years. Give a human child a semi-wooded mosaic grassland environment and his curious mind will do the rest. Depriving children of wild play is an unprecedented social experiment, a truly radical act. Tragically, our current generation of young people may be the first in our species' history to go without this basic life experience.

Since play is essential for human development, health and intelligence, play-deprivation is a major social issue for both children and adults. Play-deprived humans make bad employees, bad employers and bad leaders.

Stuart Brown, founder of The Institute for Play, has collected thousands of individual play histories and discovered that play-deprived individuals are more likely to become paranoid, violent and extremist. Not only that, play-deprived individuals are likely to be less tolerant of stress, and consequently, will tend to develop more health problems than their playful counterparts. In this sense, play-deprivation is also a public health issue.

And of course, the preservation of wild play is inextricably linked to the preservation of habitat and biodiversity. As professor Beach put it, "Children who encounter the natural world through play in their young lives are far more likely to become adults who value and understand nature's role in human ecology..." Or, to put it in the opposite sense, children who are deprived of wild play in outdoor settings are more likely to create products and policies that are environmentally hostile. Deprive a child of wild play and he may just become a developer.

PLAY ADVOCACY

Today, the creek of our childhood is no longer a place for children–or anyone else–to play. The dogs are all leashed up, the neighbor's yard has been sanitized and fenced, the greenhouses have been replaced by up-scale condos and the creek itself has been cordoned off with chain-link. There are no shortcuts to the creek anymore and no one gets in unless they're on official business. The creek is merely a topographic feature, a place for stormwater runoff to go in a heavy rain. In essence, the creek is dead.

Are we depressed by this state of affairs? Absolutely. Are we angry? There is no question. But as we begin to appreciate the primal value of play and the severe consequences of play-deprivation, we are stirred to action. We become increasingly militant play advocates, child advocates and environmental advocates. We join forces with labor unions lobbying for workers' rights and a saner work schedule, with environmentalists trying to persevere wild places and with teachers who are suffering under the Orwellian demand for test scores above all else.

Above all, we redouble our efforts towards authentic participation in wild settings. We go in search of other creeks and natural habitats that we can enjoy without supervision, coaches, flashing lights and onerous rules. Give us some rocks, some sticks and some mud. We'll know what to do.

RESOURCES

"Play as an Organizing Principle" by Stuart Brown, MD, *Animal Play: Evolutionary, Comparative, and Ecological Consequences* edited by Marc Bekhoff and John Byers, 1998 Cambridge University Press

UNDER THE AFFLUENCE

An animal may be said to be at work when the stimulus to activity is some lack, and it may be said to be at play when the stimulus is sheer plenitude of vitality.

Friedrich Schiller
German playwright

Remember how it felt the last time you found a crumpled $20 bill in a shirt pocket? How about the first day of summer vacation when school let out? What about the feeling you get when you've got a wallet full of cash, a well-stocked refrigerator or a full tank of gas?

In each of these cases, you've enjoyed a sense of abundance, even luxury. For a moment at least, you felt more relaxed and enjoyed a breath of fresh energy. You might have even felt the urge to do something creative and exuberant–go for a run, take on a new project or call up some friends. In the language of play scholarship, you were enjoying the effect of "surplus resources."

WELCOME TO SURPLUS RESOURCE THEORY

Animal play behavior is a challenging study that inspires a surprising amount of controversy and dissent, but there is one point that all animal behavior scientists agree on. That is, animals play more when they are well-fed, warm, safe and comfortable. This is one of the most conspicuous findings in animal play research. Primates, carnivores, humans–all are sensitive to resource levels and play more in times of affluence. Animal behaviorist Gordon Burghardt calls this the "surplus resource theory" of animal play.

In his book *The Genesis of Animal Play*, Burghardt describes the playful response to surplus as "...one of the most robust findings in the play literature." Not only do we observe that animals play readily in conditions of plenitude, we also see the opposite effect in times of scarcity. As Burghardt puts it, "studies confirm that play of all types is readily curtailed in times of food shortage, climatic adversity, social upheaval, and chronic stress."

We can even estimate the quality of an animal's habitat by looking at the frequency of play behaviors. That is, if animals are not playing, there is probably something wrong with their environment. In this sense, play is a barometer of environmental and cultural health. Or, to use another metaphor, play is the canary in the coal mine; when play disappears, something is seriously wrong.

DOMESTICATED SPECIES PLAY MORE

The surplus resource theory confirms what we see in our familiar animal companions. That is, domesticated animals play more frequently than their wild counterparts. In light of surplus resource theory, this makes sense. The domesticated animal gives up its wildness in exchange for a predictable food supply and in the process, gains a substantial measure of security and comfort. Free from the rigors of the wild, he can play more often and with greater abandon. His sense of surplus allows for more physical creativity. It's easier to be playful when someone is bringing you food and keeping you safe from predators and bad weather.

Animal scientists have also reported that play in young animals is more prevalent after feeding. I've observed this behavior in my dog Mojo, and he's quite reliable on this score. Every afternoon he hounds me for his dinner and then, as soon as he's finished eating, he always wants to play. He's got a sense of surplus and affluence – carbohydrates, protein and fats are flowing into his bloodstream and as far as his body is concerned, he's rich. If he had a paintbrush, he might do some art. If he knew how to type, he might write a story. Instead, he finds his teddy bear and begs me to throw it for him.

CHILDHOOD AFFLUENCE

Surplus resource theory also explains why children are so extravagantly creative. Not only do they have two large animals to look after their needs, they also have an immense sense of temporal affluence. When your entire life lies before you, the vista is incredible and the possibilities are unlimited. Inspired by this glut of time and potential, the young organism goes on a creative binge, growing, playing, drawing, singing and imagining.

In contrast, adulthood can become, for some people, a time of comparative poverty. The big animals who looked after our every need are not as omnipotent as they once were and our temporal affluence grows shorter with every passing year. Possibilities for achievement diminish and we become more "realistic." Our perceptions of affluence change and we may even come to see ourselves as impoverished, whatever the reality. When this happens, we scale back our dreams; our creativity plummets and our physical health goes with it.

HOW SURPLUS RESOURCES AFFECT THE BODY

To understand how SRT works, it's important to remember that all animals–human and non-human–live in a state of precarious uncertainty. Our bodies are perched on the edge of survival and we're alert for trends and forces that lead towards or away from life.

Instinctively, we adjust our behavior in response to perceived surplus and shortage. When resources are tight, we become more conservative and risk-averse; we hoard our physiological and psychological capabilities. When resources are abundant on the other hand, we become more liberal with our physicality. We say, "I'm safe, it's time to party."

It's easy to see how perceptions of shortage and abundance might affect the nervous system of the human animal. Remember, there are two main branches of the system, the sympathetic and the parasympathetic. Typically, the sympathetic branch is described as a "fight-flight" system that mobilizes organs and tissues for quick physical responsiveness. The parasympathetic system on the other hand, is a "feed and breed" system that stimulates relaxation, repair and regeneration.

This is an accurate description, but we can also see these branches as players in our body's responses to shortage and abundance. When an animal perceives threats or deficits, the sympathetic system initiates defensive action. It conserves, protects and defends the life core. When the body perceives surplus resources or affluence, the parasympathetic nervous system kicks into gear, undertaking what Robert Sapolsky calls "long-term rebuilding projects." In other words, when the body perceives affluence, it shifts into a creative, anabolic state. The pressure is off, and it's time to rebuild stressed organs, blood vessels and muscle tissue.

NEUROTRANSMISSION

We can also suppose that perceptions of shortage and affluence will have a real effect on neurotransmitter production in the human brain. For example, dopamine, a key neurotransmitter that influences mood, is likely to be particularly sensitive to our perception of abundance. Find a $100 bill on the sidewalk and your dopamine production is likely to go up. Have an IRS agent visit your house and feel your dopamine levels plummet while your stress hormones skyrocket. Even the most abstract, symbolic shortages and abundances can have real physical consequences.

NUTRITION

Surplus resource theory also explains why diets cause us so much grief. Not only do they give our bodies a sense of nutritional shortage and shift our metabolism into starvation mode, they do so in an environment of extravagant nutritional abundance. That is, we're starving while everyone around us is eating. Even if we do manage to bring our will power to bear over our impulses, our bodies are still going to be confused. If you want your body to feel playfully creative and active, the last thing you'll want to do is give it a sense of shortage. In other words, eat up.

Surplus resource theory even gives us a fresh perspective on what we eat. These days, it is all the rage to examine the nature of dietary fats. We go on at great length about the biochemical differences between polyunsaturated fats, monounsaturated fats, omega-3s and other variations. This is all critical knowledge in our quest to prevent disease, but from the view of surplus resource theory, we may be missing a vital point. That is, dietary fat– whatever its molecular configuration–is a prime surplus, an affluence. When we consume fat, we tell our brains that the environment is rich and that all will be well. Not only does fatty food taste great, it sends a powerful existential message to the animal brain: "This environment is rich; this is a good place to be." From this fact alone, we can predict that some measure of fat consumption will make us smarter, stronger, happier and more creative.

AFFLUENCY: RECOGNIZING ABUNDANCE

Surplus resource theory suggests that, if we want to improve our physical creativity and vitality, a good place to begin is by learning how to recognize the abundance in our lives. By adjusting our perceptions to appreciate surplus resources, we send a calming and energizing message to our bodies. We can even propose a skill called *affluency*, the art of recognizing and appreciating surplus resources.

This art begins with perception and perspective. There is no absolute affluence, of course. Beyond the basic needs of food, water and shelter, it's all a matter of interpretation. That's why rich people can feel poor and poor people can feel rich. Abundance is where you find it.

All artists live and die by their sense of affluency. In the popular imagination, we often think of the starving artist, starving musician and starving writer, struggling for scraps of recognition in a hostile world. But there's more to this picture than meets the eye. The starving artist may be eating Ramen noodles every night, but somewhere, somehow, he's found a source of affluence. It may be social support from family and friends, the richness he finds in the history of art, the raw exuberance he observes in the natural world or the possibilities of human movement. Whatever the source, artists thrive when they tap into surplus.

Most of us have been conditioned to think of affluence in financial terms, but money is only one kind of wealth. We can think of temporal, environmental, social, emotional, cultural, biophilic or spiritual affluence as well. In fact, this is the whole point of affluency; recognizing and appreciating affluence in any way we can. Your body doesn't much care about the form; any sense of surplus resource will calm the body and liberate our creative energies. Even personal experience can be a form of affluence. More years behind us mean more stories, more ideas to draw on and a better understanding of how the world works.

KEEP YOUR EYE ON THE AFFLUENCE

When times are hard, it's easy to forget the sheer magnitude of our 21st century surplus. But our affluence is truly immense, many orders of magnitude greater than that enjoyed by any other animal on the planet. Modern humans aren't simply rich, we're affluent beyond the wildest dreams of any other primate. We don't just have surplus resources, we are wallowing in wealth. We are the Microsoft of the animal world.

Our survival-oriented brains tend to focus on shortages and deficits, for these pose a more immediate concern. But if we're going to be creative—physically or otherwise—we need to get ourselves into an affluent state of mind. So count your affluences. Maybe you're short in one area, but rich in another. Work with whatever abundance you've got.

The beautiful thing about adjusting our perception is that we can sometimes get a truly free lunch. We don't have to go out and work like dogs to get rich; in all likelihood, we already are rich in one way or another. For example, Garrison Keillor gave us a profoundly affluent point of view when he said "Nothing bad ever happens to a writer; it's *all* material." By changing his outlook, he turned adversity into abundance.

POLAR OPPOSITE

By now you've probably concluded that the surplus resource theory suggests a health philosophy that is the precise opposite of the standard line in mainstream fitness culture. Some physical fitness experts like to tell us that the path to a better body and better health lies in denial, deprivation and death-defiance: Cut down on your portion sizes, resist temptation, limit your impulses. Push yourself. Master your body. Pain creates gain. Create an atmosphere of scarcity and learn to like it. This counsel is has strong ties to our macho, warrior culture and our religious beliefs about sin, temptation and the evils of the body.

The problem with such counsel is that it simply does not hold up to the reality of the biological world. Non-human animals always do better under conditions of abundance. Play, creativity and risk-taking are normal biological responses to plenitude. Intentional denial and deprivation is abnormal, which is one reason why so many people fail in their attempts to carry it out.

And so, I suggest that we adopt a health and fitness philosophy that is consistent with what we see in nature. Make your body happy by giving it a sense of abundance. Give your mind a sense of ease and exuberance. Seek pleasure in action and in rest. Celebrate the joys of robust physicality. Let your body express its enthusiasm.

A WEALTH OF IDEAS

Appropriately enough, our surplus resource theory turns out to be immensely abundant in its own right. Ponder the implications for awhile and you'll come up with a whole host of questions about human behavior, play, fitness and creativity. For example, surplus resource theory gives us some powerful ideas about the dynamics of entire cultures and civilizations. Organizations, tribes and societies are all sensitive to shortage and affluence and respond in similar ways. We also wonder about the American paradox. That is, why is it that the richest country in history has produced a population that is so spectacularly sedentary? These questions are compelling, but they'll have to wait for another day. Right now, it's time to go and play.

RESOURCES

The Genesis of Animal Play: Testing the Limits by Gordon M. Burghardt, MIT Press 2005

EXPERT OPINIONS

Mojo is regarded as one of the preeminent voices in the field of play philosophy. Widely celebrated for the depth and breadth of his play behaviors, he has created a vast repertoire of novel play forms and is largely responsible for transforming the field of play psychology. Mojo has won numerous awards for his play philosophy and his work in the field of cross-species play. He is a widely sought-after speaker on play issues and travels the world as a dedicated play advocate. The following interview took place in October, 2004, in Seattle, Washington.

"Say Mojo, I'd like to do an interview about play. Do you have a few minutes? Would you be willing to answer a few questions?"

"Can I have a biscuit?"

"You just had your dinner."

"No biscuit, no interview."

"OK."

Interviewer delivers biscuit.

"OK Mojo, I have a list of questions…"

"Can you rub my belly first?"

"Well, OK."

Interviewer rubs Mojo's belly.

"OK, can we start now?"

"You have to scratch my ears first."

Interviewer scratches Mojo's ears.

"OK, can we talk NOW?"

"OK, I'm ready. So what's up?"

"Well, I need to know a few things about play. Maybe you could start by telling me a little bit about your play history."

"Oh that's easy. I've been playing ever since I was about 4 weeks old, so that would make it about 8 years so far. I play pretty much every day, unless you drag me out on one of your stupid car trips or leave me alone in the house."

"So you consider yourself something of an authority on the subject of play."

"Well yeah, I guess I would, but I never thought of it that way before. I mean what's there to be an authority about? You just start playing and when you're finished, you stop."

"So you would say that play is an important part of your life?"

"Well obviously. I mean isn't it an important part of everyone's life?"

"Is it? What about the other animals? Do they play too? What about cats and birds and squirrels and fish?"

"Everyone plays. They just play in different ways. You can't always tell by looking, you know. It's sort of what you would call a state of mind. Although, to be honest, I don't really know about the fish."

"So what about the humans then? Do they play too?"

"Well I assume they do, but it's really hard to tell sometimes. They aren't like other animals, that's for certain. Sometimes they run and jump like normal critters, but a lot of them just sit there, for hours on end, hardly doing anything at all. I worry about them. At least the young humans are playing, but they sit around a lot too. Mostly they just look at boxes with flashing lights."

"Do you think that they might be playing in other ways?"

"No, well maybe, but even if they are, they're missing the point."

"The point?"

"Yeah."

"Well what do you mean?"

"You humans are so dense sometimes. The point is that play begins in the body and that it involves movement. That's the most important kind of play, you know. All the other forms come from that. You might say that you're playing in some other way, but if you're not moving your body, you're missing out. You might be playing with all of your objects and tools and the sounds that you make, but if you don't actually move, you're missing the best part."

"OK Mojo, now maybe you could tell me about the purpose behind your playfulness."

"The what?"

"Oh, you know. The experts are always saying that play is preparation for hunting and evasion and other behaviors that you'd be doing as an adult."

"I thought *I* was the expert."

"Well, OK, but what do you think?"

"Do you see me doing any hunting?"

"Er, well, what about all the retrieving you do?"

"That's your gig, brother, not mine. You throw all that stuff away, I'm just bringing it back."

"So you wouldn't describe play as a means to some other end, then? You're not playing to be a better hunter."

"Grrrrrrrr."

"What?!"

"You humans are so slow sometimes."

"I don't get it."

"Of course you don't. That's why you have to ask all these questions. Play isn't for anything. We do it because we like to do it. Maybe we get better at some skill or something, but that's beside the point. We'd do it no matter what. And besides, if you're an animal, you can't predict what's going to happen in the future, so how can play be *for* anything? Maybe play makes us stronger or faster or smarter, but I really don't care about any of that."

"OK then, well let's move on to some other questions."

"Do I get a biscuit when we're done?"

"It depends on how cooperative you are."

"OK, I'll be good."

"Alright, now what's going on when you play with the other dogs? It seems like sometimes you're doing the whole dance to see who's alpha, but other times you go back and forth, like you're trading off."

"I am the alpha dog, you know."

"Yes, I know that, but what about the trade-off thing? It seems like you make a deal, 'I'll chase you for awhile, then you chase me.'"

"That's the play contract, you bonehead. We all do it. You know how we bow down to each other, like we're ready to spring? That's the play position. It means, 'everything after this is pretend.' Once you make the contract, you can do whatever you want and it's OK...you didn't know this?"

"Er, well..."

"You see, once you make a play contract, you can be dominant or submissive or you can switch off. You can chase or be chased and none of it matters. It's just fun."

"I had no idea..."

"Well obviously. The play contract is really a special thing, you know. Not too many animals can do "let's pretend." It's a sign of intelligence. When we do a play contract, we can play whatever role we want and it's all OK. Somebody can be chewing on your neck or chasing you at top speed, but it doesn't matter. We also get to imagine what the other is thinking. It's not just a sign of intelligence, it also stimulates intelligence. That's why I'm so smart."

"Well yes, you are pretty smart..."

"But the thing I can't figure out is why you humans never do a play contract. I mean, you don't have a play position or anything. You hug and shake hands and things like that, but I never see anything that looks like a play contract."

"Well we used to bow to each other in martial art class."

"Maybe that's the same thing then, although it seems like anything's possible with you humans. Do you have any more of those biscuits?"

Interviewer delivers a biscuit.

"So Mojo, what about this whole idea that play is just for puppies, not adult dogs? That's what a lot of people think."

"You're kidding, right?"

"No, I'm serious. The play scholars say that young animals play, but adults don't.

"There you go with those experts again."

"Well what do you think?"

"It's total nonsense. We'd play every day if we could get away with it. If you weren't always dragging us to those field trials, obedience trials and glamour shows, we might get a chance to live a little, you know what I mean? And besides, who comes up with these ideas?"

"Well Mojo, you've got to admit that they young animals are always playing, but that the adults don't do it nearly so much."

"That's just a question of conditions. You take an animal, give him a friendly place to live and he's going to just keep on playing forever. Just like me. Play is normal. Not playing is a sign of trouble."

"OK Mojo, one last question."

"It's about time. I need to go play."

"OK, what can you tell me about the difference between the way people play and the way that animals play?"

"I don't get it."

"You know, do animals play one way and people play some other way?"

"Grrrrrrrrr."

"What?!"

"Haven't we been through this before? Your tired, old distinction between humans and animals...when are you going to wise up, primate?"

"I was just asking..."

"Is this more of your human supremacy thing? How many times do I have to tell you? We're *all* animals. Every last one of us. Your list of "unique" human qualities keeps getting shorter every day. Remember the tool using thing? The chimpanzees and their termite fishing? Your claims are all nonsense. You all think you're so special, but look at you. You're sitting here asking me questions about the most basic parts of being alive. Next thing you know, you'll be asking me for advice on how to breathe or how to have sex."

"Now wait just a damn minute!"

"Ha! Just kidding! Wanna wrestle?"

WHITE MAN'S SALVATION

The revival of dancing is imperatively needed to give poise to
the nerves, schooling to the emotions, strength to the will,
and to harmonize the feelings and the intellect with the body
which supports them.

Stanley Halt

If you're a personal trainer, physical therapist, exercise specialist, PE
teacher or physical enthusiast, I've got good news and bad news for
you.

First the bad news. I hate to break it to you, but we're late to the
party. At least eight hundred years late, but probably a lot more. We like
to think that we're at the cutting edge in working with human bodies,
but really, we're like blind infants crawling around in the dirt. We are
neophytes.

All the clever moves we've "discovered" for training and rehab? It's all
old news. All our insights into biomechanics and "correct form?" Somebody else figured this out a long time ago. All our expert knowledge
about physical education? Mostly a case of reinventing a wheel that's
been rolling along smoothly in the villages of West Africa for hundreds
of years.

IT'S ALL IN THE DANCE

The essential elements are right there on the dance floor for all to see.
Watch the dancer's shoulders and you'll see vigorous lateral rotation,
essential for juicing up the rotator cuff and keeping the shoulder joint
healthy. Watch the hips and you'll see gobs of rotational movement,
strengthening the deep muscles of the butt and nourishing the cartilage
of the hip socket. Watch the action of the spine, with it's undulating
flexion, extension and rotation, pumping the discs while it encourages
proprioceptive feedback and spinal intelligence.

Above all, watch the way the whole torso works together in an integrated fashion; hips talk to shoulders, pelvis talks to spine and so on. Modern trainers go to great length to develop these very qualities in their players and patients, but Africans were doing these things long before our culture even existed.

"PLAY A BEAT YOU CAN REPEAT"

The whole thing started with animal skins, maybe goat, cow or whatever was handy. Stretch that skin over a section of hollow tree trunk, wrap as tight as possible and you've got a drum. Bang on that drum in a rhythmic manner and it won't be long before your family and friends will gather round and start tapping their feet. Pick up the pace and their bodies will start to undulate, spines flexing, extending and rotating in harmony with your beat. Before long, your village adopts the drum dance into their culture and it becomes a regular event, filled with life and meaning. Exuberant movement becomes the social norm.

Years later, someone discovers a way to work with metal. Early applications include knives and hoes, but musical innovators take their metallurgy one step further and fashion large rings that they fit to the tops of their drums. This, in combination with a clever pattern of rope weavings, allows them to pull the skin head extremely tight. This refinement allows your drummers to produce three distinct sounds, a tone, a bass note and a slap— a GO, a GUN and a PA.

This opens up the process immensely and allows the music to grow more sophisticated. Now the link between drummer and dancer becomes even stronger. Low and high tones speak clearly to hips, shoulders and core. Powerful rhythms drive the feet as they educate the body in motion. A conversation develops; drums speak to dancers, dancers reply with movement of their own.

Over the years, rhythm is embraced into the very heart of your culture and daily life experience. When your family goes to the field, the drums go too. Rhythmic songs accompany the movements of hoeing, gathering and digging. It's all about keeping the beat, all about moving your hips and core in rhythmic oscillation. Throughout the day, your body pulses. Work is accomplished, but it doesn't feel laborious. The body learns the rhythm of sound and movement, easing the effort.

THE ORIGINAL PE

In West Africa, dancing was the original PE, the first and most powerful form of physical education. Other cultures invented valuable physical arts too, but the West African tradition stands out for its simplicity and exuberance. We can have no doubt that it worked spectacularly well.

I have no research data to back up this claim, but my guess is that back pain is rare in West African villages. African dancers have intelligent, physically educated bodies with intelligent, physically educated spines. Their hips actually work. Their neurological feedback loops are fast and efficient. Their abdomens, torsos and diaphragms actually coordinate with one another in harmonious movement. If a spinal disc gets irritated from too much work in the field, dancers can figure out a movement pattern that compensates for the irritation. Their bodies are smart.

Just as back pain is unlikely, so too for diabetes and obesity. In a dance-drum culture, muscles get worked vigorously and often. Glucose is ushered into muscle cells to power rhythmic contractions. There's no blood sugar overload and no pancreatic burn out. People get vigorous activity on most days, the precise formula that we have now "discovered" to be effective for weight-control and long life.

Drumming and dancing brought profound benefits to individual human bodies, but it also created widespread participation throughout the community. There are no try-outs or eliminations in community dance, no competitions and no pressure to win. Everyone gets invited to the dance; everyone moves. The process is fundamentally inclusive.

The dance-drum culture also obliterates the age-segregation model that we take for granted in modern PE and sport. In a West African village, anyone can dance at any stage of life. If you can stand up, you can participate. Even if you can't stand up, you can play a shaker or clap your hands. There's no anxiety about "age-appropriate developmental standards." You won't see grandstands for parent spectators or separate facilities for different age groups. It's all one community in motion.

WHITE MAN'S GRAVE?

During the era of British colonialism, explorers encountered high levels of yellow fever and malaria in West Africa and took to describing the region as a "white man's grave." This reputation of death and disease remains, but there's a lot more to this region than rampaging viruses. In fact, there are vital lessons to be learned there, lessons that we desperately need in our modern world.

Americans have displayed a spectacular level of incompetence when it comes to dealing with lifestyle disease and the decline of human physicality. Our methods and ideas simply aren't working. It is becoming increasingly obvious that the solution isn't going to come out of a research facility or a pharmaceutical laboratory. And it certainly isn't going to come out of a PE textbook. We need to look elsewhere.

When modern-day decision makers ponder the degeneration of the human body, they reflexively reach for modern-day solutions. They seek out data, analysis, accounting, measurement and assessment. At hundreds of conferences each year, experts present their data on the grim condition of the human body and conclude with the words "We need more research in this area."

I beg to differ. We don't need more research. We already know the fundamental fact. That is, people become healthy when they engage in vigorous activity on most days of the week. We don't need more knowledge or information on this score; what we need is primal participation. If the afflictions of the human body stem from modernity, it hardly makes sense to look to modernity for a solution. From the body's point of view, modernity *is* the problem.

STUPID WHITE CULTURE

Michael Moore made some good points in his book *Stupid White Men*, but he was just scratching the surface. Not only do white men have some questionable politics, they also display an astonishing level of ignorance in matters of human physicality. It may be true that white men can't jump, but the real problem is that they won't dance. And if they won't dance, it seems unlikely that they would have anything important to say about movement education. Dance, after all, is entry-level. After sex, gathering and hunting, it is the original human movement.

As a thought experiment, let's hold an open symposium on physical education and see what happens. The Africans will show up with drums, shakers and bodies pulsing with rhythmic movement. The Americans will show up with computers, pedometers, heart rate monitors and a truck load of peer-reviewed journal articles. Obviously, there's no contest; the academic Americans are dead on arrival. They can give PowerPoint presentations until the audience is comatose, but that will be the end of it. In the meantime, the African men and women will be leading actual people in actual movement sessions, doing the work that really needs to be done.

In modern America, our habit of sedentary living speaks for itself. Millions of Americans will live their entire lives completely unaware of the pleasures of robust physicality. Some of our gifted students will enjoy lifetime participation in athletics, but most drop out, frustrated by a system that is designed to eliminate the weak and the awkward. So now it's time for the white folks to give up their data mongering and get out on the open floor where they can actually do some good.

THE GOOD NEWS

By now, you may have forgotten that there's actually some good news in this story. That is, we can actually go out and dance. No matter the color of your skin, you can still participate. Most communities have some sort of drum circles and dance gigs. You can sign up, listen to the drums and learn the steps.

No aptitude for dance? Forget about it. You don't have to be a champion. No one will cut you from the team if your movements are awkward. No one will laugh at you if you swing your arms the wrong way or get your feet mixed up. No one will make you sit on the bench if your hips move in the wrong direction. No one will vote you off the island. Participation is all that matters.

And besides, anyone can do it, even inept white people. As the saying goes, "If you can talk, you can sing. If you can walk, you can dance."

MEET MR. JOY

Joy is the feeling of grinning on the inside.

Dr. Melba Colgrove

So I roll out of bed, drag a comb across my head and try to come up with a plan for the day. There's no compelling emergency staring me in the face, so I am forced to devise a course of action on my own. Where shall I begin?

Unfortunately, I have several voices in my head, each trying to seize control of my to-do list. These characters vie for my attention, yakking incessantly, each demanding access and influence over my flesh and my behavior. Sometimes they speak in the first person with "I" statements, but other times they speak in the third person, with a voice of authority. In either case, their rap has become quite familiar.

MR. SLOTH

The first voice is Mr. Sloth. As you might imagine, his voice is mellow and low to the ground. Whatever the situation, he counsels rest, relaxation and inaction. You've heard him many times...

"Better stay close to the couch today. Don't take any unnecessary risks, conserve your energy and try not to expose yourself. No point in getting worked up into a sweat. There's a couple of good shows on TV and a hot new movie coming out. A good book would be nice. And if all else fails, you can always eat another meal or have a snack. The weather doesn't look that great for running anyway and besides, you went for a walk yesterday. What's the rush? Call it a rest day. There's always time to do a workout tomorrow."

"Save your effort," says Mr. Sloth. Avoid physical exertion and slack off whenever possible. His motto: "Just do it later."

MR. SHOULD

Running on a simultaneous audio track is the demanding, monotonous voice of Mr. Should...

"You really should get some exercise today. You know that it's good for your health. You should probably do some cardio; you really need to burn some calories and lose some weight. You should do some strength training too. You need to do some ab work and some stretching. Your hamstrings are as tight as piano wires. Oh, and you probably should do some sort of stress-relief thing today, maybe some deep breathing or yoga or something. That's supposed to be good for your body too. Now get moving!"

Mr. Should's voice is dull, incessant, onerous. It carries the combined weight of every teacher, every parent, every coach, every social authority that ever told us what to do. It has no creativity or innovation, just a relentless, grinding pressure.

Even worse, it's never satisfied. "Sure," it says. "You just won the Nobel Prize for mountain biking and a MacArthur grant for ultra-marathoning, but you really should be doing something substantive and noteworthy. You should be swimming solo around Antarctica, rebuilding New Orleans and finding a cure for cancer. So what are you sitting around for?"

THE SOUNDTRACK

I used to think that this conversation was my own neurotic drama, but now I know better. These days, almost everyone is enduring a similar twin-track rap. Sloth competes with responsibility, apathy with duty, laziness with ambition. There's so much noise in the system that we feel conflicted no matter what we do.

Mr. Should has a point, of course. We know that regular movement is good for the body. We know that vigorous movement will give us profound health benefits. The facts are clear—there's no question that we SHOULD get moving.

At the same time, we've got a few million years of evolutionary history telling us to stay on the couch. Mr. Sloth speaks with an ancient, powerful voice. We love to rest and for good reason. Life in the ancestral environment forced movement upon us; insects, predators, food shortages and drought kept us on the go. In conditions like these, rest was vital and natural selection would have favored individuals who preserved their physiological resources. We are lazy today because it worked to be lazy.

If we still lived in a challenging ancestral environment, Mr. Sloth would be our best friend. But, for better and for worse, today's environment is a complete inverse of the evolutionary norm. Today, sloth is no longer adaptive because there is no longer any pressure to move. When physical movement is optional, sloth is no longer a virtue.

But Mr. Should is no friend either. Besides being a nag and an annoyance, Mr. Should saps our pleasure, satisfaction, balance and humor. His only goal is to keep the pressure on. Ultimately, Mr. Should wreaks havoc with our happiness and our bodies. He is responsible for over-use injuries, neurotransmitter depletion, adrenal exhaustion, dysfunctional relationships and a creeping sense of discontent. In short, Mr. Should can be a real prick.

MEET MR. JOY

Obviously, this bipolar conversation between Mr. Sloth and Mr. Should is getting us nowhere. Mr. Sloth is a comfortable buddy, but he's just not giving us the physical challenge that we need. Mr. Should is a loathsome and tiresome nag. What we need is another voice in the mix, someone who can get us moving without force, intimidation or compulsion. Perhaps it's time to invite Mr. Joy into the conversation.

Mr. Joy, as you might expect, is an exuberant. When he speaks up, the conversation sounds something like this:

"Hey Frank, I've got a deal for you. If you can just put down that fork for a minute, I can show you some passion and some excitement."

"What? Who was that?"

"Mr. Joy here. You remember me? I'm the guy that got you to jump off the diving board when you were 6. I'm the one that got you to ride your bike around the block for hours on end in the summer evenings. And now I've got some bouncy moves that will shake you up and give you some delight."

"Really?"

"That's right. There's some stretchy new power moves I'm thinking about that will really light up your eyes and get your juices flowing."

"Go on."

"Well, remember that time on the trampoline when you did that bouncy, twisting move? It's sort of like that. I'm thinking maybe we get the physioball, a medicine ball and couple of friends. One foot on the wobble board, some dance moves and some passing. What do you say?"

"Well, it sounds good, but I was up late last night and I drank too many beers. And besides, my knee has been acting up and I'm kinda out of shape anyway. Maybe later."

"Look, you don't have to jump right into the power moves. Once you start moving, you're going to feel better. You're going to start breathing and sweating and your body is going to wake up. You're going to feel limber and agile and powerful. You're metabolism is going to catch fire. After awhile, your neurotransmitters are going to balance out and your mood is going to improve. You're going to feel exuberant. There's a whole lot of bounce out there, you've just got to get in sync with it."

"Okay, you've convinced me. Just let me get my shoes on and we're out of here."

HECKLING FOR JOY

As you can see, Mr. Joy has his own unique style. He heckles us into action with nudges, tickles and teases. He issues occasional challenges, but these usually come in the form of wonder and curiosity. He never lays down an ultimatum, but instead poses a muse, usually beginning with the phrase "Wouldn't it be cool if..." or "I wonder if..."

In this sense, Mr. Joy is the guy at the skatepark who says "Dude, I wonder if we could ride down those stairs and then launch over the fountain?" He's the guy at the bouldering site who says "Wow, look at that blank, over-hanging face. I wonder if you could grab that pinch hold, mantle on that sloper and throw for the jug?" He's the coach who tells his players "I wonder if you guys could run backwards with the ball while you pass it between your legs?" He's the music teacher who says "I wonder if you could lay down those cords with a 12 bar blues progression?"

The thing about Mr. Joy is that he's fundamentally irrepressible. The way he sees it, there's a playful solution for almost every problem. "You're a little sluggish today? No problem. We'll start with a little bounce, add a bit of a twist and before you know it, we'll be flying."

Sure, maybe you're coming back after a junk-food binge or a sustained embrace with your couch. Maybe you feel like a block of frozen tissue and you can scarcely remember how to shoot a basket, run a lap or throw a ball. No problem. Start with something you can do. Start by wiggling your finger or getting some bounce in your step. Get some play into the system and the vigorous movement will follow.

A BROADER CONVERSATION

Mr. Should does have a place in the conversation, of course. Some sense of discipline, obligation and responsibility is essential to progress and individual happiness. But when Mr. Should tyrannizes the conversation, things eventually go bad. In the short term, we achieve impressive results, but a should-driven life is never sustainable. Mr. Should drags us down, makes us depressed and saps our energy. We wind up trudging from one task to the next, grinding out our laps, our sets, our homework, our projects. We get it done, but we eventually come to resent it. This is no way to live.

So, it's time to pay some attention to Mr. Joy and let him have his say. Let him run your day every now and then. Let him inspire some new movements and some new games. Let him heckle, tease and keep you off balance. Make him an ally in your quest for creative solutions.

Give Mr. Should the day off and have some fun.

WILDLIFE

Exuberance is an abounding, ebullient, effervescent emotion. It is kinetic and unrestrained, joyful, irrepressible.

Kay Redfield Jamison
Exuberance

WITCHES' BREW

Double, double
toil and trouble;
Fire burn, and cauldron bubble ...

Macbeth , Act IV, Scene 1
W. Shakespeare

Obesity, diabetes, heart disease, atrophy–you've heard all the disturbing statistics by now. You know that the human body is suffering from an epidemic of highly preventable disease. You know that our schools are filled with obese, attention-disordered children and that our hospitals are ready to collapse under the weight of coronary artery disease, back pain, osteoporosis, high blood pressure and a host of physical ailments that bedevil the modern human body.

If you're wondering just how our bodies got to be in such a tragic state, the true story will now be revealed to you. Before we begin, however, you must forget all the conventional explanations. Forget the editorials that appear in major medical and scientific journals. Forget the position papers cranked out by the Centers for Disease Control, the National Institutes of Health and the American College of Sports Medicine. They are completely out of the loop on this.

In fact, the whole wretched mess was actually cooked up in a dark, underground cavern, masterminded by a cabal of evil witches. By combining a diabolical mixture of noxious ingredients, they have created, in effect, a physiological witches' brew, a terrifying concoction that brings disease and unhappiness to the human body. I will reveal the recipe to you shortly.

But first, be advised that this is no knock on witches as such, because, as everyone knows, there are good witches and bad witches. Similarly, there are good witches' brews and bad witches' brews. We will do well to keep this difference in mind.

FORMULAS

As you may know, witches' brews have served a variety of purposes over the centuries: mixtures have been used for healing, clairvoyance, divination, prophecy or to enable a person to fly. And yes, some were mixed to hurt or kill people. There were thousands of recipes, many of which were customized to serve particular purposes. Ingredients in the mix may have included toads, deadly nightshade, monkshood, henbane, foxglove, hemlock, rat's blood ('slips of yew') and wolf's teeth (ergot). Crafting an effective brew would have required considerable care, knowledge and study.

In contrast, the modern witches' brew is a comparatively simple formula and the ingredients are well-known. Here is the recipe:

Start by selecting a immense, massively heavy cauldron. Fill to the halfway mark with a broth of tap water and high-fructose corn syrup. Bring to a rolling boil. Next, ladle in heaping quantities of trans-fats and white flour. Stir in massive portions of tobacco and immense quantities of ethyl alcohol. Simmer until steaming, and cast spells as desired.

Now mix in some big chunks of physical inactivity, video games, killer stress, workaholism and anxiety-provoking marketing. Sprinkle in generous portions of biophobia and urban sprawl. Season with small quantities of potent neurotoxins—lead and mercury are especially recommended. Cast more spells and inhale the vapors.

Cook the mix for several decades over a hot fossil-fuel burner, then allow to cool. Once the brew has cooled to room temperature, pour off the mixture into colorful designer bottles. Run a global marketing campaign to convince consumers—children especially—that this brew is in fact a magic elixir. Set the price as high as the market will allow and distribute widely.

If mixed properly and prepared with care, this brew will produce a full-blown public health catastrophe as well as windfall profits for the cooks. In those who consume it, the brew will produce a "metabolic syndrome" consisting of obesity, diabetes and heart disease. Other symptoms will include physical atrophy, apathy and body loathing. It may also induce an "out of body experience" in which the user loses interest in the physical world. If mixed properly, this brew will not only produce the desired effect, it will also prove to be profoundly addicting. This is truly bad magick.

THE BAD WITCHES

Naturally, we are curious about the bad witches who cooked up this satanic concoction. Who are they and how can they be stopped? Unfortunately, we have no master list. Many of the bad witches have learned how to hide in plain sight while others are masters of disguise. Nevertheless, we do know their nature. The bad witches of human health are notable for the pathology of their products, their antipathy to the human body, their utter disregard for social responsibility and above all, their naked greed. You can surely come up with a few names right off the top of your head; some candidates stand out as notably influential and pathological.

It is tempting to focus on the bad witches, to out them, to publish their names, to cast spells upon their bodies and their corporate officers. These witches certainly deserve our wrath, but this will have to wait for another day. Our task at hand is to focus on antidotes and elixirs. We're looking for physical vigor, animal health, play and wildness. We've got our own brew to cook.

ANTIDOTE AND ELIXIRS

As we have seen, the witches' brew is a potent mix, a truly dangerous poison, not only to individuals, but to entire communities. Fortunately, there are antidotes and special elixirs that we can take to counteract the effects of the witches' brew. Some of these are purely natural, others have been cooked up by the good witches.

The basic formula for the antidote is as follows:

Start with generous helpings of vigorous outdoor movement. Exuberant movement is the most powerful ingredient in the formula and must be consumed regularly. The specific form of movement is largely irrelevant, but participation is essential. You can, in some cases, substitute indoor movement for this ingredient, but this is a weaker formula.

Once you get some vigorous movement simmering on your stove, add in generous helpings of passion, play and recess. Inhale the vapors and meditate on the implications. Next, add some large chunks of wildness, beauty, biophilia and community. To serve, pour generous helpings into large mugs and hand out to your friends and family.

If mixed properly and consumed regularly, this antidote will counteract the bad witches' brew and produce an "in-body experience," a feeling of profound physicality.

At the same time, it is also a good idea to imbibe in the powerful elixirs that are made available by the good witches. Naturally, the most powerful examples are those that are taken outdoors. The list includes raft trips, backpack trips, bike trips, kayak trips, climbing trips, surfing trips, safaris and related walkabouts. These elixirs work best when consumed regularly; no overdose is possible.

GOOD WITCHES, WIZARDS AND SHAMANS

The antidotes and elixirs are given to us by the good witches, shamans and wizards. These are the individuals and groups whose magic sustains the health and vigor of the human body. Good witches are advocates of joyful physical movement, play, recess and contact with nature. They get us out, get us moving and help us take pleasure in our physicality.

Fortunately, we don't have to look too far for good witches; these people are everywhere, spreading the antidote, or at least some of the ingredients: Coaches who get their students moving, outdoor educators who take people out on the trail, teachers of all stripes who work for health and intelligence, play advocates who try to break the vicious cycle of labor. Physicians, physical therapists, and healers of all description; these are the good witches. Anyone looking for ways to get the modern body out of its funk and back into the world of vitality qualifies.

You can make up your own list of good witches, of course. My list changes from day to day, but some of my favorites are John Muir, Jane Goodall, E.O. Wilson, Henry David Thoreau, Ed Abbey, Mark Twain and Charles Darwin. Darwin is perhaps the greatest of all the good witches. By careful observation of the natural world, he managed to correct the most fundamental error of modern civilization—the notion that humans are somehow apart from the rest of the biosphere. Without Darwin, we would truly be in some vile and dangerous muck.

Whatever your list, cast your spells and hope that the good magic will prevail. Keep your eyes open for good witches and stay clear of the bad ones. Drink the antidote and the elixirs and whenever possible and avoid the bad brew. It may give you a good buzz for a while, but the hangover is a nightmare.

MY DOG IS SMARTER THAN
I AM

My dog's name is Mojo and he's really stupid. He has no grasp of the alphabet and his understanding of world affairs is almost nonexistent. Not only that, his fitness program is truly amateurish. He doesn't know anything about exercise physiology or correct training practices. He doesn't read the research and he doesn't consult with certified experts. He doesn't practice proper form or adhere to accepted guidelines. He violates all the rules.

When he exercises, he doesn't warm up or cool down. He doesn't check his heart rate and he never measures his body fat percentage. He does do occasional squats and leg lifts, but he's really sloppy about counting sets and reps. He doesn't keep a spreadsheet and he never bothers to log his progress. He has no performance objectives and seems completely indifferent to standard training protocol.

He's not interested in the details of training methodology. He has no opinion on whether it's better to run 10 wind sprints 3 times a week or 3 wind sprints 10 times a week.

As for nutrition, he's totally barbaric. He eats whatever he can get his teeth on and has no sense of portion control. He doesn't pay attention to critical nutrients, doesn't follow the food pyramid and doesn't read labels. He doesn't drink water at the proper intervals either, just visits his favorite puddles when he gets a chance. He even drinks out of the toilet!

There's no sense of discipline to his method. When he goes out on the trail, he sets whatever pace he wants. If he feels like running, he runs. If he wants to stop and sniff the bushes, he stops. On some days he walks, some days he does wind sprints, some days he goes swimming. He mixes these activities up with no regard to periodization, macrocycles, mesocycles, tapering or peaking.

He doesn't do Pilates, Yoga or Taebo. He doesn't get acupuncture treatments or spinal manipulations. He doesn't wear orthotics or drink sport drinks. He doesn't take vitamins, creatine or wear a heart rate monitor. His toys don't contain graphite, titanium or advanced composites. He doesn't have a swoosh logo on his collar.

Not only that, Mojo is completely apathetic about competition. He has no interest in pushing the envelope, setting records or winning medals. He doesn't care how fast the other dogs are or who's in the lead. If he gets tired, he rests. If he gets hot, he seeks out shade. If his paw hurts, he slows down.

In general, he pretty much does as he pleases. He sleeps about 12 hours a day and lounges around for another 6 or so. And then, when he finally does get off the couch, he just plays around. He has no motivation, no ambition and no work ethic. What a slacker.

THE RESULTS

The thing I don't understand is this: According to everything I read in the fitness and sports medicine press, Mojo ought to be in terrible condition. He should be suffering from all sorts of muscle soreness, injury, bad posture, poor performance and psychophysical grief. His unapproved and improper training practices should be sending him into early retirement at the vet hospital.

But no, it's not like that at all. When we go out on the trail, he beats me up the mountain every time. Try as I might, I just can't keep up with him. We do 10 miles on the trail and when we get back to the parking lot, he still wants to play. I'm exhausted, but he's ready for more.

Not only does he perform like an Olympian, he's also managed to achieve some impressive cosmetic results. He's got great muscle tone and a slender waist. His shoulders and neck are powerfully bulked up. It's difficult to tell with all that fur, but I think that he even has ripped, razor-sharp abs. He looks like a total stud and yet he never touches a weight machine. What gives?

A ONE-RULE DOG

Mojo may be a slacker with a bad attitude, but he does adhere to one basic rule. That is, he tries to get moderate to vigorous activity on most days of the week. That's it. Aside from his obvious preoccupation with play and pleasure, this is his only rule for fitness. It's almost as if he's read the recommendations from the American Heart Association. Maybe he got his paws on a copy of the Surgeon General's Report on Physical Activity and Health. Maybe he's following the guidelines established by the Centers for Disease Control and Prevention or the American College of Sports Medicine. They all say roughly the same thing: "to maintain physical health, individuals should participate in moderate to vigorous activity on most days of the week."

Whatever the source of Mojo's fitness philosophy, it clearly works for him; we cannot argue with his results. So the question is, "Is fitness really this simple?" Can we really disregard all the details of exercise science and reduce it down to a single guideline for physical living? Can we really ignore all the experts and their expertise? It is tempting to do exactly that.

If we're learning anything from the modern obesity epidemic it's that, whatever advanced and specialized knowledge we might happen to have, it's the fundamentals of physical living that are lacking. Sure, we can determine the precise program of mileage and resistance that will create an Olympic athlete, but if people remain sedentary, such expertise is little more than a curiosity. If we can't get people to participate in a simple program such as "moderate to vigorous activity on most days," then what good is the ability to shave another minute off the marathon? We need more fundamentals and less sophistication. We don't need higher performance, we need widespread participation.

HE'S JUST A DOG

Critics will dismiss the success of Mojo's training program, claiming that he's just a dog, a mere animal. But this objection just doesn't hold up to scrutiny. When we start looking at anatomy and physiology in detail, we simply don't find much substantive difference between canines and humans. Oh sure, my brain is slightly larger than Mojo's and I'm a lot better with abstract symbols than he is. But my neuromuscular system is almost identical to his; our tissue is almost interchangeable. Given the fact that we both evolved in similar environments, it seems unlikely that our physiological responses to movement would be significantly different. What works for terrestrial mammals works for both of us.

Looking at humans in isolation just doesn't work, especially when we start talking about the health and performance of our bodies. Human brains are capable of some remarkable things, but our bodies aren't really that different from other primates, other hominids, other mammals. If we really want to be healthier, we need to get down off our pedestal and pay more attention to the creatures around us.

CAN WE DO BETTER?

Given the impressive results that Mojo achieves with his intuitive and instinctual training program, we have to wonder why humans think that they can do better. Do we have some special knowledge? Or are we simply missing the point? Can we do better than Mojo?

DEVIANT IN AFRICA

If you're serious about studying the human body, you're eventually going to find your way to Africa. This is our ancestral homeland after all, the primal playground. It's the land where we took our first steps, spoke our first words and began our great journey. No amount of textbook study can substitute for this experience–if you're curious about your origins, this is the place to go.

So it was that I found myself in the city of Dar es Salaam, Tanzania on my way to visit the chimps at Gombe Stream. Plastered with a case of jet lag, I passed a couple of days at a simple beach hotel on the coast. The lodge was located on a slender offshore island, a short boat ride from the mainland; the setting could easily have passed for Hawaii. The main feature of the resort was a large, open-air thatched lodge with a high ceiling and ample space for meals, drinking and relaxing. A staff of local African workers cooked the meals and looked after the guests.

On the first day of my visit, I spent a casual morning in the main lodge, writing and catching up on some notes. After sitting at my table for a few hours, my body began to itch with restless energy and I felt the need to move. So I stepped off to a corner of the lodge, breathed in the ocean air and began to stretch. I went through my favorite movements, some easy lunges and some general jumping around. It felt good to move and after a few minutes, I returned to my work.

The next day I was trading stories with the lodge manager when he mentioned that some of the native staff workers had noticed my behavior. Apparently flummoxed by my odd behavior, one of them approached the manager in concern and asked, "Does that man need a doctor?"

Of course, this is not the first time that people have asked this question upon observing my behavior, but in this case, I found it particularly revealing. From the African point of view, my behavior appeared deviant in at least two key respects.

First, my behavior was markedly different from that of other guests who visited the resort. Most visitors come to relax, drink and sit by the pool; these people are sedentary by habit. In fact, many Westerners come to resorts such as this specifically to become even more sedentary than normal. In this sense, my movement behavior was a conspicuous departure for the norm and as such, a cause for concern. Apparently, the locals had never seen an American or a European exercising before.

I was different from the average Western guest, that much is certain. But my behavior also deviated from the African norm. Tanzania is not an affluent country; most of its citizens are fully occupied with the demands of making a living. Individuals reserve their physical resources for the pressing challenges of work and getting from place to place. Africans routinely walk long distances, not for pleasure or fitness, but to get to where they need to go. If you have to walk several miles to work each day, you're not going to waste your energy with optional, non-necessary movement. If you're lucky enough to have free time, you're probably going to rest. In this respect, exercise is something for the affluent, another luxury that many of us in the West take for granted.

Beyond confirming my personal eccentricity, this event reminded me that physical fitness is far more than a calculus of sets, reps, time and distance. Society and culture exert powerful influence on how we experience our bodies. Fitness is not just physical, it's physiocultural. Society shapes the way we move, how we feel about our bodies and what we do when something goes wrong. Our health and fitness are powerfully sculpted by social conditioning, mimicry, authority and conformity, not to mention economics. Thus, it's not enough to simply understand the basics of physiology and physical training practices, we also have to understand and appreciate the wider world around us.

A few days after my stay at the beach resort, I arrived in Gombe National Park, home to the chimpanzee colony made famous by Jane Goodall. Watching the chimps in their natural habitat, I could scarcely contain my curiosity and wonder. There was so much to see and so much to say—my mind was abuzz with the possibilities. Nevertheless, one simple fact was obvious—there was no taboo against public movement here. On the contrary, vigorous movement was the norm. Animals were flying in every direction, up and down tree trunks, leaping from branch to branch. I witnessed charging displays, play, patrol and exploration; there was movement of all sorts. In this environment, no chimp or baboon would ever question the health of a moving animal. On the contrary, it is a lack of movement that would attract attention and concern.

Now, before you leap to the obvious conclusion—that perhaps I would be better off living with a troop of chimps—let me remind you that these creatures are our closest animal relatives on the planet. The figure "98% genetically identical" is often cited by science writers, but that's not the only way to describe the proximity of our relationship. In terms of DNA, humans are more closely related to chimps than the horse is to the zebra, the porpoise is to the dolphin or the sheep is to the goat.

Our bodies are substantially identical to those of chimps. Our legs are longer and our brains are bigger, but beyond that, our tissue is standard-issue primate muscle, nerve and bone. We can safely assume that those things that keep the chimps healthy are likely to keep us healthy as well. Vigorous movement is a fundamental element of our heritage and is vital to our well-being. For healthy primates in natural environments, sedentary living is an abnormal exception, not the rule. In this sense, it is our culture of physical apathy that is deviant. In the West, we have created a social environment that is distinctly at odds with our physical needs.

Perhaps it's our culture that needs a doctor.

THE WORLD IS MY GYM

If you're looking to liberate yourself from entrenched ideas, static points of view and mental atrophy, a good place to begin is with comedy. Whether it's George Carlin ranting about our misuse of language, Carl Reiner and Mel Brooks working the "2,000 year old man" or Brian Regan wondering about the motivation of barking dogs, these artists provide a valuable public service that often transcends that of their serious and inhibited counterparts in university towers.

Attending a comedy show can be a truly transformational experience. When A. Whitney Brown declared, "I'm not a vegetarian because I love animals; I'm a vegetarian because I hate plants," he completely turned my world view upside down; I'll never look at a vegetable quite the same way again.

There's a lot of great talent out there these days, but for sheer mental derailment, no one can match Steven Wright. Here's a man who wonders about Houdini locking his keys in his car and how much deeper the ocean would be if sponges didn't grow there. He's got a fine collection of mutant muses, but the one that really caught my ear is this:

> "I have lots of hobbies which I pursue to the fullest. I
> have a large sea shell collection which I keep scattered on
> beaches across the world. Maybe you've seen it."

It's a funny riff, but it's a lot more than that. When we linger on this idea for a moment, our minds begin to open to some startling possibilities. If Steven Wright's shell collection is as vast as the world's beaches, what about other "collections?"

It could, for example, go like this: "Hey baby, want to see my game park? It's spread out all over the scrubby grasslands and mountains of Asia, Africa and the Americas. There are millions of animals. We can go there anytime we want." Or, "Want to see my fossil collection?" "My botanical gardens?" "My library?" "My art gallery?" "My planetarium?"

Wright's perspective has a calming effect on our minds and bodies. All the stuff that we work so hard to acquire is already out there in place, right now. We don't have to go and arrange it, dust it or polish it, although we still might want to protect it. The very idea of ownership is called into question. Suddenly, we lose the compulsion to categorize and label all the things around us. We don't have to stick pins through the butterflies or put small animals in jars. Everything is OK the way it is, right now in the present moment. No need to wall it off, set up territories or raise grant money to pay for it all. All we have to do is walk down the beach and appreciate it. What could possibly be better?

WANT TO SEE MY GYM?

Wright's shell collection and our related muses are all provocative, but for physical enthusiasts, things really come to light when we apply the same logic to places where we practice physical movement. If our shell collection lives on all the beaches of the world, then our gym consists of all the grasslands, mountains, river valleys, beaches, lakes and oceans of the planet.

Welcome to "Nature's gym." The planet itself is our training hall, our dojo, our dance studio, our playground. What a liberation this is! No dues to pay, although you will have to put some gas in your car. Lots of fresh air, diverse terrain and animals. Plus, it's really, really big, so there's always something new to see.

No treadmills, no TV's, no posters of chemically-enhanced celebrities, no contracts to sign, no special outfits to wear, no mirrors to distract us. Just diverse landscapes, habitat, creatures and incredible vistas. Once you go outside, you're there. John Muir was no comedian, but he knew this fact all along. His only question for us would be "What took you so long to figure it out?"

BEHOLD THE BEHOLDER

You can't depend on your eyes when your imagination is out
of focus.

Mark Twain

Have you noticed how ugly people are these days? They're everywhere now, right out there in public view for all to see. They're in
our shopping malls, our schools and our workplaces. Distorted features,
bad skin, yellow teeth, lumpy, grotesque, misshapen bodies. They're a
blight on the landscape.

And it's not just other people. Have you looked in the mirror lately?
If you're like me, the experience is, on a good day, shocking. That face
staring back at me is just as twisted and malformed as everyone else's,
maybe more so. We all seem to be similarly afflicted.

So what's up with this aesthetic catastrophe, this epidemic of malformed appearance? Have people really gotten uglier in the last few
decades? Or have we always been this way?

You are no doubt anxious to know the source of all this physical ugli-
ness, but you may be surprised to hear that it has nothing to do with
genetics, trans-fats, pesticide poisoning or cosmic rays. In fact, the true
source of our cosmetic misfortune lies with magazine editors and their
marketing masters.

THE BEHOLDER'S EYE

The process begins at the magazine rack. As you scan the magazines,
you've probably noticed that their covers are populated with an astonishing number of fantastically beautiful people. Perfect faces, marble skin,
ideal proportions, impossible figures, idyllic forms. These are the elite,
selected from a pool of people who have already been pre-selected for
their good looks. They are not average, they are not normal. If a Mar-
tian anthropologist came to earth and observed our magazines, he'd be

sure to notice that the images on the covers don't look anything like the creatures who purchase and read them.

Not only are these cover-models aesthetically improbable, they are also digitally manipulated to complete perfection. The formula is simple and by now, completely routine. Start with a beautiful body and a beautiful face, import the captured image into Photoshop and go to work. Adjust the colors, the hue and the saturation. Erase blemishes. Use the pucker and bloat tools to emphasize and de-emphasize particular features. Make the lashes longer and the eyes brighter. Straighten and brighten the teeth. Plump up the lips. Adjust the lighting to emphasize a skinny waist or bulging muscles. Remove any remaining flaws, sharpen the image and send to the editor for approval.

The entire process is now completely industrialized and unquestioned. A popular book on Photoshop gives simple step-by-step tutorials for "digital body sculpting." Readers learn how to shape the torso, remove love handles, slim thighs and butts, tighten flab on the back of the arms and even borrow body parts from other photographs. Simple tools allow users to remove wrinkles, sags, blemishes and other cosmetic imperfections.

Most of us are vaguely aware that magazine images are manipulated, but few appreciate just how pervasive this practice has become. In fact, wholesale image manipulation is now the norm; when you look at a magazine cover, you can assume that the image has been manipulated— *every* image in the modern magazine is manipulated. Every cover, every feature, every advertisement. None of it is real.

Get the picture? The images we see on magazine covers are not authentic; they are manufactured. The models, beautiful as they might happen to be at the outset, are simply raw material for the digital hacks who do the ultimate make-over. What we see on the magazine rack are caricatures, not real human beings. They are not us.

No wonder we are confused. No wonder our eyes are out of focus. No wonder everyone looks ugly. By comparison to magazine covers, none of us can come close to measuring up.

Contrast this state of affairs with the conditions that people have lived in for the vast majority of our experience on earth. That is, for 99.9% of our time on earth, we had no good idea of what we looked like. No mirrors, no cameras, no TV, no magazine covers, no Photoshop. We lived our lives in blissful cosmetic ignorance. Imagine the liberation.

ANXIETY MEDIA

It would be one thing if magazine cover manipulation was intended for casual entertainment, but it's not. These manufactured images cut right down into the core of who we are and how we think about ourselves. They are extremely powerful and in the end, pathological.

Manufactured images touch our bodies at the deepest level. They warp our self image and erode our self-esteem. We know that we don't look like magazine models. By comparison, we come off looking and feeling cosmetically inferior.

In turn, this feeling inspires anxiety, self-loathing and a need to compensate for the deficiency. These effects are great for business because they increase sales, but are a catastrophe for public health.

Of course, I am not the first to make these observations about body image and self-esteem. Feminists have been tracking this issue for decades. But this is no longer exclusively a woman's issue; image manipulation has now become a human issue. Men are also manipulated by impossible images of physical perfection. In fact, men's magazines have now become almost indistinguishable from women's—exceptional form and rarefied beauty grace every cover.

In each case, the subliminal message is the same: "Here is what you're supposed to look like. You don't, so now you've got a problem. But if you buy this magazine and the products advertised in this magazine, you'll have a chance of looking this way, someday." Thus the magazines give a two-pronged marketing approach: create a sense of anxiety and offer a solution, all in one stroke. The strategy is nakedly, shamelessly manipulative.

PSYCHOLOGY TODAY SURVEY

In 1997 Psychology Today conducted a major Body Image Survey showing that there's more discontent with the shape of our bodies than ever before. Among the findings:

Fifty-six percent of women say they are dissatisfied with their overall appearance. Their self-disparagement is specifically directed toward their abdomens, body weight, hips, and muscle tone. Men show escalating dissatisfaction with their abdomens, weight, muscle tone, overall appearance and chest... Body dissatisfaction is soaring among both women and men–increasing at a faster rate than ever before. This is the great paradox of body preoccupation–instead of insight, it seems to breed only discontent... The media play an important role as a cultural gatekeeper, framing standards of beauty for all of us by the models they choose. Many observers, including eating-disorder specialists, have encouraged producers and editors to widen the range of beauty standards by including models more representative of real women. But often they respond by saying that more diversity will weaken sales.

FALSE MOTIVATIONS

Magazine promoters would have us believe that we need their perfect images to "provide motivation" and "inspiration" to help us keep our exercise routines on track. This is the precise opposite of the truth. Images of physical perfection are actually disempowering. Genuine motivation comes from real people struggling against real challenges, not from airbrushed fantasies.

In fact, the claim of increased motivation is plainly contradicted by the facts: in our modern world, the proliferation of hyper-beautiful imagery has been matched by a simultaneous decrease in the numbers of people actually staying fit and healthy. We now have more magazines, but less movement. If magazine imagery really did provide motivation, we wouldn't be suffering an epidemic of diabetes and obesity.

The simple fact is that magazine publishers are not our friends; they don't want us to succeed. They want us to continue our struggles with body loathing and negative self-image. If we actually succeeded in achieving health and peace of body, we would no longer need their advice, their images or their products. We would be free, happy and independent animals.

JUST SAY NO TO PERFECTION

If we had any sense, we'd simply boycott the whole sordid enterprise. We would stop buying publications with impossible beauty. We would stop torturing ourselves. We would stop rewarding advertisers for making us feel miserable.

If you need information about exercise and fitness, read a book on the subject. Better yet, take a lesson from an authentic human trainer, coach or dance teacher. Better still, get together with friends who share your interests. Get your inspiration from real people, in real time, face-to-face.

And, if you do go shopping for magazines, approach the rack with a critical eye. These publications are not innocent entertainment, they are intentional manipulations. The magazine rack is a distorted lens, a projector of false images and bad ideas. Approach the stand with skepticism and caution.

In any case, we'd all do well to stop looking at impossible images and start looking at real people. Stop comparing your neighbors to digital illusions. You may just discover that regular people are really quite beautiful just the way they are. And so are you.

IT'S ALL IN YOUR BRAIN

Here's a thought experiment for you: A professor of exercise physiology at the local university asks you to come to his lab for an unspecified fitness test. He puts you on a treadmill, hooks you up to his sensors and gives you the following instructions: "You must run as fast as you can. The distance will be somewhere between 100 yards and 50 miles. Your performance will be rated against that of your peers. Ready, Go!"

Of course, you're likely to protest such an unreasonable demand and the professor may have to offer some substantial incentives to get you to participate. But assuming that he succeeds, imagine how this challenge might unfold. How would you manage your body? How would you set a pace? You've got to run fast, but you've got to conserve resources. You've got to be powerful, but you've got to be efficient. It's a serious conundrum, far more challenging than running a particular fixed distance.

As it turns out, this kind of fitness challenge has become a sort of Zen koan for a new generation of exercise scientists. A new body of research calls into question many of our assumptions about endurance, knowledge and the nature of fatigue. Believe it or not, fatigue is starting to become exciting.

FUEL DEPLETION AND THE "FINAL LAP PARADOX"

This modern interest in fatigue science was featured prominently in the March 20, 2004 edition of *New Scientist*. In an article titled "Running on Empty," author Rick Lovett posed the question "Can it really be possible that fatigue is all in the mind?"

For years, the standard theory has held that muscular fatigue is caused by the build up of metabolic wastes like lactic acid, accompanied by the reduction in available fuel. This is the body-as-battery paradigm, otherwise known as the "limitations theory."

But this prevailing theory has now lost favor, due in part to the "final lap paradox." The problem is that if fuel depletion and waste accumulation were really the ultimate causes of fatigue, we'd expect to see runners start fast and then gradually slow down throughout a typical race. We'd see them behave like cordless appliances, progressively losing power over time. Instead, we see brisk, well-paced movement during the early going, followed by an impressive surge of speed and power on the final lap. This tells us that there must be something else going on here.

Consequently, exercise scientists are beginning to replace the "limitations theory" with a more sophisticated idea called "central governance." This new theory holds that fatigue is not caused by distress signals coming from exhausted muscles, but is rather an emotional response which begins in the brain. Contrary to perception, it's not the muscles who are running the show. Instead, when the brain decides that it's time to quit, it creates the distressing sensations that we interpret as muscle fatigue. The most surprising consequence of this line of thought is that fatigue may scarcely be a physiological phenomenon at all. Instead, fatigue may actually be a creation of the mind.

INTERVAL TRAINING

Support for the central governance theory comes from the success of athletes who practice interval training. As you may know, intervals are surges of effort that come in the midst of sustained exercise; typically, the athlete runs, swims or bikes at a moderate pace and then adds periodic bursts of speed. Experience shows that such training practices are remarkably effective in improving performance. The traditional explanation holds that such training improves oxygen uptake and the ability to tolerate metabolic waste. But increasingly, modern coaches say that the benefits of interval training are primarily, if not exclusively, mental. Experience with intervals tells the brain that "it's safe to go faster." Once the brain becomes convinced that no harm will come to the body, it releases more resources, which in turn allows us to run, bike or swim harder than before.

BIOCHEMISTRY

Scientists have even discovered a biochemical link in the process. Researchers from the University of Cape Town in South Africa have discovered a signaling molecule called interleukin-6 that appears to play a key role in creating the fatigue response. Blood levels of IL-6 are considerably higher than normal following prolonged exercise, and injecting healthy people with IL-6 makes them feel tired. To test their theory, researchers injected trained runners with either IL-6 or a placebo and recorded their times over 10 kilometers. A week later, the experiment was reversed. On average, the IL-6 group ran significantly slower.

THE POWER OF KNOWLEDGE

We see examples of the central governor theory in almost every modern sporting event: the four minute mile, the 7 foot high jump, El Capitan in a day, deep water ocean swims, the 1,000 pound squat. All of these feats have been made possible, not so much by fitness, but by knowledge. Today's high-knowledge athletes aren't really that much "fitter" than their counterparts of the past, but they have immensely more knowledge about what they're doing. This allows them to lower the setting on their central governors.

When Sir Edmund Hillary first roped up at the base of the Khumbu icefall in his attempt on Mt. Everest, we can be sure that his brain was mightily impressed with the extremity of what he was about to do. Unfamiliar terrain and unknown demands loomed above him. His brain had no prior knowledge of this environment and no idea what to expect. Consequently, we can be sure that Hillary and his party experienced major fatigue almost as soon as they left base camp. That's one reason why they needed a series of camps up the mountain. The lack of oxygen was a challenge to be sure, but it was the lack of knowledge that really slowed their pace.

In contrast, the modern climber comes to the Himalayas armed with detailed knowledge. Mt. Everest has been mapped down to the last crevasse and even armchair mountaineers have some idea of the challenges involved. And so, today's mountaineer races up the slope, his brain comfortable in the knowledge that, however life-threatening this environment might be, it is still within the realm of the known and the possible. The body of the modern mountaineer may be somewhat fitter than Edmund Hillary's, but his brain is miles ahead. And so, today's Everest climbers manage the feat with remarkably little fatigue.

LIFE ON THE GRASSLAND

Judging from the way it creates fatigue and limits physical exertion, we can conclude that the brain's default strategy is fundamentally conservative. In effect, the brain seems to be programmed with this simple rule: "In unknown circumstances, create fatigue to limit exposure and vulnerability."

This strategy makes good evolutionary sense. After all, the human brain evolved in a hostile environment where staying alive was the first priority. If physiology was allowed to simply run amok, the organism would be exposed to excessive risk; there's no telling what might happen.

Consequently, evolution has supplied us with a governor, a neurological brake on physical exertion. In this sense, fatigue is a dampener, a restriction device that protects the organism from excessive activity. Natural selection would favor individuals with such an internal program. Individuals with a healthy fatigue-creation capability would be more likely to survive than fatigue-deficient counterparts.

THE UNKNOWN DISTANCE RUN

Our new understanding of fatigue also leads us to the inescapable conclusion that, because of their predictability, modern athletic events are completely artificial. If your event is the mile run, you know your distance down to the inch. You know that you'll be running four laps, no more, no less. You know that the running surface will be smooth and regular. There will be no obstacles and no surprises. The challenge will be utterly predictable and your knowledge level will be extremely high. Such high levels of predictability occur nowhere else in human history or in nature.

From an evolutionary point of view, a more realistic athletic event is the military's "unknown distance run." In this event, participants race against one another, but no one in the contest knows how far they're going. This makes sense in terms of military training because in combat, you never really know how long you might have to go to reach safety.

It also makes sense in terms of human history because on the grassland, anything can happen. In primal human environments, physical challenges are open-ended. When hunting, you don't know how far you'll have to walk before you score a kill. When being hunted, you have no idea which animals will chase you or for how long. There are lots of unknowns out there.

INTO THE UNKNOWN

So, the question now becomes "How can we use this new understanding of fatigue to improve our personal health and fitness? Should we seek out high-knowledge environments like sporting events or should we do our training in situations of physical mystery? What's better for your body? Perfecting your ability to perform a single, familiar movement or subjecting your body to unknown physical challenges?

Some facts are well known. When we start a training or conditioning program, almost any kind of physical challenge will give us improvements in health and fitness. As we struggle to move our bodies in some particular way, we sweat and strive and our bodies become stronger and fitter. As we run or bike or lift, we gain fitness and knowledge simultaneously.

But over time, our increased familiarity leads to a stale, less responsive physiology. If all you ever do is run the mile, your physiology will make specific adaptations to support your performance in this event. In the beginning, the challenge will be highly stimulating to your body, but as conditions become increasingly familiar, your body will begin to slack off. In this way, familiarity becomes an enemy of conditioning. The more you know, the less you grow.

Body builders and weight lifters are very familiar with this process. Start a program from scratch and you'll make solid gains over the first few weeks. Your nervous system will get smarter and faster and you'll go up in your weights. Your encounter with physical novelty will stimulate actual physical transformation. You'll be adding weight to the bar almost every session.

However, if you stay with the familiar program of sets and reps, you'll soon hit a plateau. You won't be adding weight to the bar anymore and you'll start to get frustrated. This is a familiar, well-documented pattern in gyms around the world. Trainers attempt to explain this phenomenon in physiological terms, but it may just be psychological. The reason the body stops adapting is because the challenge has become too familiar. As knowledge increases, the body begins to coast.

That's why trainers advise people to mix up their programs every six weeks or so. Introduce a fresh challenge by changing the exercises, the sets or the reps. This adds welcome diversity, but it also decreases your knowledge. You don't know what it feels like to do this new pattern and so you have to dig deeper into your physiology. As Arnold Schwarzenegger put it in *Pumping Iron*, "You must surprise the muscles."

This is good advice, not just for muscle tissue, but for all the systems of the body. Surprise your muscles, surprise your nervous system, your heart, your lungs, your sensations and your expectations. The key to sustainable, long-term physical fitness success lies in our relationship with novelty and our willingness to expose ourselves to new challenges. The less we know, the more we'll grow.

So plunge yourself into some low-knowledge situations and let your body fight its way out. At first, the challenge will be difficult and exhausting. But as knowledge and familiarity grow, your fatigue will shrink and your competence will expand.

THE NEW FITNESS GOURMET

So we must exercise ourselves in the things which bring happiness, since, if that be present, we have everything.

Epicurus

Hurry up! It's time to get moving! Get it done. Don't linger. Urges are urgent. Impulses need gratification. Grab a bite. There's a deadline coming up. Get to the gym. Achieve. Just do it. There's no time to waste. When in doubt, speed up.

Sound familiar? As everyone knows, the pace of modern living is frenetic and accelerating. In fact, you're probably scanning this essay right now, hurrying to find the salient points so that you can move on to your next urgent task. If so, you're living under the influence of Fast Culture.

SLOW FOOD

Temporal urgency has infected almost every dimension of our lives, accelerating and obscuring even our most primal needs and instincts. One obvious casualty of this culture-wide acceleration is our distorted relationship with food. Today's food is not only fast, it's almost instantaneous. Not only does it appear at the drive-up window on demand, it also arrives in our supermarkets from remote regions of the planet. In urban centers we can satisfy almost any culinary desire with a credit card and a short wait.

Critics routinely attack fast food for its poisonous ingredients, but the problem goes much deeper than trans-fats and insulin-busting carbohydrates. Environmental degradation, social dislocation and a diminished appreciation of pleasurable eating are all consequences of our instant food industry.

Determined to reverse this trend, a group of European culinary activists met in 1989 and founded an organization called Slow Food. This has now become an international movement with 77,000 members in 48 countries. The mission of Slow Food is to return to our nutritional roots by emphasizing quality ingredients, pleasure, community and sustainability.

SLOW FOOD , SLOW FITNESS

Just as we see the effects of the Fast Life on our eating practices, we see similar effects on our movement and exercise practices. Just as we are consumed by Fast Food, we are also afflicted by Fast Fitness, a frenzied, desperate rush to achieve weight loss, youthful appearance and athletic performance. Like fast food, fast fitness leads to a host of negative consequences including distorted relationships with our bodies, overuse injuries, denial of sensation, obsessive competition, steroid abuse and paradoxically, an epidemic of exercise avoidance and obesity.

The obvious solution is to propose a parallel movement called Slow Fitness, a philosophy of exercise that emphasizes sustainability, pleasure, participation and quality of movement. The idea is to develop health and performance gradually over the course of years and decades, enjoying ourselves along the way.

It's important to recognize that Slow Fitness is a philosophy, not a training technique. The specifics of your movement program aren't particularly important here. You might be a biker, a swimmer or a power-lifter. You might favor high reps with low weight or low reps with high weight. These things don't matter much. What's important is your outlook. If you're training for the long term, you're practicing Slow Fitness.

DUELING CLAIMS

The difference between fast and slow fitness comes into stark relief when we examine the claims made by their advocates. We are all familiar with the claims made by fast fitness:

"Shape your body in just 10 minutes!"
"Get rid of those extra pounds fast!"
"Build your biceps in just six weeks with this new program!"

In contrast, Slow Fitness claims are pointedly modest.

"Develop a long-term relationship with your body."
"Discover health and vigor gradually over the course of your life-time."
"Manage your weight by participating in consistent, regular move-ment."

Obviously, none of these claims are flashy enough to make it onto magazine covers. And yet, these slow fitness claims are completely consistent with what we know about exercise physiology and athletic training. If we practice vigorous movement on most days of the week and maintain this kind of lifestyle for many years, success and satisfac-tion are almost inevitable.

PUBLIC HEALTH

Slow Fitness offers a viable antidote to our modern health crisis. As you surely know, America is mired in an epidemic of obesity and other inactivity-related disorders. In early December, 2003, *Newsweek* ranked obesity as the number one health story of the year and called for sub-stantive lifestyle change:

"Obesity, the biggest health crisis facing the country, may be a disease, but curing it will require not just a new gen-eration of pills, but changes in our own lives."

That same week, *Time* magazine reported on the diabetes epidem-ic and concluded that "something in our way of life has gone terribly wrong." Obviously, we need a new orientation towards long-term health and sustainable movement practices.

HEALTH AND PERFORMANCE

Slow fitness is clearly a path to improved health for average Ameri-cans. If people would simply savor the joys of modest movement over the course of their lives, we could reduce the incidence of diabetes, obe-sity and heart disease by enormous measure. But Slow Fitness also turns out to be a powerful path to athletic excellence, especially at elite levels. It takes many years of dedicated effort to develop the skills and biomotor capabilities required to compete at world-class levels; this requires sustainability. Olympic coaches now recognize that motivation, pleasure and joy are essential to maintaining interest, focus and intensity. Slow Fitness not only makes Homer Simpson healthier, it also makes elite athletes even better.

COMMON THEMES

SENSORY EDUCATION:

One of the main interests of the slow food movement is sensory education or, shall we say "sensory fitness." When we eat well, we learn to recognize subtle distinctions between flavors and textures; over time, our senses become more intelligent. Similarly, the slow fitness movement places great emphasis on educating the sensory receptors and pathways of the body. This time however, we're not talking about taste, we're talking about proprioception.

Proprioception is our sense of body position and movement in space. It's a genuine sense, just as real as taste, sight or smell. Nerve cell receptors in muscles, tendons and joints relay a constant stream of information to the spinal cord where it is processed and used to coordinate movement. If the system is slow or the signal is weak, our physical movement becomes clumsy and awkward. Fortunately, this system is trainable; we can increase our sensitivity with playful, functional movement.

This orientation gives new meaning to our experience in the gym or on the track. We aren't going out just to pump muscles or challenge our cardiovascular system; we're going there to make our bodies more sensitive and more intelligent. This, of course, flies in the face of our macho athletic tradition where insensitivity is worshipped as the highest good. Modern athletes know better. If you want your body to work well, you'd better have some appreciation of physical position and motion.

SUSTAINABILITY:

Another core idea for the Slow Food movement is sustainability. Clearly, fast food is hard on the environment and cannot be maintained indefinitely. Production, transportation and packaging all exact a heavy toll on the biosphere. Industrial agriculture promotes deforestation, depletes soil and groundwater and increases pressure on already marginal farmlands. The Slow Food movement recognizes the fact that human beings are dependent on the environment for sustenance and health. By promoting food that is local, seasonal and organically grown, we can prosper. By caring for the land and protecting biodiversity, we give future generations a chance to thrive.

In Slow Fitness, we look for similar sense of sustainability. Obviously, highly-concentrated, short-term physical efforts can give us improvements in strength and endurance, but such sprints cannot last and if maintained, will eventually wreak havoc with the body. By concentrating maximum physical intensity in a short span of conditioning, we effectively rob the future to maximize the present.

Therefore, Slow Fitness seeks to create an orientation towards movement that lasts a lifetime. The idea is to create movement practices that are fun and interesting enough so that people will continue to practice them throughout their lives. With this philosophy, people will continue to practice regular movement, not for any extrinsic reward, but because it offers intrinsic payoffs. If it's fun, people will keep on doing it.

INCLUSIVENESS:

Slow Food philosophers are dedicated to ideals of inclusiveness and community. Good food is produced in cooperation and shared in fellowship. Slow Food advocates believe that social context is just as important as the nutritional substances contained within our food.

Slow Fitness also seeks to build community. It begins by de-emphasizing competition and eschewing dominance hierarchies whenever possible. There are no eliminations in Slow Fitness—no brackets, no playoffs, no standings, no medals, no records and no trophies. There may be movement teachers and apprentices, but only as necessary to support the goal of broad-based, community-wide physical education.

In a Slow Fitness environment, everyone plays with everyone else. There is little movement specialization and little stratification. Beginning students and elite athletes find ways to train with one another. Individuals of diverse shapes, sizes and abilities invent games and movements that can be shared. The tribe sweats together and plays together.

EMPHASIS ON PLEASURE AND QUALITY:

Slow Food puts an intentional emphasis on pleasure and quality, relishing the complete experience of a wholesome meal. The aesthetic qualities of the food experience –growing, harvesting, preparing and eating–are considered extremely important. A good meal is truly a celebration.

In the same way, Slow Fitness celebrates the pleasures of physical movement and play. Participation feels good. The sweat, the muscle fatigue, the challenge–all of these offer pleasure to be savored.

Slow Fitness emphasizes pleasure by abandoning the idea of the "work-out." The phrase "working out" implies labor which in turn implies ends over means. We work, in most cases, to achieve some end. Work can sometimes be pleasant and even sustainable in some contexts, but in general, the whole point of work is to get something different from what you've got. Instead, Slow Fitness emphasizes play and movement sessions. We get together to play because it is enjoyable to do so. Participation is its own reward.

SENSE OF HISTORY, CONTEXT AND PLACE:

When we eat slow food, we establish a connection to history, context and place. Every dish has a story to tell. Food is grown in a bioregion, a place with a unique culture, a climate and a history. The recipes were created by authentic, creative individuals who lived in relationship to the land and one another.

In contrast, fast food is context-free. We don't know where it comes from. It simply appears and we dig in. There is no meaning, no sense of history or place, no connection to anything of consequence. Fast food tells no story (or a story that we'd rather not hear).

Like fast food, fast fitness is also context-free. The quick weight loss plan promises instant results, but it is also devoid of anything that might tell a story. The prescribed movements come out of thin air, without history or meaning; their only purpose is to burn calories. We perform them as instructed, but boredom is inevitable. There's no fascination here, no story and thus, no reason to stick with it.

In contrast, when we practice Slow Fitness, we establish a relationship with history. The movements of our bodies are the product of millions of years of mammalian, primate and hominid history. When we take the time to study these origins, we find ourselves rooted in an ancestral environment that is friendly to our bodies. Suddenly, the movements of our bodies take on a much deeper meaning. Our ability to walk and run is important, not just for burning calories, but because it gave us survival as hunters and gatherers. Every time we do a movement session, we are recreating an ancient experience that goes to the very roots of humanity.

DIVERSITY:

For Slow Food philosophers, diversity of food and taste is essential. There are literally millions of taste and texture combinations that we can enjoy. Not only that, diverse tastes in food also reflect cultural diversity. When we eat a new dish, we gain an appreciation for the people who created it.

Similarly, Slow Fitness advocates value a diversity of movement practices. There are millions of movement combinations to explore; the permutations are endless. A few strength activities, a few endurance experiences, some skill challenges and a little stretching: this is the biodiversity of fitness. A slow fitness practitioner is unlikely to be a specialist. Not only is specialization ultimately boring, it also tends to be unsustainable. If we stress the same tissues of the body repeatedly in the same way, they will ultimately break down. Diversity of movement promotes health by giving stressed tissues a rest.

IT'S MORE THAN CHEMISTRY

Slow Food and Slow Fitness philosophers are united in the belief that there's a lot more to the human body than chemistry. In the world of nutrition, some of us become obsessed with measuring the chemical content of our food, but this calculation is destined to prove inadequate. There is more to our food than grams of protein, fat and carbohydrates.

So too with fitness. There's a lot more to health than some ideal combination of sets and reps. Like food, fitness is personal, social and cultural. The physiology of muscle tissue is a subset of the complete movement experience. Placebo effects are inevitable and widespread. Movement means different things to different people. It's embedded in personal history, culture and social relations. You might get the sets and the reps right, but that's only a small part of the picture. If we want to see the truth of food or fitness, we have to broaden our view.

SAVOR THE FITNESS EXPERIENCE

Unfortunately, our efforts to practice slow food or slow fitness are likely to meet substantial resistance. Both food and fitness are deeply influenced by a marketing industry that intentionally amplifies and exaggerates normal desires. We're hungry, but when we watch TV, we get even hungrier. We feel uneasy about our bodies, but when we look at the magazine rack, we feel anxious and desperate. This is the whole point of modern advertising; create enough anxiety and consumers will feel compelled to buy more products.

Thus there is a rebellious streak to both the Slow Food and Slow Fitness movements. We have had enough of Fast Culture; we want to live our lives at our own pace. We want our food back; we refuse to participate in the obliteration of our senses. We want our bodies back; we're tired of being told how to look. We're sick of being compared to gifted athletes and super-models. Movement is our birthright and we demand a lifetime of play and sustainable pleasure.

Eventually, Americans will see the folly of speed culture and reject the outrageous claims of fast food and fast fitness. In the meantime, we will have to do what we can. As we move into a slow fitness orientation, we learn to savor the details of our movement experience.

Become a connoisseur of exercise, a fitness gourmet. Taste your movements the way a slow food philosopher tastes a fine meal. Take pleasure where you can. As you'll discover, there is a world of pleasure in movement. This is something to be relished.

RESOURCES

Slow Food International: http://www.slowfood.com/
Slow Food USA: http://www.slowfoodusa.org

SAPIENCE

...the use of our intelligence quite properly gives us pleasure. In this respect the brain is like a muscle. When we think well, we feel good. Understanding is a kind of ecstasy.

Carl Sagan

BODY LANGUAGE

I can't remember not being suspicious of words. I treat them as I do any approaching shadows on a half-lit street in a city.

T.E. Tucker

The beginning of wisdom is the definition of terms.

Socrates

The new year is time for a fresh start. As the calendar flips over, millions of us will vow to turn our lives around, especially with resolutions about the state of our bodies. Finally, we're going to quit messing around and get back in shape. We're going to get on a program, start eating right and lose some weight. Unfortunately, these resolutions will fail more often than they succeed.

Part of the problem lies in the words that we use. Resolutions are, of course, composed of words. If you choose the wrong words, your resolution isn't likely to give you what you're looking for.

Everyone thinks that physical conditioning begins with the muscles or the cardiovascular system. I say that it begins with the tongue. After all, if we can't get our language working right, we're going to have a hard time setting intelligent objectives or making sensible choices. It's essential that we choose our language carefully: our words will sculpt our thoughts, our decisions, our experience and in turn, our bodies. I suggest we begin the new year with a look at some "body language."

WORKOUT

The first word that we need to talk about is *workout*. I have yet to uncover the original use of this word, but until I do, we will have to assume that it is, like work itself, a product of the industrial age. Obviously, primal humans never would have thought of doing a workout; they didn't even think of work. It was only with the dawn of agriculture and industry that labor became a fact of human life.

Given the fact that so many of us are chronically overworked in the modern world as it is, it hardly makes sense to practice yet another activity with nearly the same name and connotations. In fact, the word *workout* suggests some of the same industrial values that are currently eating away at our sense of happiness: a relentless quest for speed, efficiency and productivity over pleasure, for example. If you're trying to protect yourself from the ravages of overwork, you're crazy to do a *workout* when you get home. You may as well throw gasoline on the fire of your over-stressed life.

The only way that the word *workout* makes sense is if we use it in an ironic way, as an antidote to the work that we are compelled to perform each day. In this sense, we'd go to the gym, the track or the dojo, not to perform additional labor, but to somehow get the work *out* of our bodies and *out* of our lives. Vigorous movement can in fact do this, purging the body and the mind of the toxic, deadening constraints that we are forced to labor under. If this is how you like to use the word, go ahead. But beware. Most people will miss the point and will continue to bring their work-oriented values to the gym, the pool, the studio and the track. Maybe a different word would be a better choice.

FITNESS

The word *fitness* also deserves our scrutiny. The biggest problem here is that many people confuse physical fitness with the idea of biological fitness. In fact, the word *fitness* only became popular after Darwin's *Origin of Species* was published in 1859. The phrase "survival of the fittest" eventually became "physical fitness."

But people have always misinterpreted Darwin's writings and the entire concept of natural selection. When casual observers talk about "survival of the fittest" they tend to assume that animals survive in the wild because of their ability to move and run like Olympic athletes. Yes, lots of non-human animals are strong, fast and agile, but for the serious biologist, the word *fitness* refers to the overall relationship of the organism to its environment. The animal's "fit" to the environment may have nothing at all to do with its athleticism, speed, power or strength. An animal or species might be considered well-adapted or "fit" because of its ability to retain heat, digest certain plants, see in the dark, function without water or hide from predators. In this sense, even a sloth can be "fit."

When serious biologists talk about fitness they are not talking about animals with rippling muscles or low body fat percentages. Instead, they are talking about a set of physical traits that allow an animal to live to reproductive age and generate viable offspring. Natural selection is a process of differential reproduction, not an athletic competition. Thus, a capable immune system, a good nose or the ability to hear low-frequency sound may have as much to do with "fitness" as speed or strength.

This ambiguity between biological fitness and physical capability seriously undermines the usefulness of the word *fitness* in physical training programs. The confusion has become so great that it's time for us to look elsewhere for descriptive language. Perhaps it's time to quit using the biologist's language and come up with some of our own.

WELLNESS

Next we have the perplexing and mystifying word *wellness*, a word with many possible definitions, or no definition at all. While the word does have legitimacy in some quarters, it also tends to be vague, vaporous and not particularly illuminating. Some wellness advocates do good work in promoting stress-relief and integrated living, but the word has now become a marketing buzzword that says more about style than it does about substance. In short, all is not well with wellness.

Not only that, the very existence of the word *wellness* suggests some alternate or superior state of being that is somehow separate from or beyond *health*. *Wellness* suggests that it's possible to be more than healthy, or to be healthy, but not well.

But do we really need another concept here? Isn't *health* good enough? Hippocrates would have been completely mystified by our insistence that there is some other state of being that is somehow beyond or outside of health. In fact, *health* is a perfectly good word. We generally agree on what it means: freedom from disease, good physical and mental function, synchronization of the body's systems and perhaps a sense of happiness. This is a good, workable concept.

IN SHAPE

Then there's the compound construction *in shape*, as in "This year, I'm determined to get in shape." This usage calls to mind a visual image, a cosmetic ideal, an appearance. We want to get in shape because we want to look a certain way.

This is all well and good, but it puts the cart in front of the horse. That is, it puts cosmetics at the forefront of our attention. But as modern trainers, coaches and physical therapists agree, the superior approach is to concentrate on practical movement skills that lead to sustainability. If we focus on quality movement, we'll enjoy the process, build injury-resistance and craft a lifestyle that lasts for decades.

The way to lose weight is to move consistently and vigorously, year in and year out. So, if you want to get in shape, forget about your shape. Concentrate instead on the quality of your movement. Develop your functional performance. Stoke your exuberance with fun activity. Seek pleasure. Ultimately, your shape will go along for the ride.

EXERCISE AND MOVEMENT

The next word that we need to examine is *exercise*. This is another modern construction. That is, we can be sure that no primal humans ever even conceived of doing exercise. When you live in a hostile environment, your first priority is to conserve your physical resources. If conditions are good, you might hunt, gather, wrestle, play or dance for pleasure, but that would be the end of it.

In today's world, *exercise* is recognized as physical repetition intended to improve conditioning, skill or biomotor performance. Exercises are stereotyped fragments that are extracted from a larger range of possible movements. In other words, *exercise* is a subset of a much larger class of human *movement*.

Movement is a broad, general term that encompasses a wide range of physical action. It includes many physical behaviors that are not normally thought of as exercise. You might climb up a ladder to clean out the gutters on your house; you are engaging in physical movement, but unless you intentionally run laps up and down the ladder, we wouldn't really consider it to be exercise. The same holds true for dance; it's obviously movement, but it's unlikely that we'd call it exercise.

If we look at exercise and movement across history, we see a profound and intriguing difference. That is, while the idea of physical *exercise* only goes back to ancient Greece and Asia, *movement* goes all the way back to the Cambrian explosion, that incredible flowering of animal life that took place some 500 million years ago. When we *exercise*, we place ourselves in the ranks of modern athletes and fitness buffs, but when we do *movement*, we join forces with the entire animal kingdom and participate in an activity that is as old as animal life itself. In this sense, exercise and movement are of entirely different orders. *Exercise* is a modern innovation but *movement* is primordial.

We also see a profound difference between ourselves and other animals. That is, while all animals engage in physical movement, only modern humans exercise. During daylight hours, the chimps at Gombe are moving vigorously, climbing trees and chasing one another around the forest. But they are not exercising, nor is it likely that we could persuade them to do so. In fact, in the entire history of zoology, no naturalist has ever observed a non-human animal doing sets, reps or abstracted exercises. This fact suggests that *exercise* is profoundly unnatural.

The distinction becomes even clearer when we look at the way human children respond to movement and exercise. While it is often difficult to convince children to engage in repetitive exercise, it is almost impossible to keep them from moving. While children take to movement without instruction of any kind, they must be conditioned and persuaded to engage in exercise.

MOVEMENT IS ESSENTIAL, EXERCISE IS OPTIONAL

When we consider this distinction between exercise and movement in the context of human health, we come to yet another surprising conclusion. That is, while movement is obviously essential for health, exercise is optional. It is perfectly possible to live a life entirely without exercise and remain healthy; non-human animals have been doing this for hundreds of millions of years. On the other hand, it is inconceivable that we could live a life without movement and retain our vigor. Exercise is optional, movement is mandatory.

Over the last several years, health and fitness pundits have been pontificating on the need for Americans to get more exercise. But our distinction suggests that this advice is off the mark. Americans are not suffering from a lack of exercise, they are suffering from a lack of movement. This is made abundantly clear by recent studies of Amish communities. As you have surely heard by now, the Amish have almost no obesity, diabetes or similar health problems. Nor do they engage in exercise. Instead, they get lots of vigorous movement each day, typically walking several thousand more steps than the average American.

The distinction between exercise and movement is also reflected in recent public health recommendations that come to us from institutions such as the Centers for Disease Control, the National Institutes of Health and the American College of Sports Medicine. In general, these recommendations for improving public health have little to say about exercise. Rather, they emphasize movement. The idea is to get "vigorous activity on most days of the week."

FOCUS ON MOVEMENT

The key to improving the health of Americans lies in finding an approach that's sustainable. Because it is fundamentally unnatural, exercise lacks the authenticity to pull us off our couches. When exercise is imposed or prescribed, it becomes artificial. And because it's artificial, it's easy to quit doing it. An inclination towards vigorous movement, on the other hand, is something that is more likely to stick. As health columnist Laura Jones put it, "Exercise is a habit you break, movement is something you do forever."

GOING FORTH

So, as we look ahead into the future, let's start by getting our language cleaned up, detoxed and straightened out. Be suspicious of *workouts, fitness, in shape, wellness* and *exercise*. Instead, put your emphasis on *health* and *movement*. You might even phrase your resolution like this:

"This year, I'm going to get lots of vigorous, challenging movement and seek out exuberant health at every opportunity."

This is one resolution that just might be sustainable.

LEARNING LEARNING

The organism will not absorb the fruits of the task unless its powers of apprehension are kept fresh by romance.

Alfred North Whitehead

The philosopher and the neuroscientist walked into the pub one day, intent on some stimulating conversation. Friends and colleagues for years, they'd been coming to this bar for the better part of a decade, always eager to share their insights about brains, minds and the state of the universe. Both were fitness nuts in their own way–the neuroscientist a runner, the philosopher a climber–both were passionate about the human body, albeit in a slightly different way.

The philosopher ordered a Guiness and grabbed a bowl of peanuts. The neuroscientist ordered a blueberry protein shake and a double espresso and they retreated to a booth. They talked about their training, their injuries and then, the latest in their fields.

"So, what's the latest in neuro? asked the philosopher.

"It's really an exciting time right now," his friend replied. "We're on to some hot new ideas about how the brain works and how people learn."

"Oh really?" said the philosopher. "Tell me more, I'd like to learn some new things."

"Well, you see, we've got a whole bunch of amazing new tools that allow us to see deep into the brain. Our functional MRI machine is incredible. We're coming up with some solid, practical conclusions about human learning. This is going to revolutionize education at every level. We'll be able to design programs and methods that are consistent with the way the human body actually works. This is some really exciting stuff."

The philosopher took a sip of his brew and urged his friend to continue.

"Yes," said the neuroscientist. "It turns out that the brain works sort of like a topiary bush in a garden. Growth, then pruning, then more growth and trimming, all mediated by the simple act of use. 'Use-dependent plasticity' they call it. Seems like the whole process works in discrete phases. It's a simple system, but extremely powerful. And, it may just have implications for how we train and educate people—mentally and physically."

"Oh," said the philosopher. He paused for a long moment, composing his words carefully. "That all sounds very interesting and I hate to break it to you this way, but we were on to this a long time ago."

"Oh come on," the neuroscientist shot back, challenging his friend's assertion. "This is the latest, cutting-edge stuff. Our imaging technologies have only been around for a couple of decades. We're only just now starting to map the circuits. Nobody knew this stuff before. It was all just guesswork. How can you claim prior knowledge? We're at the forefront on this one, I'm afraid."

The philosopher grinned, anticipating a friendly sparring match. "Well," he began, "it may not be precisely the same thing, but there's an uncanny coincidence here, a convergence you might say. Ever hear of Alfred North Whitehead?"

"Sure," said the neuroscientist. "Wasn't he a Brit? A mathematician, right? Late 19th, early 20th century? Logic and philosophy?"

The philosopher nodded, encouraging his friend's recollection.

"Can't say that I remember his contribution exactly. I didn't get over to your end of campus much as an undergrad you know. But what has he got to do with this? Back then, we didn't know anything about the nervous system. People were still arguing over whether it was composed of distinct cells or was one vast entity. The synapse wasn't even discovered until around the turn of the century. We couldn't see down to that level until we developed more powerful microscopes."

"Ahh yes, the microscope" mused the philosopher. "But surely you don't think that the microscope is the only instrument for observing how the human organism works. Perhaps there are other ways to approach these things."

The neuroscientist braced himself. He was used to attacks on his reductionist approach and he was well armed with a good selection of retorts. Ever since those books by Fritjof Capra—*The Turning Point* in particular–people had been lining up to take their shots at the scientific method. "So, what exactly are you getting at?"

The philosopher sipped his drink, delighted to be capturing his friend's attention. "You see, Whitehead was like every other Western philosopher. Lived most of his life in the stratosphere. Never met an abstraction he didn't like. Confused the hell out of most of his students. You know the type." He winked. "But Whitehead was also a Taoist of sorts, a real yin-yang kind of guy."

The neuroscientist rolled his eyes, fearing that his normally level-headed friend was lapsing into a state of New Age mysticism. He postulated a sub-clinical brain disorder; maybe a neurotransmitter imbalance. This could be bad, he thought.

"You see," said the philosopher. "Whitehead was intrigued with the learning process and he was fascinated by arguments about educational style. In his day, as in ours, teachers of every stripe were arguing constantly about the merits of freedom and discipline in the schools. The conservatives wanted to tighten the screws, and the liberals wanted to give the students more room to breathe."

"Sounds like some of our department meetings," remarked the neuroscientist.

"Exactly. An eternal controversy. And it's not just in academics; every learning environment suffers the same debate. We see it in everything from phys ed to doctorate programs. But Whitehead refused to get caught up in the whole thing. He was kind of a meta-guy, he figured out a way to get beyond the controversy. From this point of view, both freedom and discipline are essential elements. You've got to have freedom to develop your curiosity, but you've got to have discipline to master the facts, sequences and elemental knowledge. Education without freedom is intellectual dictatorship. Education without discipline is anarchy."

The neuroscientist was intrigued now. "I know what you're saying. I run into this with my students all the time. There's always this tension. They want to play with the material, but I have to keep them on track. So how did Whitehead do it?"

The philosopher smiled. "He set up an oscillation. In fact, his pivotal essay is called 'The Rhythmic Claims of Freedom and Discipline.' By alternating perspectives, you reconcile the opposites and have it both ways. In practice, it's really quite simple. Just set up a dynamic curriculum that swings back and forth between the poles; if you do it right, the method is always in motion. For Whitehead, the whole thing starts with romance."

"Romance?" asked the neuroscientist with another skeptical eyebrow.

"Absolutely. No question. Romance is the first phase of the cycle. This is the time for engagement, for passion, for curiosity and wonder. This is the time for speculation, daydreaming and lateral thinking. The teacher's job in this phase is not to 'teach' as we normally think of it, but to stimulate the imagination. Success is achieved when students find passion in the material. This is a time of play and exploration, not of tests or grades."

"Sounds like fun," observed the neuroscientist.

"Sure is, but once the romance stage has run its course, it's time to move into the precision stage. This is the time for narrowing the field of attention and tightening the focus. This is the time for right answers, sound logic and perfect reps. This is the time for grades, exams and evaluations. This is the time for discipline and rigor."

"Now you've got my attention," said the neuroscientist. "I'm starting to see where you're going with this."

"I thought you would," said the philosopher. "It's really quite intriguing. But it doesn't end there. The final period is what Whitehead calls the 'Stage of Generalization.' This is closely related to the romance phase, except that now the student sees his field with a new set of facts or tools. The process returns to passion, curiosity and interest, but with the ability to go deeper than before."

"A cycle," said the neuroscientist.

"Absolutely. That's the rhythmic phrasing of education. And for my money, it makes perfect sense. I try to structure all my courses this way. But like I said, this method should succeed in any educational discipline, inside or outside the classroom. It should work in phys ed, in industry, in childhood ed, grad school and adult ed. Keep the rhythm going and you'll stimulate learning. Oscillate back and forth between romance and precision and you'll turn out some really bright students."

The neuroscientist was silent now, his brain working furiously, making connections, forming new pathways, rewiring his circuitry. He felt a nearly palpable sensation, as if some great gears had suddenly clicked into place.

"This is amazing," he remarked, suddenly captivated by an expanding field of possibility. "You are right, of course. But you may not realize just how truly right you are."

The philosopher grinned. "Well please, go on. I'm all ears."

"It goes like this," began the neuroscientist, adjusting his posture and settling in for a protracted explanation. "After Darwin, everyone in the sciences began to think in terms of selection, not just at the level of populations, but at every level. Obviously, Darwin was right about the process in terms of species. Big reproduction, variation, scarce resources, lots of death, that sort of thing. But suddenly we began to think about other levels. Natural selection became a metaphor for all kinds of processes and suddenly we began to see it in unlikely places. You see, a lot of people in my field are starting to talk about this thing called neural Darwinism."

"I believe I've heard the term," said the philosopher, "although I'm not sure what you guys are driving at."

"Well, let me explain it this way. One of the big players in this has been Joseph LeDoux, a neuro guy out at NYU. He's got a couple of great books on the brain, *Synaptic Self* and *The Emotional Brain*. He's really into emotion and fear responses, but he's also curious about learning and get this, he's identified three distinct phases of neurological activity that take place in learning."

The philosopher's eyes widened. "Of course. I knew it. It had to be this way. I'd be amazed if it was anything else. Please continue."

"OK, well according to LeDoux, the first phase is called exuberance. During this time, there's a lot of neural proliferation. Lots of new synapses are being made and there's even a lot of neurogenesis going on. You're on board with this idea of neurogenesis?"

"Sure," said the philosopher. "The old dogma held that we don't make new brain cells. You've got what you're born with and that's the end of it. But now it turns out that we really do make new brain cells, thank God."

"Yes, that's neurogenesis and it's crucial. But wait, you'll love this. In the old days, everyone believed in a static nervous system, a static brain. Now we call it *neural fatalism*; you're born with a set of nerve cells and that's the end of the story. But now we know that the brain—the nervous system—constantly remodels itself to adapt to changing circumstances.

We call this *neural optimism*; you get to keep changing yourself as long as you live."

"Astounding," said the philosopher, his mind abuzz with the implications.

"Anyway," continued the neuroscientist. "During the phase of exuberance, or romance as you would call it, the brain goes on a sort of growth binge, sprouting new dendrites and reaching out for fresh connections."

"It's like springtime in the brain," said the philosopher.

This observation derailed the neuroscientist for a brief moment. "Er yes, sure. I guess you could say that. But anyway, next comes the phase of active use or exercise. The individual practices the movement or concept in question and in the process, solidifies connections between active cells. By using the circuits, the circuits become stronger. As they say in the business, cells that fire together wire together."

"Snappy phrase," observed the philosopher.

"The exercise phase is followed closely by a phase of subtraction, in which connections that are not used die off. This is basically cell death by disuse. You lose the ones you don't use. And then, the cycle comes back round again and so on and so forth, as the brain continually tunes itself to meet whatever challenges are imposed upon it."

The philosopher was captivated by the possibilities. "So, what we're talking about is essentially the same thing..."

"It would appear so, my friend. You figured it out by observing the macro level, we figured it out by looking at the micro level. Each finding confirms the other."

"It's all so organic too," replied the philosopher. "Call it what you will–neural Darwinism, rhythmic learning–it's got a swing to it, just like every other living process. Lots of role models out there too."

"Yeah, and we can apply this everywhere. Romance then precision in the classroom and the gym. Exuberance, then pruning in the workplace and in home study. Grow a bunch of dendrites then keep the ones you're using. It all makes such good sense."

"Sure does," replied the philosopher. "But the question remains, why are so few educators doing it this way? I look at classrooms and gyms and seminars and they all look the same to me. No rhythm. They might have gobs of romance or gobs of precision, but hardly anyone oscillates. The average educational experience in the modern age is a flat-line monotony. Each day looks pretty much like every other day. Where's the romance?"

"I don't know," said the neuroscientist. I fell in love with my field decades ago and never looked back. But not everyone is so lucky. I've seen lots of students who never get the spark. Others have the spark, but it gets drilled out of them with endless boring reps. Things have just gotten so narrow these days."

"I hear you," agreed the philosopher. "The specialists have run amok. They do one thing really well, but they can never get to the other side of the oscillation. Fragmented disciplines, isolated studies. One-trick ponies. No one goes meta anymore. Conservatives are tightening the screws at every level. Multi-disciplinary studies are out of fashion and so no one can see the big picture. When you're a specialist, taking the big view just isn't part of your job description. And if you can't see the big picture, you're not going to adopt a rhythm. More likely, you'll live and teach in a rut."

"So, the key is not to be a disciplinarian, but to be a multi-disciplinarian?"

"Yes, that's it exactly."

The philosopher pondered this thought and drained the last of his brew. "It all gets back to the body, right? Rhythm is everything. Breathing, sleep-wake cycles, you know how your training goes. Run hard, then rest big. Push the envelope for a few months, then have an off season. Try a new sport and fall in love with movement all over again."

"It all fits doesn't it? Let's meet up tomorrow and go for a run."

RESOURCES

The Aims of Education by Alfred North Whitehead 1967 Free Press

The Emotional Brain: The Mysterious Underpinnings of Emotional Life by Joseph LeDoux 1996 Touchstone

DANGER IN NUMBERS

while you and I have lips and voices which
are for kissing and to sing with
who cares if some oneeyed son of a bitch
invents an instrument to measure spring with?

e.e. cummings

We're so happy we can hardly count.

Pink Floyd
Have a cigar

The whole thing started with Pythagoras, I suppose. Sitting there on the stairs of a Greek temple, plucking on his proto-guitar string, he realized that the tones he was playing corresponded to numbers. He then got carried away with this observation and jumped to the conclusion that numbers are "the very essence of things," the key to understanding the cosmos.

Pythagoras got some good press for his observation, but it was the big dogs of the Renaissance that really pushed numbers into the headlines. Newton, Kepler, Copernicus and Galileo provided a vivid demonstration of just how powerful numbers could be. By successfully predicting planetary motions and eclipses, they gained the respect of every other discipline within earshot. This led to the ascendance of physics and inspired a profound case of physics envy that continues to this day.

PHYSICS ENVY AND THE BODY

Today, physics envy has infected almost every level of human life and culture. Of course, hardly anyone actually understands physics, but we know that physicists use lots of numbers and so we try to follow suit. We now assume that measurement is essential to success and we try to count everything within arm's reach.

Physics envy has not only infected disciplines like psychology and sociology, it has also infected medicine, physical education, coaching, physical therapy and almost every other discipline that touches the human body. We too aspire to match the precision and success of the physicists. The key to health and fitness, we assume, must lie in quantification.

And so we proceed to count every feature of the body that we possibly can. We count reps and laps, heart rates, breathing rates, lactic acid concentrations and glucose levels. We count pounds lifted, miles run, distance jumped and records broken. We count body mass index, joint ranges of motion, lung capacity and oxygen uptake. Armed with calipers, stopwatches, lap counters and the ever-present clipboard, we put the body on the laboratory bench and start counting. Measure and record: this is how we do it.

OUR OVER-MEASURED WORLD

Measurement has now become an unconscious reflex action that we apply to almost every human endeavor, regardless of necessity. Armies of accountants have descended on every institution and activity, all declaring the mantra of modernity, "If in doubt, count."

In this environment, quantification brings the appearance of rigor and precision, and thus, credibility. Numbers lend an air of legitimacy to almost any profession; numbers, we believe, are serious tools used by serious people. The more you measure, the more expertise you can claim.

Unfortunately, this compulsive counting leads to disordered vision, a kind of blindness. Our metricentric philosophy overvalues things that can be measured while simultaneously obscuring and devaluing everything else. In such an environment, if you can't measure it, for all practical purposes, it doesn't exist.

Numbers offer exactitude and precision about things that, in many cases, are not really worth knowing in the first place. Just because we can measure something doesn't mean that such information is valuable. In many cases, it is the unmeasurable aspects of our experience that are really the most important. As Einstein himself put it, "Sometimes what counts can't be counted and what can be counted doesn't count."

When we extend the reach of our metricentric value system, the perversities soon become obvious. Would we judge a writer by the speed with which he types? Would we judge a musician by the number of notes that he can squeeze into a song? Would we judge a doctor by the number of patients that he sees in a day? A student's education by his score on a standardized test?

Apparently, a lot of people would. In fact, I frequently run into exactly this orientation on my hikes in the North Cascades. No matter how beautiful the conditions, no matter how fresh the air or expansive the view, no matter how complete the sense of alpine rapture, there's always someone in the parking lot whose first and only question is "How long did it take?"

This is precisely the same orientation that we hear from grade-obsessed students who complete long courses of study in subjects ranging from biology to philosophy. After supposedly engaging their minds in a transformational learning experience, their only question is "What did I get?"

NUMERICAL IDENTITIES: I AM MY NUMBERS

The dangers of metricentrism become obvious as soon as we realize just how often we define ourselves numerically. Everyone now seems to have a favorite "identity stat" that they use to secure their place in the world. For some it's their IQ or SAT score. For others, it's their hourly or yearly income. Some of us keep a firm grip on "hours worked per week" or "hours billed per year." And of course, many of us define ourselves by body weight or Body Mass Index. These numbers give us a sense of identity and rank; we are very much aware of how our numbers stack up in comparison to others.

And of course, identity stats are an obsession in the world of sports. Runners, swimmers and rock climbers are particularly prone to this practice. "I'm a 2:30 marathoner," "I swim a :48 hundred," "I climb 5.12." Even decades after retirement, many athletes cling to their numerical identity and remember every split. Fans gleefully participate in this obsession, learning to tick off the stats down to the last decimal point.

But what happens when human beings define themselves, not with ideas, experience or relationships, but by digits? We may gain extremely precise social order, but we lose quality, depth and meaning. With numbers, there are really only two directions to go—higher or lower, slower or faster. Your position in the hierarchy can only go up or down. In a numerically dominated world, there can be no creativity, no ambiguity, no nuance. By taking away subtlety, numbers strip away our intelligence, our inspiration and our passion. They give us precision blindness.

TRAINING BY NUMBERS

Unfortunately, our cultural obsession with counting has come to dominate the world of physical training and movement. When a beginner signs up for a program at a commercial fitness facility, the certified trainer now says "Let's start by getting some numbers." There may be some talk of the client's objectives, but these too are cast in numbers, usually weight loss. Then, once a baseline data set is established, the client is periodically re-measured to determine his or her progress. Success or failure is determined by the client's chart, not by the quality of his or her experience.

Meanwhile, out in the world of sport, we see the modern, metrically obsessed athlete, compulsively tracking all his or her performance biometrics. The triumph of numbers over experience reaches its peak with modern counting gadgets, most conspicuously the runner's watch and heart rate monitor. Many participants now assume that these devices are essential to success, but from the body's point of view, they are completely redundant. The human body already has highly sophisticated internal sensors (interoceptors) to detect heart rate, blood pressure and chemical concentrations. In fact, these internal sensors are immensely more sensitive than any digital device that you can strap around your wrist or chest.

6 MILLION YEARS OF INNUMERACY

Data-heads like to say that numbers are crucial for physical health and fitness. True die-hards have even made the claim "I've got data proving that data is essential!" Nevertheless, such an assertion fails in the face of evolutionary reality. For the overwhelming majority of human history, there was no counting at all and it has only been in the last half century that people have begun to apply numbers to movement and exercise. So what are we to make of the millions of healthy, pre-numerate humans who hunted and gathered their way across Africa, Asia and the Americas? Are we to assume that their physical experience was somehow inferior to our own? Last time I checked, it seemed that we are the ones with the obesity and diabetes problem.

And by the same token, what are we to make of the spectacular health and performance of non-human animals over the last 500 million years? We can be sure that no dinosaur ever counted a rep or a lap. And of the four thousand species of mammals in today's world, three thousand nine hundred and ninety nine manage to stay healthy without counting any dimension of their physical experience whatsoever.

SENSATION FIRST!

When it comes to making our bodies healthier and happier, the most important element is vigorous, frequent participation and authentic physical experience. Period. All other considerations are secondary.

In fact, numbers are completely unnecessary for physical education and conditioning. If some alien power swept over the planet and destroyed all of our physical counting methods, we could still move our bodies vigorously and train effectively. We could still do physical education and we could do it well. With a little creativity, we could create classes, movements and challenges that are completely independent of numbers.

So, if you're looking to deepen the quality of your fitness experience, resist the urge to quantify; look for quality instead. Get out of your head and into your body. Pay attention to sensation and use your words to describe your experience. How does it feel when you pump the big weight, run the fast sprint or climb the big mountain? If you work with quality, you'll make progress.

In the end, we need to pay more attention to a playful, sustainable process and less attention to a performance product. Education critic Alfie Kohn said it best in his book *No Contest: The Case Against Competition*:

> Play is not concerned with quantifying because there is
> no performance to be quantified...the process-oriented
> individual gladly gives up precision–particularly precision
> in the service of determining who is best–in exchange for
> pure enjoyment.

In other words, "He who plays does not ask the score."

SAFE EMERGENCIES, FRIENDLY ENEMIES

> To enhance creativity, merge two previously separate concepts that are in conflict with one another. For example, combinations such as 'friendly enemy' and 'healthful illness.' The more discrepant the concepts, the more likely they are to result in novel properties.
>
> Tom Ward
> Journal of Creative Behavior

If you're interested in physical training and fitness, you're naturally interested in change and transformation. You might be trying to lose a few pounds, increase your strength or build your aerobic capacity. Maybe you're trying to develop your nervous system for better sports performance or rehab your body back into condition after a foolish episode of over-training.

In any case, you're looking for physical change. But how are you going to stimulate that transformation? After all, your body isn't going to simply change on its own. Why should it? Unless there's some immediate need, your body will be perfectly content to float along in its current condition.

In order to stimulate change, we need to provoke the organism in some fashion. In other words, we've got to apply some stress. Of course, we can't simply apply that stress indiscriminately. Stress hormones have a paradoxical effect of dose and benefit. A little stress can be highly beneficial and transforming, but too much or too long an exposure can be extremely damaging, not only to the brain itself, but to the entire quest for change.

So, the challenge is to hold both possibilities in hand so that we don't go too far in either direction. We want to apply stress, but we want to give ourselves the chance to back away if it becomes too intense or dangerous. We want to position ourselves so that each alternative is within our grasp; one hand advancing the challenge, the other offering support and safety.

As it turns out, this is also a central theme in the world of psychotherapy. Like physical trainers, psychotherapists are looking to stimulate transformation in their clients. They're trying to relieve depression, anxiety or phobias. In the popular imagination, we tend to think of these afflictions as something exclusively "in the mind." But these things are also "in the body," and an emerging school of thought now holds that psychotherapists are really creating physical transformations in their patient's nervous systems. Physical therapists and psychotherapists simply approach the organism from different directions.

As you might expect, psychotherapists have a long history of studying the therapist-patient relationship. Naturally, there are many opinions on this score, but one common theme emerges. That is, the most effective relationship seems to be a paradoxical, hybrid approach that utilizes both challenge and safety. Frederick S. (Fritz) Perls (1893 - 1970) a noted German-born psychiatrist and psychotherapist used the term "safe emergency" to describe the ideal experience.

A safe emergency is a predicament that challenges the organism, but the consequences for failure are not severe. Safe emergencies provoke the animal towards change and transformation, but do not push them over the edge into exaggerated fear and stress responses.

Louis Cozolino described the relationship in his book, *The Neuroscience of Psychotherapy: Building and Rebuilding the Human Brain*:

> Research across most forms of therapy supports the
> hypothesis that positive outcomes in psychotherapy are
> related to the combined engagement of thought and
> affect, utilizing both support and challenge... A safe
> emergency is a challenge for growth and integration in the
> context of guidance and support.

So it turns out that we're all in the same business. The athletic coach, the executive coach, the personal trainer, the psychotherapist—all these people are doing essentially the same thing. That is, stimulating a transformation in their clients by creating safe emergencies. The details may be different, but the relationship is nearly identical. Provocation and support, challenge and care–these define the transformative relationship. It doesn't matter what the material is, nor the level. If you're in the transformation business, this is the kind of relationship you're after.

HOW THE BODY RESPONDS

To understand the psycho-physical nature of the safe emergency, think of it this way: If you walk the tightrope without a net, it's a genuine emergency; if you walk it with a net, it's a safe emergency. Similarly, rockclimbing with a rope (sport climbing) is a safe emergency. Rockclimbing without a rope is an actual emergency.

Just imagine how the human body would respond to this predicament: Take a beginning climber and put him on a steep rock face without a rope. The stress would be so overwhelming that he'd be lucky to function at all. His fight-flight-freeze response would kick into high gear and stress hormones would flood his bloodstream. In these conditions, no transformation would be possible. The organism would be content merely to survive.

But now put a rope on that beginner and show him how it will catch him if he falls. And, to make the experience even safer, give him an attentive partner and a good course of preparatory training. Tell him what's going to happen on his climb and run through a bunch of "what-if" scenarios. Give him a host of alternatives and options. Then, send him up on the climb.

Things are entirely different now. His adrenal glands will still pump out stress hormones, but only in moderate levels, not enough to derail his concentration or enjoyment. In fact, he will probably feel exhilarated. And, under these conditions, physical and psychological transformation becomes not only possible, but likely.

ANIMAL PLAY BEHAVIOR

Animal play behavior offers a conspicuous example of a safe emergency. When a pair of dogs perform a "play bow" at the onset of play, they form a kind of contract that says "everything after this is pretend." Or in other words, "This is safe. I might bite your ears or try to knock you over, but it's all for the sake of fun and exuberance." At this point they become friendly enemies, challenging each other to higher levels of physical engagement. Their bodies experience stress and produce stress hormones, but only in moderate amounts. This yields an ideal experience that is simultaneously stimulating, transformative and a hell of a lot of fun.

SPORTS

We also see safe emergencies in the world of athletic competition. Victory and defeat are meaningful to the participants, but in most cases, there is little in the way of actual physical danger. There's plenty of pressure to perform, but that pressure is largely abstract; the consequences of defeat and failure are not likely to be catastrophic. This is why sport can be so incredibly transformative. Pressure to perform at a high level gets results, especially when it's backed up by the support of coaches, teammates, friends and family.

And, just as a sporting competition is a safe emergency, a good opponent is a friendly enemy, especially if he subscribes to the ethic of good sportsmanship. He'll knock you silly on the playing field, but help you up if you fall down. He'll point out your weaknesses with skillful counter-moves, but he'll help you off the field if you get hurt.

MARTIAL ART

Martial art is also famous for creating safe emergencies with friendly enemies. Face off against a talented sensei and he'll tap your weaknesses with his fists or the bottom of his feet. You're in no real danger, but it sure feels like it and your body remains on high alert. There's good stimulation here, but the stress and fear are exhilarating, not disabling. Your body responds.

IN THE EXERCISE WORLD

Unfortunately, modern conditioning programs miss a golden opportunity to create safe emergencies or develop friendly enemies. The problem begins, as it so often does, with machine-based training. Users simply wander from one machine to the next, never part of a human relationship, never challenged or supported. It's just you, your clipboard and the pin on the machine. Or, if you're on a cardio machine, it's you and your computer display. But computer displays, even with creative programming, can never substitute for genuine human relationship. Your time on the treadmill can never be a safe emergency. Your stair machine can never be a friendly enemy; it's simply an appliance with flashing lights. Transformation is highly unlikely.

"TO HECKLE AND PROTECT"

In Exuberant Animal classes, we make an intentional effort to create safe emergencies and train students specifically to become friendly enemies. The process begins with an explicit expression of support and safety. New students are welcomed to class with this introduction:

> Everything here is optional. All our fitness games and movements are at your discretion. Participate to whatever level you like. If you want to adjust your movements or sit out entirely, you're welcome to do so. We'll back you up. That said, we'll also hound you and heckle you to put in a good effort. We'll encourage you because we want to see you succeed. We'll cheer your good efforts and applaud your good moves. The better you do, the better we all do.

Once the introductions are complete, we establish a sense of physical safety and support with spotting drills. This fits right into the content of the class. If you've done some functional training, you know that there's a big emphasis on balance and agility work. People are spending a lot of time on one foot and they're pushing the limits of stability with wobble boards, bosu balls and other devices.

This puts students in danger of falling, but it also gives us an opportunity to spot one another. Practice this by gathering in a circle and designating an experienced person as the "faller." His job is to approach the perimeter of the circle and do some gentle "falls" into his classmates. He might feign a stumble, for example, and allow a portion of his body weight to fall forward. His classmates respond by breaking his fall and keeping him upright. The technique is simple—use your hands to break the momentum of the torso. Catch the fall if you can, or at least get your body in the way to absorb some of the momentum.

At a minimum, do a few minutes of spotting practice every now and then. Not only is it fun, it's also a good team-builder. And, it sends a simple message: members of the class are expected to look out for one another.

Once you've established some spotting skills and a spotting ethic, you can move on to creating challenge. Now is the time to heckle, provoke and challenge. On the simplest physical level, heckling consists of light nudges to your partner's torso, hips or shoulders. Ask for a volunteer to stand in the center of your circle, on one foot. Friendly enemies step up with light heckles, just enough to challenge balance, not enough to set off a stress reaction. As you develop a rapport and a sense of ease, gradually increase the challenge, but be ready to back off if stress and frustration begin to build. And don't forget that, as a heckler, you're still responsible for spotting. Heckle the hip or the shoulder, but be there to break a stumble or prevent a fall. You're a friendly enemy after all.

REMEMBERING HOW TO PLAY

Safe emergencies, friendly enemies: This is how people are supposed to play. This is what makes play so productive and rewarding. This is what more of our training programs should look like.

Unfortunately, many of us never learned how to play this way, or maybe we forgot. But in any case, it's still within our reach. Start by creating the right culture in your studio, your gym, your clinic or your dojo. Make it a safe, challenging place filled with friendly opponents.

You'll be amazed how transformative the experience can be. And you'll be delighted with how much fun you can have.

STOP DRAWING HORSES

Art teachers have some fascinating stories to tell about the varieties of human aptitude that they encounter in their classrooms. Each year, students show up for drawing courses with a wide range of talent. But in each new class, a few students demonstrate a strange kind of capability that defies normal description.

These students can draw one thing extremely well, but only one thing. In many cases, that one thing is a horse. Fascinated with horses through-out childhood, these students have done thousands of practice drawings and have mastered the practice. Unfortunately, they can scarcely draw anything else; their landscapes, portraits and human figures are car-toonish hacks. If you visited an exhibit of their horse work, you'd hail the artist as a master, but if you looked at the rest of their portfolio, you'd say that they needed to go to art school.

So what's going on here? These students aren't afflicted with some rare neurological disorder that allows for horse-drawing but inhibits ev-erything else. They aren't autistic or idiot savants. No, these are normal students with a high degree of nervous system specialization. They are adept at duplicating the anatomical structure of the horse, but that's the limit of their expertise. Their repertoire may be deep in horse variants, but it remains narrow. We might be impressed with their horse draw-ings, but we'd be hard-pressed to call them artists.

THEY'RE EVERYWHERE

The horse-artists strike us as odd curiosities, but their condition is symptomatic of a larger theme in human experience and education. That is, in this modern age of specialization, we see horse-artists everywhere, especially in the world of sports and athletics. Every year, students show up at high schools, colleges and pro ranks with fragmented, narrow movement specialties that may be spectacular in their own right, but are nowhere near complete. One is a 40 yard specialist. Another has a great jump shot. Another can bench press three times his body weight. But are they athletes or are they just horse-artists?

It's not just sports either; we see such specializations everywhere these days. You probably know someone from your youth who took up the guitar and, through long hours of excruciating toil, managed to pick out the entire sequence of notes in "Stairway to Heaven." At parties, he can pull off a passable performance, but by no stretch can we call him a musician. He's a one-song pony, another kind of horse-artist.

We see the same thing in the world of martial art. One guy practices a single sword cut to perfection, another learns to break boards, another devotes thousands of hours to catching arrows in flight. All of these are impressive feats, but all remain specialties. And because they are specialties, they are also vulnerabilities. Bruce Lee saw this clearly and so refused to limit his repertoire. For him, the ultimate style was a completely spherical capability that could respond in any form required. Specializations, however strong, ultimately become weaknesses.

MAKING IT WHOLE

So what are we to do with these horse-artists, these one-dimensional athletes and these one-song wonders? As teachers, educators and coaches, our job is to round them out, to diversify their expertise, to stretch their capability across a broader range. Traditionally, we do this by the time honored method of "working the weakness." We figure out what the student or athlete does poorly and then devise drills and exercises to bring that skill up to speed. In other words, make them draw something besides horses.

Examples of this strategy abound. Early in Michael Jordan's career, a jealous critic foolishly remarked, "Well, Michael's pretty good on offense, but he's weak on defense." That assessment was probably bogus, but Michael took it as a challenge and went to work on his defensive game. Before long, he became a league leader in blocks, rejections and steals. He applied the same attention to every possible weakness in his performance. Ultimately, his game became almost perfectly spherical, his only flaw being a passing interest in baseball.

And speaking of baseball, we can cite the career of Sadarahu Oh, the legendary "Japanese Babe Ruth." As an obscure minor leaguer, Oh tried everything to raise his game to the next level, finally coming to the conclusion that his balance at the plate was his primary weakness. To resolve this flaw, he spent the entire off-season practicing his swing exclusively on one foot. When he finally returned to a normal two-footed stance in the regular season, he was fearsomely effective and set new records for power and home runs.

In the world of fantasy boxing, we saw the same principle when Rocky Balboa's trainer forced him to practice for months with his non-dominant hand (his right). Naturally, Rocky hated the process, but ultimately it proved successful. Late in the title match, after suffering the requisite beating, Rocky's coach allowed him to switch to his dominant hand, a change that completely mystified and defeated his opponent. Fiction yes, but the principle is sound.

STRAYING FROM THE PATH

Unfortunately, modern trainers often stray from the time-honored principle of "working the weakness" and try instead to "strengthen the strength." Coaches, teachers and parents often become conspirators in this process. We keep a sharp eye out for early signs of student aptitude and then sign them up for additional, specialized training. If a student is good at drawing horses, we send him to a horse drawing camp or an Institute of Horse Drawing, hoping for a scholarship or a lucrative professional contract.

In some cases, it all works out. The strength gets stronger and the specialization becomes a life asset. If the student or athlete is lucky, he'll get some extracurricular experience along the way, round out his skill set and become a complete player, artist or scholar. But if not, the whole thing can come crashing down into irrelevance or injury. The horse artist might get lucky, but if things change, he's sunk. The one-dimensional athlete or musician might find a place to thrive, but if the environment shifts, he's out of options.

The folk wisdom is right, of course. It's crazy to put all your neurological, fitness or educational eggs in one basket. In a dynamic environment, it's better to spread them out across a whole bunch of baskets.

THE INJURY CONNECTION

The perils of specialization are obvious in the way that our bodies respond to narrow experience. Simply put, intensive movement specialization is a recipe for tissue break down. The over-use injury is best described as a specialization injury or, to put it another way, a horse-drawing injury. Too much micro-trauma in one place ultimately leads to trouble.

If you're a sporting specialist, it should come as absolutely no surprise when some part of your body starts to break down. Inflammation and pain are the price we pay for drawing nothing but horses. In fact, if you're really dedicated to a single sport or movement type, you should plan on injury. It's only a matter of time. The more refinement you develop, the deeper your physical rut, the greater the accumulated stress on tissue.

In contrast, we never hear much about diversification injuries. People who play a variety of movements spread out the physical stress. Micro-trauma gets a chance to heal when we practice across a broader spectrum. In the short term, diversists fail to develop the incredible powers of the specialist, but they also have longer careers. For these players, diversity wins in the end.

WHAT'S YOUR WEAKNESS?

So the burning question of the moment is "What's your weakness?" Are you trapped in a single specialization? If you've been drawing nothing but horses for the last few years, you might want to think about the flip side. What are the things you never draw? What are the moves you never do?

If you're serious about developing a comprehensive fitness or skill set, you'll want to start working your weaknesses. Try a bunch of physical arts, find out what you're really bad at, and practice that thing. If you discover that you're really bad at yoga, do yoga. If you're really bad at distance running, do distance running. If you're really bad at dancing, dance. Look to the opposite side of your capability. If you're strong on cardio, work strength. If you're strong on strength, work cardio. If you're strong on power, work flexibility.

At some point, you've got to stop drawing horses. You've got to stop playing Stairway to Heaven. You've got to stop running that same route and distance that you've been doing for the last decade.

Find out your awkwardness. Figure out what you're good at and then—Just Do the Opposite. Go towards your awkwardness, go towards your fear, go towards your instability, your errors and your ignorance.

Of course, most people do precisely the opposite, which is precisely the problem. We look for games, sports and skills that we're already good at. We sample some activities in our youth, then settle on the one that we have the most success. Why? Because it gives us pleasure to do well. A good reason, but not an altogether sustainable one.

THE ROLE OF THE COACH

So what of the teacher and the coach? Contrary to popular opinion, the role of the teacher/coach is not to recognize and reward aptitude. Any amateur can hand out carrots for good execution. No, the teacher-coach is there to recognize ineptitude and train it away.

Yes, good teachers and coaches can inspire, but their first duty is a somewhat unpleasant one: "Here's the flaw in your performance. Let's work on it." A poor teacher and coach will help you strengthen your strengths. A good teacher and coach will help you identify your weaknesses and eliminate them.

In this sense, the English teacher, the basketball coach and the martial art sensei are all doing essentially the same thing. "Your language, your movement, your skill set, lacks this particular quality. Here's an exercise to increase that quality in your repertoire."

In the popular imagination, the teacher and the coach are sometimes held up as friends, even buddies, but this is not good teaching or good coaching. In fact, the coach and the teacher are best thought of as benevolent enemies. "You are weak here, here and here" the teacher-coach will say, pointing to the vulnerable spots in your performance. "You are slow in this movement, your vocabulary is weak, your strength is insufficient and you can't draw a landscape to save your life."

The problem with this "work the weakness" philosophy is that it's both physically and psychologically demanding. We love proficiency and mastery and cling to it. If we're good at drawing horses, we take pleasure from that process. It's our meditation, our outlet, our fascination. Drawing landscapes seems like drudgery. And of course, the same holds true for physical artistries. If I'm a good distance runner, I'll take my pleasure there. If I've got an aptitude, I want to exercise it.

So therein lies the conundrum of training, teaching and coaching. If you want your students to improve, you've got to work their weaknesses. It's essential. But if you're too zealous, you'll take away the one thing that sustains the process.

And so we make yet another case for balance and proportion. Yes, work the weakness by all means. Find the flaws in your skill set and flog them good. But don't deprive yourself of your pleasure either. If you're good at drawing horses and it gives you pleasure, draw some horses too.

WHEN IN DOUBT, ROUND IT OUT

No matter what your situation, work towards comprehensive capability. If you've been drawing horses or playing Stairway to Heaven for the last 20 years, it's time to get with a teacher or a coach who will stand you up in front of your weaknesses and get you working on them. Listen to this coach and cherish his advice. Draw something new. Play something different. Horses are great, but a comprehensive skill set is even better.

WHAT'S UP DOC?

Rewards and punishments are the lowest form of education.

Chuang Tzu

Who would have thought that play could be turned into work
by rewarding people for doing what they like to do?

Rosemarie Anderson

What's the biggest substance abuse problem in our culture today?
Is it alcohol, heroin, crack or tobacco? Is it trans-fats or high-fructose corn syrup? I submit that it's none of the above. You may be
surprised to hear that it's carrots.

By this I don't mean to suggest that millions of people are lying
comatose in dark bedrooms for days at a time, intoxicated by some mind-altering properties of a common root vegetable. No, I use the vegetable
figuratively, as a stand-in for our cultural strategy of manipulating be-havior through rewards. Grades, incentive programs, even praise–they're
all carrots. These carrots sometimes produce short-term compliance, but
ultimately they distract people from what's truly important.

PUNISHED BY CARROTS

The definitive statement on the social pathology of carrots is Alfie
Kohn's *Punished by Rewards: the trouble with gold stars, incentive plans,
A's, praise and other bribes.* In a series of powerful arguments, Kohn ex-poses the fundamental problem with carrots. As he puts it, what passes
for education these days is really little more than behavioral manipula-tion, all based on the simple prescription: "Do this and you'll get that."
We frame learning as something one does in exchange for a prize rather
than something intrinsically valuable. Kohn cites a series of fascinat-

ing studies demonstrating not only that carrots are manipulative and coercive, they also don't really work very well; in many cases, rewards actually undermine performance.

THE BEHAVIOR MOD SQUAD

Kohn's observations are aimed at the classroom and the workplace, but they apply equally to matters of PE, fitness, athletic training and public health. Health and fitness experts everywhere point to our epidemic of sedentary living and agree that we need to get people moving. Unfortunately, the most commonly proposed solutions fall into two basic classes, carrots and sticks, the first-line tools of behavior modification. The general idea is simple: we'll impose some sort of punishment for sloth and some sort of reward for exercise. That way, behavior will change and in turn, our obesity crisis will be solved. End of analysis.

This approach has a long history in educational circles where the implicit lesson plan has nothing to do with education itself. Rather, the hidden objective is to "teach" students to start thinking in terms of sticks and carrots. If you're a student in such a program, the background message is clear: Ignore the passions and curiosity you might feel. Look instead for the sticks and carrots and adjust your behavior accordingly. If you're good at avoiding sticks and getting carrots, you'll get good grades. You'll be a success.

THE PROBLEM WITH STICKS

As physical educators, trainers and coaches, we also use carrots and sticks. Of course, most of us are reluctant to use actual sticks on our students, players and clients. We don't beat them outright, but we sometimes use abstract sticks—words, images and ideas of negative consequence:

"Do this workout because if you don't, you'll get obesity
and diabetes! You'll get heart disease and cancer. You'll be
a burden to society and a drag on the economy!"

If such medical sticks are deemed inadequate, some of us turn to cosmetic sticks:

"You'd better exercise because if you don't, you'll end up looking fat and disgusting and no one will want to date you or marry you. You'll be a social outcast. Give me another lap and another set of push ups."

The problem with these "motivators" is that they create a poisonous atmosphere of fear, guilt and anxiety. And besides that, they just don't work. They may generate temporary compliance, not long-term transformation. As soon as the stick goes away, we go back to our default behaviors.

THE PROBLEM WITH CARROTS

When sticks don't work, many of us turn to carrots. In an effort to get people moving, we offer "motivation" in the form of high grades, perks and outright payouts. Lose a pound, earn a treat. Run a lap, get a reward. Eat a carrot, get a "carrot." This may work for a few days or weeks, but in the end, carrots may be just as damaging as sticks, maybe even more so.

Carrots are good at producing short term compliance but they are notoriously ineffective at developing sustainable habits of living. Yes, we can give Johnny some gold stars and reward pellets for running a mile a week, but this will only get results as long as the pellets hold out. If we really want to create lifetime habits of movement, we need to find something more compelling.

Carrot advocates insist that we need to offer motivation to get people to run their laps and do their reps. But what exactly are people learning here? In fact, rewards completely transform and distort the original enterprise; they change the nature of the game. Kohn puts it this way— "Do rewards motivate people? Absolutely. They motivate people to get rewards."

The biggest problem with carrots is that they are demeaning—literally—in the sense that they strip away all meaning of the enterprise beyond that necessary to achieve the reward. Once you set up a carrot-based incentive program, the carrot itself takes on the meaning and obscures whatever else might be involved. As educator A.S. Neil put it, promising a reward for an activity is "tantamount to declaring that the activity is not worth doing for its own sake."

Carrots shift our attention and distort our sense of values. In an ingenious experiment, a social psychologist visited a preschool classroom and noted that the children loved to draw with both felt-tip pens and also with pastel crayons. He then divided the class into two groups. He told the first group that "before you can draw with the pens, you have to spend some time drawing with the crayons." He told the other group the reverse. When he returned two weeks later, he found that whichever activity had been the prerequisite for the other was now something the children were less interested in doing.

As for the classroom, so too for the playground, the gym and the athletic field. If I'm aiming for a grade that will go on my permanent record, I'm going to do whatever is necessary to get that score and ignore everything else. I'll run hard today if that's what it takes, but once my score is recorded, I'll do as I please.

Not surprisingly, carrots also discourage risk taking, play and exploration. As Kohn puts it, "when we are working for a reward, we do exactly what is necessary to get it and no more." No side trips, no diversions, no exploration, no bushy exuberance. The path to an "A" is straight, narrow and above all, economical. "Risks are to be avoided whenever possible because the objective is not to engage in an open-ended encounter with ideas; it is simply to get the goody." Another psychologist puts it bluntly "Rewards are the enemies of exploration."

A NATION OF RABBITS

Worst of all, gold stars, grades and perks are all instruments of domestication. They deprive us of our freedoms and our independence. They distract us from authentic engagement with the world and turn our minds to externalities. Once we become addicted to carrots, we lose our capacity for truly creative experience. Carrots, as Karl Marx would have put it, are an opiate of the masses.

Naturally, some will reject this entire line of reasoning. They point to professional sports, a system that offers lavish carrots to those who push themselves to new levels. Carrots, they might even say, are responsible for all human advancement, especially in the world of physical movement. If it weren't for carrots, people would simply sit on their back porches, eating barbecue and swilling beer for the rest of their lives. If it weren't for yellow jerseys, Lance Armstrong would still be riding a coaster bike around his neighborhood. If it weren't for the NBA championship ring, Michael Jordan would have grown up to be a playground dabbler with a few good hops.

But I reject these claims. Carrots are a distraction, especially for those who are intrinsically motivated. Armstrong and Jordan were driven, not by carrots, but by the idea of excellence. Sure, the money is great, but it's mostly a side-show. This is precisely the story of Jim Thorpe's life as one of the greatest athletes in history. There is no question that he craved money and respect, but his core motivation was always the exuberance of playful sporting movement.

CARROT-FREE CREATORS

The most obvious question for carrot advocates is "Why do we feel the need to provide "motivation" for behaviors that are intrinsically compelling in their own right?" After all, no one had to offer reward pellets to Socrates, Hippocrates, Newton, Galileo, Copernicus or daVinci. In the modern era, no one had to give carrots to Carl Sagan, Steven Jay Gould, Richard Feynman or Richard Dawkins. These are people who pursued their interest because it fascinated them, completely independent of any carrots that administrators might have thrown their way. In fact, their passion was so complete that it would have survived even under the lash of administrative sticks. When creativity is flowing, you don't need sticks *or* carrots.

By the same token, no one had to offer reward pellets to the millions of pre-modern dancers and hunter-athletes who moved their bodies for the sheer joy of doing so. These people moved their bodies because it felt good. If a time-traveling administrator were to show up in a Pleistocene village and offer reward pellets for physical movement, his offer would be met by uncomprehending stares.

And, even more to the point, no one needs to offer carrots to non-human animals to motivate movement and play. A healthy dog is going to play regardless of any external reward he might receive. Play itself is the reward.

DO IT FOR LOVE: THE EXPERIENCE IS THE CARROT

For the healthy human animal, physical movement is intrinsically pleasurable and self-rewarding. (The buzz word here is autotelic.) What we need to do is strip away the incentives and get back to the core educational experience–the intrinsic pleasure of vigorous movement. In other words, we need to return to our amateur status. (The word *amateur* is from French and the Italian *amatore*, from the Latin *amator* 'lover' and *amare* 'to love.') Go for a run or hit the weights because the sensation pleases you, not because of some externality.

Physical educators will be most effective when they emphasize the intrinsic motivations and pleasures of joyful movement. Of course, for this model to work, coaches and teachers have to actually demonstrate the pleasures that they're trying to awaken in their students; it makes no sense to speak of the intrinsic joys of movement if you've got a death grip on the clipboard. If you don't find human movement intrinsically fascinating, you're in the wrong field. But if you're walking the talk and enjoying movement for its own sake, students will get the idea.

SLOW, STEADY AND SUSTAINABLE

There are only two rules to change: One is to begin; the second is to continue.

unknown

Patience is also a form of action.

Auguste Rodin

So whatever happened to the tortoise? Last time I heard, he was am-bling along at a leisurely pace, making incremental progress and ultimately defeating the impulsive and over-confident hare. Adults told us that the tortoise was the smarter creature and that by exercising pa-tience, we'd all end up winners. "Slow and steady," they said gravely, "wins the race."

Well apparently we've chosen to disregard that advice because these days it's all about speed. The hare and his hare-brained philosophy is proliferating into every corner of modern life. Fast diets, fast fitness, fast careers, fast machines, fast business, fast relationships. The tortoise has been forgotten. Seized with a compulsive, unquenchable need for instant gratification, we have become a nation of desperate, over-reach-ing, maniacal rabbits.

It would be one thing if this frenzied rushing and lurching actually made us happy and healthy, but it doesn't. Our bodies are spectacularly stressed, atrophied, obese and diabetic. The latest report from the World Health Organization tell us that 1 billion people on the planet are now overweight or obese. The current trajectory of diabetes and heart disease promises a future of increasing physical disease and disability.

We know there's a problem, but frantic for quick resolution, we revert to our habitual hare-styles and lunge for the instant gratification. "Hurry Up! Let's solve our fitness problem right now!"

You've seen it all in the checkout line at the supermarket. Every diet and fitness claim is tagged with a hare-brained claim for speed:

"Get into that bathing suit by summer!"
"Shape your hips in just 10 minutes!"
"Get rid of those extra pounds fast!"
"Build your biceps in just six weeks with this new program!"

Of course, it's all hype. Every last word of it. Hare-brained diets, hare-brained fitness, hare-brained health; it's all bunk. There is no accelerated formula for weight-loss, fitness or athletic excellence. Every responsible physician, trainer and coach knows that speed fails. The only thing that really, truly works is frequent, vigorous movement combined with a sensible, food-based diet, sustained over years and decades.

MEET THE HARE (STYLE)

He who wishes to be rich in a day will be hanged in a year.

Leonardo da Vinci
The Archetype of Human Potential

Our children's books never went into much detail about the hare's personality, so let's take a closer look. Obviously he's impatient, but there's a lot more to the story. In the world of modern health and fitness, the hare is a frantic and obsessive short-termer. Desperate for instant gratification, he becomes a physical extremist, either training or dieting to excess. Fueled by anxiety, he lunges for instant achievement. When his strategies fail, he redoubles his efforts. Ultimately, he becomes frustrated, manic and possessed.

Adding to his difficulties, the hare has little tolerance for ambiguity and is a compulsive black and white thinker. In the depths of the rabbit brain, all qualities fall into either one category or the other. There is no overlap and no middle ground. You're either fat or skinny, either fit or atrophied. You're either in training or on the couch. A champion or a loser. On a diet or on a binge. All or nothing.

Not surprisingly, this polarized thinking style leads to a life of frenzied and erratic behavior. We've all heard about yo-yo diets, but what really characterizes the hare is his yo-yo psychology. Radical swings in thought and disposition lead to jagged swings in physiology, an exaggeration of the normal oscillation and rhythmicity of life.

Not only that, the hare is also a notorious unrealist. A desperate dreamer, he shoots the moon and goes for broke in both weight loss and fitness. He invokes radical measures in a wild lunge for a final solution. But in the end, his utopian measures fall short and he is left with nothing. As Andre Maurois sagely observed, "He who wants to do everything will never do anything."

MEET THE TORTOISE

> Patience and perseverance have a magical effect before
> which difficulties disappear and obstacles vanish.
>
> John Quincy Adams

So what of the tortoise? Children's books tell us only that he is patient, but in fact this critter is a sophisticated, relaxed and dedicated long-termer. His style is one of minimal urgency.

Above all, the tortoise is process-oriented. That is, he is primarily interested in the quality of his experience. His efforts are sustained, not by what he might get at the end of the race, but by the rewarding properties of the experience itself. Consequently, he looks for joy and exuberance, pleasure and playfulness at every opportunity.

Outwardly, the tortoise may appear perfectly calm, but he does have his share of difficulties in life. Challenges, complications and confusion come his way, but he remains tolerant of insecurity and ambiguity. The tortoise understands that uncertainty is an essential part of the creative process. There's no big rush to solve every problem because when you're moving forward, many difficulties simply fall by the wayside.

It comes as no surprise to find that the tortoise is also a flexible, "both-and" thinker. As a highly intelligent animal, he can hold two contradictory statements in mind at the same time and still function. Never a slave to either-or thinking, he is fluent with the word *both*.

Above all, the tortoise is a realist. He knows the power of habit and the trajectory of human development. He knows that drastic changes are likely to backfire. He knows that the failure rate for diet and exercise programs is legendary. Artificially pushing the pace ultimately means going slower, so why rush? There's plenty to be enjoyed at this moment; as long as you keep moving, you'll eventually get what you're after.

THE SLOW LANE TO SUCCESS

> You may be capable of great things,
> But life consists of small things.
>
> Den Ming-Dao

In his wisdom, the tortoise rejects speed as an organizing principle of his life. Yes, there are times to quicken the pace, but in general, fast food, fast diets and fast fitness are recipes for failure. Thus the tortoise practices slow food and slow fitness.

Slow Food is an international movement founded by a group of European culinary activists in 1989. The mission of Slow Food is to return to our nutritional roots by emphasizing quality ingredients, pleasure, community and sustainability. The Slow Food philosophy rejects the high-speed rabbit pellets that are doled out from vending machines and drive-up windows. Food is something to be grown, prepared, shared and relished.

Similarly, we see the emergence of a parallel movement called Slow Fitness, a philosophy of exercise that emphasizes sustainability, pleasure, participation and quality of movement. The idea is to develop health and performance gradually over the course of years and decades, enjoying ourselves along the way.

A LITTLE BIT OF SOMETHING...

> If you add a little to a little, and then do it again, soon
> that little shall be much.

> Hesiod

The hare is so engrossed in his pursuit of ultimate solutions that he finds it almost impossible to fit his perfectionist program into the messy reality of daily life. Unable to accomplish his utopian plan, he eventually gives up and does nothing at all. In contrast, the tortoise recognizes the simple fact that when it comes to seizing opportunities for health and fitness, a little bit of something is far better than a whole lot of nothing.

Maybe you don't have time to train for a marathon. Maybe you only have time for 2 miles per week. It's not much, but it's something. After one year you'll have run 104 miles. Keep at it and after ten years you will have logged 1040 miles. After 40 years, 4,160 miles. That puts you far ahead of any all-or-nothing conditioning program.

Hike 30 miles each summer, an easily achievable goal. After 40 years, that's 1,200 miles of hiking. Ride your bike just 10 miles each week; after 40 years that's 20,800 miles. Fifty push ups per week; that's 104,000 in 40 years. Stretch for thirty minutes each week: that's 1,040 hours of stretching in 40 years. It's not Olympian, but it is significant.

The same kind of calculation holds true for nutrition. Eliminate that tasty trans-fat treat from your Friday office routine, multiply by 52 weeks and after a year you'll have avoided a bucket-full of artery-clogging calories. Such small changes in diet ultimately add up to some serious relief for the tissues of your cardiovascular and nervous system.

VICTORY DANCE

If you're facing in the right direction, all you have to do is keep walking.

Buddhist saying

Ultimately, the tortoise wins the health and fitness race in a most paradoxical, zen-like way. That is, she wins, not by racing, but by not racing. In fact, she has little interest in the outcome and little interest in achieving any external award. She's motivated by the intrinsic pleasures she finds in the process. She does vigorous movement on most days because it's fun. She trains hard because she likes the physical challenge of resistance and endurance. She eats good food on most days because it tastes better and makes her feel great.

The moral to this parable is simple: Win by not racing. Win by loving the process. Win by living well. Let the hare race on ahead and drive himself into a frenzy. Let him make his frantic, desperate lunge for a utopian body. Let him wrap himself up in a knot of frustration and chase his tail with yo-yo living. We've got better things to do.

TALKIN' ABOUT OUR GENERATIONS

Death is more universal than life; everyone dies but not everyone lives.

A. Sachs

While it is true that the unexamined life is not worth living, it is just as true that the unlived life is not worth examining.

Swami Beyondananda

The chief danger in life is that you may take too many precautions.

Alfred Adler

This week I celebrate the passing of a milestone birthday. Another year gone by, another lap around the sun; more past to reflect on, less future to dream about. Naturally, the event gets me thinking about my mortality, the aging process and the inevitable degeneration of my tissue. In a few short decades, my body will be wrinkled, weak, slow and deformed. With good food and vigorous movement, I'll be able to moderate the worst of it, but these measures simply blunt the inevitable; time flows on and the body breaks down.

I run and I run to catch up with the sun
But it's sinking
Racing around to come up behind me again
The sun is the same in a relative way
But I'm older
Shorter of breath and one day closer to death

The realization fills me with dread and anxiety. I loathe the prospect of physical breakdown. On good days, I rationalize it away and get absorbed in the tasks of daily living, but other times, my mind drifts back to 1966. That year, young people were speaking out, filled with anger and premature cynicism. The war in Vietnam was raging and death by nuclear annihilation loomed ever-present in the background. Not surprisingly, we were furious at the lot we were being handed. It was in this year that The Who put their angst to music in their landmark piece, "My Generation."

People try to put us down,
Just because we get around...

If you're of that era, you probably played the air guitar yourself, pounding out the power chords and savoring the taste of rebellion. We were exuberant and defiant and we saw no promise in adulthood. In fact, we were determined to avoid the fate entirely.

Things they do look awful cold
I hope I die before I get old.

The lyrics rang true in our hearts. We had no desire to participate in the grim conservatism of adulthood, the constant worries about money and order, power and security. Adults raised armies and built bombs, worked like dogs, kept a death-grip on power and then claimed omniscience and righteousness on top of it all. If this was the kind of life that lay in store for us, well, we'd just as soon be dead. Not only would our bodies be worthless, we'd be mean-spirited authoritarians without heart or soul. There was no future here; somehow, we would have to escape.

The Who's lyrics rebelled against adult imperialism and war, but they also spoke to our fear of aging and disability. And in this respect, the words were a reflection of not just My Generation, but every generation. All of us look at the aged bodies around us and desperately seek an escape from a similar fate. We're too polite to mention it in mixed company, but we all share The Who's point of view. Outwardly, we remain calm, but inside, we'd do anything to avoid the wrinkles, the deformity and the weakness.

Things they do look awful cold.
We hope we die before we get old.

The Who's rant had great authenticity and remains a vital expression of rage and discontent. Nevertheless, it is hardly a sensible long-term solution for effective living. Some would even call it a celebration of incompetence. Better if we could find an intelligent and exuberant way to live in harmony with our predicament. But how shall we celebrate when physical breakdown looms just over the horizon?

THE WAR ON DEATH

Unfortunately, many of us approach aging in the same way that we approach other unpleasant realities. That is, we declare war on it. We already have a war on terror, a war on drugs and a war on cancer. We have yet to make it explicit, but our hyper-medicalized culture is now constructing a vast and intricate "War on Death," carried out in hospitals, clinics and gyms across the country. We now treat every affliction of the body as opponent to be vanquished, an enemy to be defeated. Even processes and changes that are perfectly normal are now labeled as medical conditions and attacked with every available resource. When we lose the war, as we inevitably do, we come to see it as a defeat and a tragedy.

Even physical movement itself has been drafted into the war effort. Unnerved by the prospect of aging and death, some of us turn to the promise of exercise. Surely exercise, if practiced with enough dedication and focus, will protect us from the ravages of time. The right combination of sets, reps, mileage, nutrition and stress reduction will defeat the reaper, so we believe. So we lace up our shoes and hit the road with grim resolve, determined to beat the system.

Initially, it all seems possible. The young animal body compensates quickly and progress comes in waves; we just keep getting better. Our strength, speed and endurance improve and we begin to feel impervious to harm. We've found the solution now and nothing can stop us.

You're gonna fly high,
You're never gonna die
You're gonna make it if you try
They're gonna love you.

Of course, it's all a delusion. Exercise does work wonders; it's probably the most effective medicine ever discovered. It may very well tack on a few years to our lifespans. But physiology has some fundamental limitations that, as far as we know, cannot be defeated. Death itself is a 3 billion-year-old creation of life; without it, there would be no evolution, no diversity, no biological exuberance. When we try to beat this system, we set ourselves up for frustration. In fact, the belief that exercise will defeat death reminds us of other, similarly futile quests. A geologist's bumper sticker sums up the human predicament and the folly of trying to resist natural forces that are far more powerful than ourselves. It says quite simply, "Stop Plate Tectonics."

THE WAR ON RISK

Closely related to our War on Death is our accelerating War on Risk. Intimidated by our fragile existence and our impending demise, many of us turn towards security in all its forms, especially in this post-9/11 world. Consciously or not, we warn ourselves about the hazards of the world: "Don't take chances. You might get sick. Play it safe. You might get injured. You might even *die.*"

So we try to rig the game with infrastructure, social institutions and a gargantuan medical-industrial complex. Chart all the possibilities, eliminate the unknowns, plan for every contingency–given enough computing power, we can figure it all out. Decode the human genome and then, when you're done with that, take on the holy grail of physiology, the proteome. (This is the immense set of proteins that constitute the form and function of the human body.) Once we know the codes, it will be a simple matter of splicing a few genes and all will be well–so we believe.

Of course, such a risk-hostile approach to life is destined to backfire. No amount of insurance or infrastructure will protect us from the reality of death. No amount of exercise, supplements or medical care will free us from our predicament. Animal life is what it is; death is part of the package.

Ultimately, our war on risk becomes a kind of suicide. In our effort to kill risk and achieve perfect security, we simultaneously destroy the dynamic quality that defines life. In his landmark book *The Wisdom of Insecurity*, Zen philosopher Alan Watts pointed out the absurdity of our quest for risk-free living:

There is a contradiction in our desire to be secure in a
universe whose very nature is fluidity and movement...If I
want to be secure, that is, protected from the flux of life,
I am wanting to be separate from life. Yet, it is this very
sense of separateness that makes me feel insecure. In other
words, the more security I can get, the more I shall want...

DEATH IN AMERICA

Aging is not a disease, nor is it a catastrophe. All animal bodies age;
all creatures perish. All species ultimately go extinct. The earth itself has
its own lifespan, its own mortality. It is hubris to suggest that we are
exceptions. Aging, and all its attendant transformations, is utterly normal. Every organism on this planet is aging at this moment. The fittest
carnivore, the most athletic predator, all are but moments away from
degeneration. No one, with the possible exception of viruses, escapes
this game.

The tragedy is not that human bodies age. The tragedy is not that the
flesh becomes weak. These transformations are inevitable. Rather, the
tragedy is that people wake up late in life and realize that they haven't
really lived in the first place.

This, of course, is precisely what is happening with so many modern
human lives. Trapped in sedentary habits that are fundamentally alien
to the human body, millions of Americans are physiologically alive, but
not really living. Sedated by entertainment, oppressed by a workaholic
culture and caged by a pedestrian-hostile infrastructure, modern Americans have little sense of animal health or authentic living. Many of us
are technically alive, but not really prospering. We have vital signs, but
no signs of vitality. Wrapped in a cocoon of security and pampered by
labor-saving machinery, the best that many Americans can hope for today is a near-life experience.

TAKE THE WORLD IN A LOVE EMBRACE

So maybe The Who had it backwards. Maybe the positive solution is
to turn the whole thing around and look for an authentic, passionate life
experience. Instead of wishing for an early demise and an escape from
the horrors of old age, wish instead for vigorous experience and exuberance for as long as we can manage it, in whatever way we can. There is a

world of difference between the statements "I'm exercising to avoid the ravages of old age" and "I'm exercising because I'm celebrating my life as a vigorous animal."

Unfortunately, "I hope I live before I get old" sounds weak, passive and inadequate for our purposes. What we need is something with guts, something like Born to be Wild, the 1968 release by Steppenwolf.

Yeah Darlin' go make it happen
Take the world in a love embrace
Fire all of your guns at once
And explode into space
Like a true nature's child
We were born, born to be wild...

3 BILLION BEATS...

A physiology textbook tells us that the average human heart beats about 3 billion times over the course of a typical lifespan. Give or take a few million beats for variations in cardiovascular health, this is what we get. So how will you spend your 3 billion beats? Will you squander them and then wish for more?

A lot of people surely will. According to one calculation, the average American will spend roughly 2 years of his or her life watching TV commercials. And yet, those same Americans will wish desperately for a longer life. Why? What would they do with such excess?

George Carlin likes to remind us that "Life is not measured by the number of breaths we take, but by the moments that take our breath away." To put it another way, we might say that "Life is not measured by the number of times your heart beats but by the times your heart wants to explode with passion, desire and joy." Better a short life of passion than a long life of passivity. In the grand scope of human experience, quality is far more important than quantity.

AND IN THE END...

In keeping with our classic rock theme for the day, it's fitting that The Beatles get the last word. The final lyrics on their final album went like this:

And in the end
The love you take
Is equal to the love you make.

A grand and wonderful exit line to be sure, but had the Fab Four pondered the predicament of aging and the paradox of security, they might have given their lyrics a slightly different twist:

And in the end,
The life you make
Is equal to the risk you take

Embrace it all. Take a chance. Dance while you can.

FURTHER ADVENTURES

JOIN THE EXUBERANT ANIMAL NETWORK

Animals that play together tend to stay together.

Marc Bekhoff

Beyond the immediate goal of sharing ideas through the pages of this book, GoAnimal® is seeking to create culture, conversation and community around these themes of exuberant physical experience. We invite like-minded partners to join us in creating new programs, games, exercises and ideas.

Naturally, this will be a bushy creation, all organized around a philosophy that is primal, practical and playful. If you are involved in physical training and education at any level, you may want to be involved in this process. Join our network of exuberants. Contact GoAnimal® for details regarding partnership and affiliation.

Frank Forencich
9112 32nd Ave. NE
Seattle, WA 98115
frank@exuberantanimal.com

Seminars and workshops are available. For more information, see www.exuberantanimal.com.

RECOMMENDED READING

A History and Philosophy of Sport and Physical Education: From Ancient Civilizations to the Modern World
Robert A. Mechikoff, Steven G. Estes
WCB/McGraw-Hill 1998

Animal Play: Evolutionary, Comparative and Ecological Perspectives
Marc Bekoff and John Byers
Cambridge University Press 1998

Becoming Human: evolution and human uniqueness
Ian Tattersall
Harcourt Brace and Company 1998

Biophilia: The human bond with other species
Edward O. Wilson
Harvard University Press 1984

Evolving Health: The Origins of Illness and How the Modern World is Making Us Sick
Noel Boaz
John Wiley 2002

Exuberance
Kay Redfield Jamison
Knopf 2004

Feeling Good is Good For You: How Pleasure Can Boost Your Immune System and Lengthen Your Life
Carl J. Charnetski and Francis X. Brennan
Rodale 2001

In the Age of Mankind: A Smithsonian Book of Human Evolution
Roger Lewin
Smithsonian Books 1988

Lucy: the beginnings of humankind
Donald Johanson and Maitland Edey
Warner Books 1982

Our Inner Ape
Frans de Waal
Riverhead 2005

Physical Activity and Health: A Report of the Surgeon General
U.S. Department of Health and Human Services
Centers for Disease Control and Prevention
National Center for Chronic Disease Prevention and Health
Promotion 1996

Punished by Rewards: The Trouble with Gold Stars, Incentive Plans, A's, Praise and Other Bribes
Alfie Kohn
Houghton Mifflin 1993

Tao of Jeet Kune Do
Bruce Lee
Ohara Publications 1975

The Aims of Education
Alfred North Whitehead
The Free Press 1957

The Biophilia Hypothesis
Edited by Stephen R. Kellert and E.O. Wilson
Island Press / Shearwater Books 1993

The End of Stress as We Know It
Bruce McEwen
The Dana Press 2002

The Genesis of Animal Play: Testing the Limits
Gordon Burghardt
MIT Press 2005

The Origin of Humankind
Richard Leakey
BasicBooks, HarperCollins 1994

The Paleolithic Prescription: A Program of Diet and Exercise and a Design for Living
S. Boyd Eaton, Marjorie Shostak, Melvin Konner
Perennial 1988

The Play Ethic: A Manifesto for a Different Way of Living
Pat Kane
Macmillan 2004

The Status Syndrome: How Social Standing Affects Our Health and Longevity
Michael Marmot
Times Books 2004

The Third Chimpanzee: The Evolution and Future of the Human Animal
Jared Diamond
HarperPerennial 1992

Walking with Cavemen (book/DVD)
John Lynch and Louise Barrett
BBC production
DK Publishing 2003

Why Johnny Hates Sports: why organized youth sports are failing our children and what we can do about it
Fred Engh
Avery Publishing Group 1999

Why Zebras Don't Get Ulcers (third edition)
Robert Sapolsky
Henry Holt 2004

Printed in the United States
57786LVS00004B/1-90